Thomson

John from R... ♡ P9-AZX-123
Christmas 1982

THE SCOTS BOOK
OF LORE
AND FOLKLORE

THE CLANS OF SCOTLAND

THE SCOTS BOOK
OF LORE
AND FOLKLORE

Compiled by
RONALD MACDONALD
DOUGLAS

BEEKMAN HOUSE
New York

The illustrations on pages 15, 54, 65, 87, 95, 105, 219, 265 and 285 are by Douglas Percy Bliss, and those on pages vi, 1, 21, 34, 53, 57, 79, 83, 94, 161, 207, 229, 231, 241, 247, 257, 291, 293, 313, 317, 323 and 337 are by Betty Aylmer.

The Gaelic map of Scotland on page 162 is by the Author. The map of Clans and families, facing the title-page, is by Betty Aylmer.

Copyright © 1982 by Crown Publishers, Inc.

This edition is published by Beekman House, distributed by Crown Publishers, Inc., One Park Avenue, New York, New York 10016

h g f e d c b a

BEEKMAN HOUSE EDITION 1982

Manufactured in the United States of America

Library of Congress Cataloging in Publication Data

Main entry under title:

The Scots book of lore and folklore.

Includes indexes.
1. Folklore—Scotland.   2. Clans and clan system—Scotland—Folklore.   3. Scotland—Social life and customs.   I. Douglas, Ronald MacDonald.
GR144.S35   398'.09411   81-15555
ISBN: 0-517-366037

CONTENTS

PART IV

PART V

MAPS

SHIELDS

FOREWORD

Lay the proud usurpers low!
Tyrants fall in every foe!
Liberty's in every blow!
Let us do, or die!

From "Bruce Before Bannockburn" by Robert Burns, the above verse illustrates the national loyalty and pride ingrained in Scottish culture. It was at Bannockburn that Scotsmen under King Robert the Bruce defeated the English King Edward II in 1314.

To understand the Scots, a knowledge of their poetry, history, and folklore is essential. They are a people steeped in tradition and proud of their heritage; through pride they derived the strength to endure the tumultuous history of their land. Cold, rainy, buffeted by the sea, rocky and mountainous, Scotland is, by design, unforgiving. Her history has been one of struggle; from invasions by the Norsemen in the eighth through twelfth centuries, up to the present nationalist movement, the Scots have always fought to preserve their liberty and their dignity. Time has bred a tenacious people.

The following compilation by Ronald Macdonald Douglas provides an excellent selection of poetry, prose, folklore, and other delights of Scottish origin. If you are a Scot, you may discover much to be proud of—if you are not, you may wish you were.

G.W.O.

THE WHEREFORE OF THE WHY ...

When Paul Gauguin wrote his *Intimate Journals* he did his best to confound the critics at the outset by declaring : ' This is not a book ! ' I might try a similar trick ; but, I am afraid in my case, it wouldn't work. Neither can I take refuge behind some such utterance as Montaigne used when he wrote : ' I have here only made a garland of choice flowers ; I bring nothing but the threads that bind them.' And that simply because it would not be true—but whether the one or two posies of my own growing are flowers or nothing but weeds is another matter. Nor yet, leaving the metaphor behind, do I feel disposed to adopt the customary apologetic attitude of most anthologisers, collectors of analecta, and writers of odds and ends.

And so, without apologies or qualifications, I accept the full responsibility for bringing out yet another Scottish book which, I hope, may be of interest to Scots and lovers of Scotland ; but which, I feel, will be attacked by the too-clever-by-half brigade. (*Why is this included ?   And why is that missed out ?   And where, oh where, is dear Mr. So-and-so ?*) Well, battle is half the joy of life to the Scot ; so, here's to it !

There is a lot of cauld kail het again in this pot—sometimes I have stirred it with a stick of sugarolly, but more often with the business end of a claymor—but, in the hotch-potch, there are two or three things that have never appeared before. And, if I seem to be mixing up flowers and

ix

vegetables, what does it matter ?—kail may be made from a mixture of almost anything, provided there is a little salt in it !

I take pleasure in having provided at least one new ingredient—the Gaelic map—and that, not because it is a good map—for it isn't—but because it is the very first Gaelic map of Scotland ever to appear. And if the hypercritical among the Gaels (and that means all of them !) find the map to be all wrong, I have at anyrate given them the hint, and there is nothing to prevent any of them from making a better one. I shall be among the first to applaud.

But this is not a book for the critical, nor is it a book for students and scholars : it is a book for the general reader, a book for the ordinary man and woman, and, in particular, for the ordinary Scot—if there is such a thing as an ordinary Scot. It is more thoroughly Scottish than it may appear to be on the surface : it is as Scottish as any book can be that is written, perforce, in a language not Scottish. However, I have managed, I hope, to avoid the ' wha's like us ? ' attitude. That can be left to the Burns Nighters !

And now, before I give thanks to those who have helped me, there is just one other little thing : to those who, having read the book of stories I was fortunate enough to have published a few months ago, and who have been kind enough to say that they would look forward to the appearance of my next book—this is not my ' next book ' ! My next book is yet to come.

I have to thank my learned Gaelic friend, John N. MacLeod, for putting me right whenever I blundered in the true and ancient tongue of Alba—for my Gaelic is most ungrammatical, and can be at times amusing—but, even then, I have occasionally gone over his head : if there are any errors, they are mine—they are certainly not his. To those copyright-holders who have given permission for the reprinting of copyright material I offer grateful thanks ; and to my friend and publisher, Alexander MacLehose, I raise my bonnet in token of appreciation for all the help that he has given me, but more particularly do I thank him for his having put a firm, but none the less most kindly, skid on some of my wilder efforts and attempts. At first, whenever he said 'No!' to anything I wished to include, I flashed my dirk, but he only smiled and stood his ground ; and now that the book is shaped I see that on every occasion he was right and I was wrong.

MONADH CHLUAINE,
    CNOC MHOIRE,
      INBHIR-NIS.

Gordon

Read these faint runes of mystery,
O Celt, at home and o'er the sea ;
The bond is loosed—the poor are free—
The world's great future rests with thee !

Till the soil—bid cities rise—
Be strong, O Celt—be rich, be wise—
But still, with those divine grey eyes,
Respect the realm of Mysteries.

THE BOOK OF ORM : *Robert Buchanan*

PART I

POEMS

Macdonald

PART I

THOMAS THE RHYMER

True Thomas lay on Huntlie bank;
  A ferlie he spied wi' his e'e;
And there he saw a ladye bright,
  Come riding down by the Eildon Tree.

Her shirt was o' the grass-green silk,
  Her mantle o' the velvet fyne;
At ilka tett of her horse's mane,
  Hang fifty siller bells and nine.

True Thomas, he pull'd aff his cap,
  And louted low down to his knee,
' All hail, thou mighty queen of heav'n!
  ' For thy peer on earth I never did see.'

' O no, O no, Thomas,' she said;
  ' That name does not belang to me;
' I am but the queen of fair Elfland,
  ' That am hither come to visit thee.

' Harp and carp, Thomas,' she said;
  ' Harp and carp along wi' me;
' And if ye dare to kiss my lips,
  ' Sure of your bodie I will be.'

' Betide me weal, betide me woe,
  ' That weird shall never danton me.'
Syne he has kissed her rosy lips,
  All underneath the Eildon Tree.

' Now, ye maun go wi' me,' she said ;
   ' True Thomas, ye maun go wi' me ;
' And ye maun serve me seven years,
   ' Thro' weal or woe as may chance to be.'

She mounted on her milk-white steed ;
   She's ta'en true Thomas up behind :
And aye, whene'er her bridle rung,
   The steed flew swifter than the wind.

O they rade on, and farther on ;
   The steed gaed swifter than the wind ;
Until they reached a desart wide,
   And living land was left behind.

' Light down, light down, now, true Thomas,
   ' And lean your head upon my knee ;
' Abide and rest a little space,
   ' And I will shew you ferlies three.

' O see ye not yon narrow road,
   ' So thick beset with thorns and briers ?
' That is the path of righteousness,
   ' Though after it but few enquires.

' And see not ye that braid braid road,
   ' That lies across that lily leven ?
' That is the path of wickedness,
   ' Though some call it the road to heaven.

' And see not ye that bonny road,
   ' That winds about the fernie brae ?
' That is the road to fair Elfland,
   ' Where thou and I this night maun gae.

'But, Thomas, ye maun hold your tongue,
  'Whatever you may hear or see;
'For, if you speak word in Elflyn land,
  'Ye'll ne'er get back to your ain countrie.'

O they rade on, and farther on,
  And they waded through rivers aboon the knee,
And they saw neither sun nor moon,
  But they heard the roaring of the sea.

It was mirk mirk night, and there was nae stern light,
  And they waded through red blude to the knee;
For a' the blude, that's shed on earth,
  Rins through the springs o' that countrie.

Syne they came on to a garden green,
  And she pu'd an apple frae a tree—
'Take this for thy wages, true Thomas;
  'It will give thee the tongue that can never lie.'

'My tongue is mine ain,' true Thomas said;
  'A gudely gift ye wad gie to me!
'I neither dought to buy nor sell,
  'At fair or tryst where I may be.

'I dought neither speak to prince or peer,
  'Nor ask of grace from fair ladye.'
'Now hold thy peace!' the lady said,
  'For as I say, so must it be.'

He has gotten a coat of the even cloth,
  And a pair of shoes of velvet green;
And, till seven years were gane and past,
  True Thomas on earth was never seen.

CANADIAN BOAT SONG

Listen to me as when ye heard our father,
　Sing, long ago, the song of other shores;
Listen to me, and then in chorus gather
　All your deep voices as ye pull your oars:

Fair these broad meads—these hoary woods are grand,
But we are exiles from our fathers' land.

From the lone shieling of the misty island
　Mountains divide us, and a waste of seas;
Yet still the blood is strong, the heart is Highland,
　And we in dreams behold the Hebrides.

We ne'er shall tread the fancy-haunted valley,
　Where, 'twixt the dark hills, creeps the small clear stream;
In arms around the patriarch banner rally,
　Nor see the moon on royal tombstones gleam.

When the bold kindred in the time long vanished,
　Conquered the soil and fortified the keep,
No seer foretold the children should be banished,
　That a degenerate lord might boast his sheep.

Come foreign rage! let discord burst in slaughter!
　O then for clansmen true, and stern claymore!
The hearts that would have given their blood like water,
　Beat heavily beyond the Atlantic's roar.

Fair these broad meads—these hoary woods are grand,
But we are exiles from our fathers' land.
　　　　　　　　　　　　　　Authorship disputed.

TO EXILES

Are you not weary in your distant places,
  Far, far from Scotland of the mist and storm;
In drowsy airs, the sun-smite on your faces,
  The days so long and warm?
When all around you lie the strange fields sleeping,
  The dreary woods where no fond memories roam,
Do not your sad hearts over seas come leaping
  To the highlands and the lowlands of your Home?

Wild cries the Winter, loud through all our valleys,
  The midnights roar, the grey noons echo back;
About the scalloped coasts the eager galleys
  Beat for kind harbours from horizons black:
We tread the miry roads, the rain-drenched heather,
  We are the men, we battle, we endure!
God's pity for you people in your weather
  Of swooning winds, calm seas, and skies demure!

  .   .   .   .

Let torrents pour then, let the great winds rally,
  Snow-silence fall, or lightning blast the pine;
That light of Home shines warmly in the valley,
  And, exiled son of Scotland, it is thine.
Far have you wandered over seas of longing,
  And now you drowse, and now you well may weep,
When all the recollections come a-thronging
  Of this old country where your fathers sleep.

They sleep, but still the hearth is warmly glowing,
  While the wild Winter blusters round their land:
That light of Home, the wind so bitter blowing—
  Look, look and listen, do you understand?

Love, strength, and tempest—oh, come back and share
    them !
    Here is the cottage, here the open door;
Fond are our hearts although we do not bare them,
    They're yours, and you are ours—for evermore.

                                        Neil Munro.

HAME

> *Hame, hame, hame, hame fain wad I be,*
> *O, hame, hame, hame, to my ain countrie !*

When the floo'er is i' the bud and the leaf is on the tree,
The larks shall sing me hame in my ain countrie.
Hame, hame, hame, hame fain wad I be,
O, hame, hame, hame, to my ain countrie !

The green leaf o' loyaltie's begun for to fa',
The bonnie white rose it is witherin' an' a';
But I'll water't wi' the blude o' usurpin' tyrannie,
An green will it graw in my ain countrie.

O, there's nocht frae ruin my country can save
But the keys o' kind heaven to open the grave :
That a' the noble martyrs wha died for loyaltie
May rise again an' fecht for their ain countrie.

The great are now gane, a' wha ventured to save,
The new gress is springin' on the top o' their grave ;
But the sun thro' the mirk blinks blythe in my e'e—
' I'll shine on ye yet in your ain countrie.'

> *Hame, hame, hame, hame fain wad I be,*
> *Hame, hame, hame, to my ain countrie !*
>   *Allan Cunningham.*

HOME THOUGHTS FROM ABROAD

Aifter the war, says the papers, they'll no be content at hame,
  The lads that hae feucht wi' death twae 'ear i' the mud and
    the rain and the snaw ;
For aifter a sodger's life the shop will be unco tame ;
  They'll ettle at fortune and freedom in the new lands
    Far awa.

No me !
By God ! No me !
Aince we hae lickit oor faes
And aince I get oot o' this hell,
For the rest o' my leevin' days
I'll mak a pet o' mysel.

I'll haste me back wi' an eident fit
And settle again in the same auld bit.
And oh ! the comfort to snowk again
The reek o' my mither's but-and-ben,
The wee box-bed and the ingle neuk,
And the kail-pat hung frae the chimley-heuk !
I'll gang back to the shop like a laddie to play,
Tak doun the shutters at skreigh o' day,
And weigh oot floor wi' a carefu' pride,
And hear the clash o' the countraside.
I'll wear for ordinar' a roond hard hat,
A collar and dicky and black cravat.
If the weather's wat I'll no stir ootbye
Wi' oot an umbrella to keep me dry.
I think I'd better no tak a wife—
I've had a' the adventure I want in life.—
But at nicht, when the doors are steeked, I'll sit,

While the bleeze loups high frae the aiken ruit,
And smoke my pipe aside the crook,
And read in some douce auld-farrant book ;
Or crack wi' Davie and mix a rummer,
While the auld wife's pow nid-nods in slum'er ;
And hark to the winds gaun tearin' bye
And thank the Lord I'm sae warm and dry.

When simmer brings the lang bricht e'en,
I'll daunder doun to the bowling green,
Or delve my yaird and my roses tend
For the big floo'er show in the next back-end.
Whiles, when the sun blinks aifter rain,
I'll tak my rod and gang up the glen ;
Me and Davie, we ken the püles
Whar the troot grow great in the howes o' the hills ;
And, wanderin' back when the gloamin fa's
And the midges dance in the hazel shaws,
We'll stop at the yett ayont the hicht
And drink great wauchts o' the scented nicht,
While the hoose lamps kin'le raw by raw
And a yellow star hings ower the Law.
Davie will lauch like a wean at a fair
And nip my airm to mak certain shüre
That we're back frae yon place o' dule and dreid,
To oor ain kind warld—

But Davie's deid !
Nae mair gude nor ill can betide him.
We happit him doun by Beaumont toun,
And the half o' my hert's in the mools aside him.

                                    John Buchan.

SCOTLAND OUR MITHER

Scotland our Mither—this from your sons abroad,
Leavin' tracks on virgin veld that never kent a road,
Trekkin' on wi' weary feet, an' faces turned fae hame,
But lovin' aye the auld wife across the seas the same.

Scotland our Mither—we left your bieldy bents
To hunt wi' hairy Esau, while Jacob kept the tents.
We've pree'd the pangs o' hunger, mair sorrow seen than
mirth,
But never niffer'd, auld wife, our rightfu' pride o' birth.

Scotland our Mither—we sow, we plant, we till,
But plagues that passed o'er Egypt light here an' work their
will.
They've harried barn an' basket till ruin claims us sure ;
We'd better kept the auld craft an' herdit on the muir.

Scotland our Mither—we weary whiles and tire ;
When Bad Luck helps to outspan, Regret biggs up the fire ;
But still the hope uphaulds us, tho' bitter now the blast,
That we'll win to the auld hame across the seas at last.

Scotland our Mither—we've bairns you've never seen—
Wee things that turn them northward when they kneel
down at e'en ;
They plead in childish whispers the Lord on high will be
A comfort to the auld wife—their granny o'er the sea.

Scotland our Mither—since first we left your side,
From Quilimane to Cape Town we've wandered far an' wide;
Yet aye from mining camp an' town, from koppie an' karoo,
Your sons richt kindly, auld wife, send hame their love to you.

                                        Charles Murray.

LOCHINVAR

O, young Lochinvar is come out of the west,
Through all the wide Border his steed was the best;
And save his good broadsword he weapons had none,
He rode all unarmed, and he rode all alone.
So faithful in love, and so dauntless in war,
There never was knight like the young Lochinvar.

He staid not for brake, and he stopp'd not for stone,
He swam the Esk river where ford there was none;
But ere he alighted at Netherby gate,
The bride had consented, the gallant came late:
For a laggard in love, and a dastard in war,
Was to wed the fair Ellen of brave Lochinvar.

So boldly he entered the Netherby Hall,
Among bride's-men, and kinsmen, and brothers, and all:
Then spoke the bride's father, his hand on his sword,
(For the poor craven bridegroom said never a word)
' O come ye in peace here, or come ye in war,
Or to dance at our bridal, young Lord Lochinvar?'

' I long woo'd your daughter, my suit you denied;—
Love swells like the Solway, but ebbs like its tide—
And now I am come, with this lost love of mine,
To lead but one measure, drink one cup of wine.
There are maidens in Scotland more lovely by far,
That would gladly be bride to the young Lochinvar.'

The bride kissed the goblet: the knight took it up,
He quaffed off the wine, and he threw down the cup.
She looked down to blush, and she looked up to sigh,

With a smile on her lips, and a tear in her eye.
He took her soft hand, ere her mother could bar,—
' Now tread we a measure ! ' said young Lochinvar.

So stately his form, and so lovely her face,
That never a hall such a galliard did grace ;
While her mother did fret, and her father did fume,
And the bridegroom stood dangling his bonnet and plume ;
And the bride-maidens whispered, ' 'Twere better by far,
To have matched our fair cousin with young Lochinvar.'

One touch to her hand, and one word in her ear,
When they reached the hall-door, and the charger stood
    near ;
So light to the croupe the fair lady he swung,
So light to the saddle before her he sprung !
' She is won ! we are gone, over bank, bush, and scaur :
They'll have fleet steeds that follow,' quoth young
    Lochinvar.

There was mounting 'mong Graemes of the Netherby clan ;
Forsters, Fenwicks, and Musgraves, they rode and they ran :
There was racing and chasing on Cannobie Lee,
But the lost bride of Netherby ne'er did they see.
So daring in love, and so dauntless in war,
Have ye e'er heard of gallant like young Lochinvar ?

                                                    Scott.

THE DOUGLAS TRAGEDY

'Rise up, rise up, now, lord Douglas,' she says,
  'And put on your armour so bright;
'Let it never be said, that a daughter of thine
  'Was married to a lord under night.

'Rise up, rise up, my seven bold sons,
  'And put on your armour so bright,
'And take better care of your youngest sister,
  'For your eldest's awa the last night.'

He's mounted her on a milk-white steed,
  And himself on a dapple grey,
With a bugelet horn hung down by his side,
  And lightly they rode away.

Lord William lookit o'er his left shoulder,
  To see what he could see,
And there he spy'd her seven brethren bold,
  Come riding o'er the lea.

' Light down, light down, lady Marg'ret,' he said,
  'And hold my steed in your hand,
'Until that against your seven brethren bold,
  'And your father, I mak a stand.'

She held his steed in her milk-white hand,
  And never shed one tear,
Until that she saw her seven brethren fa',
  And her father hard fighting, who lov'd her so dear.

'O hold your hand, lord William!' she said,
  'For your strokes they are wond'rous sair;
'True lovers I can get many a ane,
  'But a father I can never get mair.'

THE DOUGLAS TRAGEDY

O she's ta'en out her handkerchief,
　　It was o' the holland sae fine,
And aye she dighted her father's bloody wounds,
　　That were redder than the wine.

' O chuse, O chuse, lady Marg'ret,' he said,
　　' O whether will ye gang or bide ? '
' I'll gang, I'll gang, lord William,' she said,
　　' For ye have left me no other guide.'

He's lifted her on a milk-white steed,
　　And himself on a dapple grey,
With a bugelet horn hung down by his side,
　　And slowly they baith rade away.

O they rade on, and on they rade,
　　And a' by the light of the moon,
Until they came to yon wan water,
　　And there they lighted down.

They lighted down to tak a drink
　　Of the spring that ran sae clear ;
And down the stream ran his gude heart's blood,
　　And sair she gan to fear.

' Hold up, hold up, lord William,' she says,
　　' For I fear that you are slain ! '
' 'Tis naething but the shadow of my scarlet cloak,
　　' That shines in the water sae plain.'

O they rade on, and on they rade,
　　And a' by the light of the moon,
Until they cam to his mother's ha' door,
　　And there they lighted down.

'Get up, get up, lady mother,' he says,
  'Get up, and let me in!—
'Get up, get up, lady mother,' he says,
  'For this night my fair lady I've win.

'O mak my bed, lady mother,' he says,
  'O mak it braid and deep!
'And lay lady Marg'ret close at my back,
  'And the sounder I will sleep.'

Lord William was dead lang ere midnight,
  Lady Marg'ret lang ere day—
And all true lovers that go thegither,
  May they have mair luck than they!

Lord William was buried in St. Marie's kirk,
  Lady Marg'ret in Marie's quire;
Out o' the lady's grave grew a bonny red rose,
  And out o' the knight's a brier.

And they twa met, and they twa plat,
  And fain they wad be near;
And a' the world might ken right weel,
  They were twa lovers dear.

But bye and rade the Black Douglas,
  And wow but he was rough!
For he pull'd up the bonny brier,
  And flang't in St. Mary's loch.

Old Ballad.

STANZAS FROM 'THE KINGIS QUHAIR'

. . . And therewith cast I doun mine eyes again,
Whereat I saw, walking under the tower,
Full secretly, now comen here to plain,
The fairest or the freshest younge flower
That e'er I saw, methought, before that hour:
For which sudden abate, anon astart
The blood of all my body to my heart.

And though I stood abasit for a lite,
No wonder was; for why? my wittis all
Were so o'ercome with pleasance and delight—
Only through letting of my eyen fall—
That suddenly my heart became her thrall
For ever of free will, for of menace
There was no token in her sweet face.

King James I.

MARGARET DRUMMOND

The blossoms that were blicht and bricht
    By her were black and blue,
Scho gladit all the fowl of flicht
    That in the forest flew.
Scho micht haif comfort king or knicht,
    That ever in countrie I knew,
As wale and well of warldly wicht
    In womanly virtúe.

Her colour clear, her countenance,
    Her comely crystal een,
Her portraiture of most plesance,
    All picture did prevene;

Of every virtue to avance,
   When ladies praisit been,
Richtest in my remembrance
   That rose is rootit green.

This mild, meek, mansuet Mergrit,
   This pearl poleist most white,
Dame Natouris dear dochter discreet,
   The diamond of delight,
Never formit was to found on feet
   Ane figure more perfite,
Nor none on mould that did her meet
   Micht mend her worth a mite.

The poem from which these verses are taken, beginning ' When Tayis bank was blumit bricht,' probably refers to Margaret Drummond, the one woman whom James IV certainly loved. She was poisoned when it was feared that he might marry her, and an alliance with Margaret Tudor, daughter of the English king Henry VII, was arranged for him. It was this alliance that eventually brought about the union of the Crowns of Scotland and England.

The poem may probably have been written by King James IV himself.

THE JOLLY BEGGAR

There was a jolly beggar, an' a-beggin' he was boun' ;
An' he took up his quarters intil a lan'wart toun—

    An' we'll gang nae mair a-rovin',
      A-rovin' in the nicht,
    An' we'll gang nae mair a-rovin',
      Let the müne shine e'er sae bricht.

He wad neither lie intil the barn, nor yet wad he in byre,
But in ahint the ha' door, or else ayont the fire.

The beggar's bed was made at e'en, wi' guid clean strae an'
    hay,
Juist in ahint the ha' door, an' there the beggar lay.

Up raise the guidman's dochter, an' a' tae bar the door,
An' there she saw the beggar man was standin' on the flüre.

He took the lassie in his airms, an' tae the neuk he ran,
' O ! hooly, hooly wi' me, sir, ye'll wauken oor guidman.'

He took a horn frae his side, an' blew baith lood an' shrill,
An' four an' twenty belted knicht cam skippin' ower the hill.

An' he took oot his braw wee knife, loot a' his duddies fa',
An' he stood the brawest knichtly man that was amang
    them a'.

> *An' we'll gang nae mair a-rovin',*
>   *A-rovin' in the nicht,*
> *An' we'll gang nae mair a-rovin',*
>   *Let the müne shine e'er sae bricht.*
>   *Attributed to King James V.*

SUMMONS TO LOVE

Phoebus, arise !
And paint the sable skies
With azure, white, and red :
Rouse Memnon's mother from her Tithon's bed
That she may thy career with roses spread :
The nightingales thy coming each where sing :
Make an eternal spring !

THE JOLLY BEGGAR

Give life to this dark world which lieth dead;
Spread forth thy golden hair
In larger locks than thou wast wont before,
And emperor-like decore
With diadem of pearl thy temples fair:
Chase hence the ugly night
Which serves but to make dear thy glorious light.

—This is that happy morn,
That day, long-wishéd day
Of all my life so dark,
(If cruel stars have not my ruin sworn
And fates my hopes betray),
Which, purely white, deserves
An everlasting diamond should it mark.
This is the morn should bring unto this grove
My Love, to hear and recompense my love.
Fair King, who all preserves,
But show thy blushing beams,
And thou two sweeter eyes
Shalt see than those which by Peneus' streams
Did once thy heart surprize.
Now, Flora, deck thyself in fairest guise:
If that ye winds should hear
A voice surpassing far Amphion's lyre,
Your furious chiding stay;
Let Zephyr only breathe,
And with her tresses play.
—The winds all silent are,
And Phoebus in his chair
Ensaffroning sea and air

Makes vanish every star :
Night like a drunkard reels
Beyond the hills, to shun his flaming wheels :
The fields with flowers are deck'd in every hue,
The clouds with orient gold spangle their blue ;
Here is the pleasant place—
And nothing wanting is, save She, alas !

W. Drummond of Hawthornden.

SONNET

Frae bank to bank, frae wood to wood I rin,
  Owrehailit with my feeble fantasie ;
  Like til a leaf that fallis frae a tree,
Or til a reed owreblawn with the win'.
Twa gods guides me : the ane of them is blin',
  Yea and a bairn brocht up in vanitie ;
The next a wife ingenrit of the sea,
And lichter nor a dauphin with her fin.

Unhappy is the man for evermair
  That tills the sand and sawis in the air ;
  But twice unhappier is he, I lairn,
That feedis in his heart a mad desire,
And follows on a woman throw the fire,
  Led by a blin', and teachit by a bairn.

Mark Alexander Boyd (1563-1601).

GLENLOGIE

Four-and-twenty nobles sits in the king's ha' ;
Bonnie Glenlogie is the flower amang them a'.

In cam Lady Jean skippin' on to the flair,
And she has chosen Glenlogie 'mang a' that was there.

She turned to his footman, and thus did she say :
' Oh, what is his name, and where does he stay ? '

' His name is Glenlogie when he is frae hame,
He's o' the gay Gordons, and John is his name.'

' Glenlogie, Glenlogie, an you will prove kind,
My love is laid on you : I'm telling my mind.'

He turned about lightly, as the Gordons does a',
' My thanks, Lady Jean—my love's promised awa.'

She called on her maidens her bed for to make,
Her rings and her jewels all from her to take.

In cam Jeanie's father, a wae man was he ;
Says : ' Ye'll wed with Drumfendrich—he's mair gold than
    he.'

Her father's own chaplain—a man of great skill,
He wrote him a letter—indited it weel.

The first line he looked at, a licht laugh laughed he ;
But ere he read through it, the tears blinded his e'e.

Oh, pale and wan looked she when Glenlogie cam in,
But e'en rosy grew she when Glenlogie sat doun.

' Turn round, Jeanie Melville, turn round to this side ;
And I'll be the bridegroom, and you'll be the bride.'

Oh, 'twas a merry wedding, and the portion doun told,
Of bonnie Jeanie Melville—scarce sixteen years old !

Anonymous.

THE BIRKS OF INVERMAY

The smiling morn, the breathing spring,
Invite the tuneful birds to sing;
And while they warble from each spray,
Love melts the universal lay.
Let us, Amanda, timely wise,
Like them improve the hour that flies,
And in soft raptures waste the day
Among the birks of Invermay.

For soon the winter of the year,
And age, life's winter, will appear ;
At this, thy living bloom will fade,
As that will strip the verdant shade :
Our taste of pleasure then is o'er ;
The feathered songsters love no more ;
And when they droop, and we decay,
Adieu the birks of Invermay.

David Malet (1700-1765).

TELL ME HOW TO WOO THEE

If doughty deeds my lady please,
  Right soon I'll mount my steed:
And strong his arm, and fast his seat,
  That bears frae me the meed.
I'll wear thy colours at my brow,
  Thy picture in my heart;
And he that bends not to thine eye,
  Shall rue it to his smart.

    Then tell me how to woo thee, love,
      O tell me how to woo thee!
    For thy dear sake, nae care I'll take,
      Though ne'er another trow me.

If gay attire delight thine eye,
  I'll dight me in array;
I'll tend thy chamber-door all night,
  And squire thee all the day.
If sweetest sounds can win thine ear,
  These sounds I'll strive to catch;
Thy voice I'll steal to woo thysel,
  That voice that nane can match.

    Then tell me how to woo thee, love,
      O tell me how to woo thee!
    For thy dear sake, nae care I'll take,
      Though ne'er another trow me.

But if fond love thy heart can gain,
  I never broke a vow;
Nae maiden lays her skaith to me;
  I never loved but you.

For you alone I ride the ring,
  For you I wear the blue ;
For you alone I strive to sing—
  O tell me how to woo !

Graham of Gartmore.

OWER THE MUIR

Ower the muir amang the heather,
Ower the muir amang the heather,
There I met a bonnie lassie
Keepin' a' her ewes thegither.

Comin' through the craigs o' Kyle,
  Amang the bonnie bloomin' heather,
There I met a bonnie lassie,
  Keepin' a' her ewes thegither.

Says I, My dear, where is thy hame ?
  In muir or dale, pray tell me whether ?
Says she, I tent the fleecy flocks
  That feed amang the bloomin' heather.

We laid us doon upon a bank,
  Sae warm and sunnie was the weather ;
She left her flocks at large to rove
  Amang the bonnie bloomin' heather.

While thus we lay, she sang a sang,
  Till echo rang a mile and further ;
And aye the burden o' the sang
  Was, Ower the muir amang the heather.

She charmed my heart, and aye sin syne
  I couldna think on ony ither ;

By sea and sky ! she shall be mine,
　The bonnie lass amang the heather.

　Ower the muir amang the heather,
　Ower the muir amang the heather,
　There I met a bonnie lassie
　Keepin' a' her flocks thegither.

Jean Glover.

TO YOU LET SNOW AND ROSES...

To you, let snow and roses
　And golden locks belong.
These are the world's enslavers,
　Let these delight the throng.
For her of duskier lustre
　Whose favour still I wear,
The snow be in her kirtle,
　The rose be in her hair !

The hue of highland rivers
　Careering, full and cool,
From sable on to golden,
　From rapid on to pool—
The hue of heather-honey,
　The hue of honey-bees,
Shall tinge her golden shoulder,
　Shall gild her tawny knees.

Robert Louis Stevenson.

THE ROVER O' LOCH RYAN

The rover o' Loch Ryan he's gane,
  Wi' his merry men sae brave;
Their herts are o' the steel, an' a braver, better keel
  Ne'er bowled ower the back o' a wave.
It's no when the loch lies deid in its troch,
  When naethin' disturbs it ava;
But the rack an' the ride o' the restless tide,
  Or the splash o' the grey sea-maw.

It's no when the yawl an' the licht skiffs crawl
  Ower the breist o' the siller sea,
That I look to the west for the bark I lo'e best,
  An' the rover that's dear to me;
But when the clùd lays its cheek to the flood,
  An' the sea lays its shouther to the shore;
When the wund sings high, an' the sea whaups cry,
  As they rise frae the whitenin' roar.

It's then that I look to the thickenin' rook,
  An' watch by the midnicht tide;
I ken the wund brings my gallant rover hame,
  An' the sea that he glories to ride.
O merry sits he 'mang his gallant crew
  Wi' the helm-heft in his hand;
An' he sings alood to his lads in blue,
  As his een are on Galloway's land.

' Unstent an' slack each reef an' tack,
  Gie her sail, lads, while it may sit;
She has roared through a heavier sea afore,
  An' she'll roar through a heavier yit.

When landsmen sleep, or wake an' creep,
    In the tempest's angry moan
We dash through the drift, an' sing to the lift
    O' the wave that heaves us on.'

                                    Hew Ainslie.

THE GAY GOSS HAWK

' O Waly, waly, my gay goss hawk,
    ' Gin your feathering be sheen ! '
' And waly, waly, my master dear,
    ' Gin ye look pale and lean !

' O have ye tint, at tournament,
    ' Your sword, or yet your spear ?
' Or mourn ye for the southern lass,
    ' Whom you may not win near ? '

' I have not tint, at tournament,
    ' My sword, nor yet my spear ;
' But sair I mourn for my true love,
    ' Wi' mony a bitter tear.

' But weel's me on ye, my gay goss hawk,
    ' Ye can baith speak and flee ;
' Ye sall carry a letter to my love,
    ' Bring an answer back to me.'

' But how sall I your true love find,
    ' Or how suld I her know ?
' I bear a tongue ne'er wi' her spake,
    ' An eye that ne'er her saw.'

' O weel sall ye my true love ken,
    ' Sae sune as ye her see ;

'For, of a' the flowers of fair England,
    'The fairest flower is she.

'The red, that's on my true love's cheik,
    'Is like blood drops on the snaw;
'The white, that is on her breast bare,
    'Like the down o' the white sea-maw.

'And even at my love's bour door
    'There grows a flowering birk;
'And ye maun sit and sing thereon
    'As she gangs to the kirk.

'And four-and-twenty fair ladyes
    'Will to the mass repair;
'But weel may ye my ladye ken,
    'The fairest ladye there.'

Lord William has written a love letter,
    Put it under his pinion gray;
And he is awa' to Southern land
    As fast as wings can gae.

And even at that ladye's bour
    There grew a flowering birk;
And he sat down and sung thereon
    As she gaed to the kirk.

And weel he kent that ladye fair
    Amang her maidens free;
For the flower, that springs in May morning,
    Was not sae sweet as she.

He lighted at the ladye's yate,
    And sat him on a pin;
And sang fu' sweet the notes o' love,
    Till a' was cosh within.

And first he sang a low low note,
   And syne he sang a clear ;
And aye the o'erword o' the sang
   Was—' Your love can no win here.'

' Feast on, feast on, my maidens a',
   ' The wine flows you amang,
' While I gang to my shot-window,
   ' And hear yon bonny bird's sang.

' Sing on, sing on, my bonny bird,
   ' The sang ye sung yestreen ;
' For weel I ken, by your sweet singing,
   ' Ye are frae my true love sen.'

O first he sang a merry sang,
   And syne he sang a grave ;
And syne he peck'd his feathers gray,
   To her the letter gave.

' Have there a letter from lord William ;
   ' He says he's sent ye three.
' He canna wait your love langer,
   ' But for your sake he'll die.'

' Gae bid him bake his bridal bread,
   ' And brew his bridal ale ;
' And I shall meet him at Mary's kirk,
   ' Lang, lang ere it be stale.'

The lady's gane to her chamber,
   And a moanfu' woman was she ;
As gin she had ta'en a sudden brash,
   And were about to die.

' A boon, a boon, my father deir,
  ' A boon I beg of thee ! '
' Ask not that paughty Scottish lord,
  ' For him you ne'er shall see.

' But, for your honest asking else,
  ' Weel granted it shall be.'
' Then, gin I die in Southern land,
  ' In Scotland gar bury me.

' And the first kirk that ye come to,
  ' Ye's gar the mass be sung;
' And the next kirk that ye come to,
  ' Ye's gar the bells be rung.

' And when ye come to St. Mary's kirk,
  ' Ye's tarry there till night.'
And so her father pledged his word,
  And so his promise plight.

She has ta'en her to her bigly bour
  As fast as she could fare;
And she has drank a sleeping draught,
  That she had mix'd wi' care.

And pale, pale grew her rosy cheek,
  That was sae bright of blee.
And she seemed to be as surely dead
  As ony ane could be.

Then spak her cruel step-minnie,
  ' Tak ye the burning lead,
' And drap a drap on her bosome,
  ' To try if she be dead.'

They took a drap o' boiling lead,
  They drapp'd it on her breast;

' Alas ! alas ! ' her father cried,
  ' She's dead without the priest.'

She neither chatter'd with her teeth,
  Nor shiver'd with her chin ;
' Alas ! alas ! ' her father cried,
  ' There is nae breath within.'

Then up arose her seven brethren,
  And hew'd to her a bier ;
They hew'd it frae the solid aik,
  Laid it o'er wi' silver clear.

Then up and gat her seven sisters,
  And sewed to her a kell ;
And every steek that they put in
  Sewed to a siller bell.

The first Scots kirk that they cam to,
  They gar'd the bells be rung ;
The next Scots kirk that they cam to,
  They gar'd the mass be sung.

But when they cam to St. Mary's kirk,
  There stude spearmen all on a raw;
And up and started lord William,
  The chieftane amang them a'.

' Set down, set down the bier,' he said;
  ' Let me look her upon : '
But as soon as lord William touched her hand,
  Her colour began to come.

She brightened like the lily flower,
  Till her pale colour was gone;
With rosy cheik, and ruby lip,
  She smiled her love upon.

' A morsel of your bread, my lord,
  ' And one glass of your wine :
' For I hae fasted these three lang days,
  ' All for your sake and mine.

' Gae hame, gae hame, my seven bauld brothers !
  ' Gae hame and blaw your horn !
' I trow ye wad hae gi'en me the skaith,
  ' But I've gi'en you the scorn.

' Commend me to my grey father,
  ' That wish'd my saul gude rest;
' But wae be to my cruel step-dame,
  ' Gar'd burn me on the breast.'

' Ah ! woe to you, you light woman !
  ' An ill death may you die !
' For we left father and sisters at hame
  ' Breaking their hearts for thee.'

                                        Old Ballad.

QUEEN MARY'S ESCAPE

Put off, put off, and row with speed,
For now is the time and the hour of need!
To oars, to oars, and trim the bark,
Nor Scotland's queen be a warder's mark!
Yon light that plays round the castle's moat
Is only the warder's random shot;
Put off, put off, and row with speed,
For now is the time and the hour of need!

Those pond'rous keys shall the kelpies keep,
And lodge in their caverns dark and deep;
Nor shall Lochleven's towers or hall,
Hold thee, our lovely Queen in thrall,
Or be the haunt of traitors, sold,
While Scotland has hands and hearts so bold;
Then oarsmen, oarsmen, on with speed,
For now is the time and the hour of need!

Hark! the alarum bell hath rung,
And the warder's voice hath treason sung!
The echoes to the falconet's roar,
Chime sweetly to the dashing oar.
Let tower and hall, and battlements gleam—
We steer by the light of the taper's beam;
For Scotland and Mary, on with speed,
Now, now is the time and the hour of need!

Robert Allan.

TO KING JAMES IV

My prince in God gife thee guid grace,
Joy, glaidness, comfort, and solace,
Play, pleasance, mirth, and merrie cheer,
In hansel of this guid new year.

God gife to thee ane blissed chance,
And of all virtue abundance,
And grace aye for to persevere,
In hansel of this guid new year.

God gife thee guid prosperitie,
Fair fortoun and felicitie,
Evermair in earth while thou be here,
In hansel of this guid new year.

The heavenlie Lord his help thee send,
Thy realm to rule and to defend,
In peace and justice it to steer,
In hansel of this guid new year.

God gife thee bliss wherever thou bounes,
And send thee many Frauncè crounes,
Hie liberal heart, and handis nocht sweir,
In hansel of this guid new year.

William Dunbar.

TO QUEEN MARY

Welcome, illustrate Ladye, and our Queen ;
Welcome, our Lion with the Fleur de Lys ;
Welcome our Thistle with the Lorraine green ;
Welcome our rubent Rose upon the rise ;
Welcome our Gem and joyful Genetrice ;
Welcome our Belle of Albion to bear ;
Welcome our pleasant Princess maist of price !
God give you grace against this guid New Year.

This guid New Year we hope, with grace of God,
Shall be of peace, tranquillity, and rest ;
This year shall Right and Reason rule the Rod,
Which so long season has been sore supprest ;
This year firm Faith shall freely be confesst,
And all erroneous questions put arrear ;
To labour that this Life among us lest,
God give you grace against this guid New Year.

                                        Alexander Scott.

KINMONT WILLIE

O have ye na heard o' the fause Sakelde ?
    O have ye na heard o' the keen Lord Scroope ?
How they ha'e ta'en bauld Kinmont Willie,
    On Haribee to hang him up ?

Had Willie had but twenty men,
    But twenty men as stout as he,
Fause Sakelde had never the Kinmont ta'en,
    Wi' eight score in his companie.

They band his legs beneath the steed,
 They tied his hands behind his back,
They guarded him, fivesome on each side,
 And they brought him owre the Liddel-rack.

They led him through the Liddel-rack,
 And also through the Carlisle sands;
They brought him to Carlisle castle,
 To be at my Lord Scroope's commands.

'My hands are tied, but my tongue is free,
 And wha will dare this deed avow?
Or answer by the Border law?
 Or answer to the bauld Buccleuch?'

'Now haud thy tongue, thou rank reiver!
 There's never a Scot shall set thee free:
Before ye cross my castle yett,
 I trow ye shall take farewell o' me.'

'Fear na ye that, my lord,' quo' Willie:
 'By the faith o' my body, Lord Scroope,' he said,
'I never yet lodged in a hostelrie,
 But I paid my lawing before I gaed.'

Now word is gane to the bauld Keeper,
 In Branksome Ha', where that he lay,
That Lord Scroope has ta'en the Kinmont Willie,
 Between the hours of night and day.

He has ta'en the table wi' his hand,
 He gar'd the red wine spring on hie—
'Now Christ's curse on my head,' he said,
 'But avengèd of Lord Scroope I'll be!

' O is my basnet a widow's curch?
    Or my lance a wand of the willow-tree?
Or my arm a lady's lily hand,
    That an English lord should lightly me?

' And have they ta'en him, Kinmont Willie,
    Against the truce of Border tide?
And forgotten that the bauld Buccleuch
    Is Keeper here on the Scottish side?

' And have they e'en ta'en him, Kinmont Willie,
    Withouten either dread or fear?
And forgotten that the bauld Buccleuch
    Can back a steed, or shake a spear?

' O were there war between the lands,
    As well I wot that there is none,
I would slight Carlisle castle high,
    Though it were builded of marble stone.

' I would set that castle in a lowe,
    And sloken it with English blood:
There's never a man in Cumberland,
    Should ken where Carlisle castle stood.

' But since nae war's between the lands,
    And there is peace, and peace should be;
I'll neither harm English lad or lass,
    And yet the Kinmont freed shall be!'

He has called him forty marchmen bauld,
    I trow they were of his ain name,
Except Sir Gilbert Elliot, called
    The Laird of Stobs, I mean the same.

He has called him forty marchmen bauld,
   Were kinsmen to the bauld Buccleuch;
With spur on heel, and splent on spauld,
   And gloves of green, and feathers blue.

There were five and five before them a',
   Wi' hunting-horns and bugles bright:
And five and five came wi' Buccleuch,
   Like warden's men, arrayed for fight.

And five and five, like a mason gang,
   That carried the ladders lang and hie;
And five and five, like broken men;
   And so they reached the Woodhouselee.

And as we crossed the Bateable land,
   When to the English side we held,
The first o' men that we met wi',
   Wha should it be but fause Sakelde?

'Where be ye gaun, ye hunters keen?'
   Quo' fause Sakelde; 'come tell to me!'
'We go to hunt an English stag,
   Has trespassed on the Scots countrie.'

'Where be ye gaun, ye marshall men?'
   Quo' fause Sakelde; 'come tell me true!
'We go to catch a rank reiver,
   Has broken faith wi' the bauld Buccleuch.'

'Where are ye gaun, ye mason lads,
   Wi' a' your ladders, lang and hie?'
'We gang to herry a corbie's nest,
   That wons not far frae Woodhouselee.'

'Where be ye gaun, ye broken men?'
   Quo' fause Sakelde; 'come tell to me!'
Now Dickie of Dryhope led that band,
   And the never a word of lear had he.

'Why trespass ye on the English side?
   Row-footed outlaws, stand!' quo' he;
The never a word had Dickie to say,
   Sae he thrust the lance through his fause body.

Then on we held for Carlisle toun,
   And at Staneshaw-bank the Eden we crossed;
The water was great and meikle of spate,
   But the never a horse nor man we lost.

And when we reached the Staneshaw-bank,
   The wind was rising loud and hie;
And there the laird gar'd leave our steeds,
   For fear that they should stamp and neigh.

And when we left the Staneshaw-bank
   The wind began full loud to blaw;
But 'twas wind and weet, and fire and sleet,
   When we came beneath the castle wa'.

We crept on knees, and held our breath,
   Till we placed the ladders against the wa';
And sae ready was Buccleuch himsel'
   To mount the first before us a'.

He has ta'en the watchman by the throat,
   He flung him down upon the lead—
'Had there not been peace between our lands,
   Upon the other side thou hadst gaed!

' Now sound out, trumpets ! ' quo' Buccleuch ;
  ' Let's waken Lord Scroope right merrilie ! '
Then loud the warden's trumpet blew—
  O wha daur meddle wi' me ?

Then speedily to wark we gaed,
  And raised the slogan ane and a',
And cut a hole through a sheet of lead,
  And so we wan to the castle ha'.

They thought King James and a' his men
  Had won the house wi' bow and spear ;
It was but twenty Scots and ten,
  That put a thousand in sic a steir.

Wi' coulters, and wi' forehammers,
  We gar'd the bars bang merrilie,
Until we cam to the inner prison,
  Where Willie o' Kinmont he did lie.

And when we cam to the lower prison,
  Where Willie o' Kinmont he did lie—
' O sleep ye, wake ye. Kinmont Willie,
  Upon the morn that thou's to die ? '

' O I sleep saft, and I wake aft ;
  It's lang since sleeping was fley'd frae me !
Gi'e my service back to my wife and bairns,
  And a' gude fellows that speir for me.'

Then Red Rowan has hent him up,
  The starkest man in Teviotdale—
' Abide, abide now, Red Rowan,
  Till of my Lord Scroope I take farewell.

‘ Farewell, farewell, my gude Lord Scroope !
    My gude Lord Scroope, farewell ! ’ he cried ;
‘ I’ll pay you for my lodging mail,
    When first we meet on the Borderside.’

Then shoulder high, with shout and cry,
    We bore him down the ladder lang ;
At every stride Red Rowan made,
    I wot the Kinmont’s airns played clang.

‘ O mony a time,’ quo’ Kinmont Willie,
    ‘ I have ridden horse baith wild and wud ;
But a rougher beast than Red Rowan
    I ween my legs have ne’er bestrode.

‘ And mony a time,’ quo’ Kinmont Willie,
    ‘ I’ve prick’d a horse out owre the furs ;
But since the day I backed a steed,
    I never wore sic cumbrous spurs ! ’

We scarce had won the Staneshaw-bank,
    When a’ the Carlisle bells were rung,
And a thousand men on horse and foot,
    Cam wi’ the keen Lord Scroope along.

Buccleuch has turned to Eden Water,
    Even where it flowed frae bank to brim,
And he has plunged in wi’ a’ his band,
    And safely swam them through the stream.

He turned him on the other side,
    And at Lord Scroope his glove flung he—
‘ If ye like na my visit in merry England,
    In fair Scotland come visit me ! ’

All sore astonished stood Lord Scroope,
    He stood as still as rock of stane ;

He scarcely dared to trow his eyes,
  When through the water they had gane.
' He is either himsel' a devil frae hell,
  Or else his mother a witch maun be;
I wadna have ridden that wan water
  For a' the gowd in Christentie.'

Ballad.

THE TRIBUTE OF GASK TO THE KING (1364)

Noo ken ye the gift Gask has brocht to the King?
'Tis an offering sae regal, sae perfect and fair,
Than jewels o' siller mair dainty and rare,
A croun for a maid or a monarch to wear.
The courtier's tribute is but a puir thing ;
For what can he offer, and what can he bring
Like the croun o' white roses frae Gask to the king ?

Noo ken ye the service Gask does for the King ?
A' for his sake in the sweet o' the year,
In the gardens o' Gask the white roses appear,
The royal white roses to Scotland sae dear.
Then far ower Strathearn let the praise o' them ring,
Let them live once again in the sang that we sing :
The croun o' white roses frae Gask to the King !

Noo ken ye what Gask will still do for the King ?
In the days that may come when the roses are dead,
When the pledge is forgotten, the vows left unsaid,
What then shall be found for an offering instead ?
O then at his feet his heart will he fling,
Truth, honour, devotion as tribute will bring
For the Croun o' White Roses frae Gask to the King !

Margaret Ethel Blair-Oliphant.

BRUCE BEFORE BANNOCKBURN

Scots, wha hae wi' Wallace bled,
Scots, wham Bruce has aften led,
Welcome to your gory bed,
   Or to victorie.

Now's the day, and now's the hour ;
See the front of battle lour ;
See approach proud Edward's power—
   Chains and slaverie !

Wha will be a traitor knave ?
Wha can fill a coward's grave ?
Wha sae base as be a slave ?
   Let him turn and flee !

Wha for Scotland's King and Law
Freedom's sword will strongly draw,
Free-man stand, or free-man fa' ?
   Let him follow me !

By Oppression's woes and pains !
By your sons in servile chains !
We will drain our dearest veins,
   But they shall be free !

Lay the proud usurpers low !
Tyrants fall in every foe !
Liberty's in every blow !
   Let us do, or die !

                       Burns.

THE BATTLE OF THE RED HARLAW

' Now haud your tongue, baith wife and carle,
   And listen, great and sma',
And I will sing of Glenallan's Earl
   That fought on the red Harlaw.

' The cronach's cried on Bennachie,
   And doun the Don and a',
And hieland and lawland may mournfu' be
   For the sair field of Harlaw.—

' They saddled a hundred milk-white steeds,
   They hae bridled a hundred black,
With a chafron of steel on each horse's head,
   And a good knight upon his back.'—

' They hadna ridden a mile, a mile,
   A mile, but barely ten,
When Donald came branking down the brae
   Wi' twenty thousand men.

' Their tartans they were waving wide,
   Their glaives were glancing clear,
The pibrochs rung frae side to side,
   Would deafen ye to hear.

' The great Earl in his stirrups stood
   That Highland host to see :
" Now here a knight that's stout and good
   May prove a jeopardie :

' " What wouldst thou do, my squire so gay,
   That rides beside my reyne,
Were ye Glenallan's Earl the day,
   And I were Roland Cheyne ?

' " To turn the rein were sin and shame,
   To fight were wondrous peril,
What would ye do now, Roland Cheyne,
   Were ye Glenallan's Earl ? "

' " Were I Glenallan's Earl this tide,
   And ye were Roland Cheyne,
The spur should be in my horse's side,
   And the bridle upon his mane.

' " If they hae twenty thousand blades,
   And we twice ten times ten,
Yet they hae but their tartan plaids,
   And we are mail-clad men.

' " My horse shall ride through ranks sae rude,
   As through the moorland fern,
Then ne'er let gentle Norman blude
   Grow cauld for Highland kerne." '

THE ANTIQUARY, *Scott.*

KILLIECRANKIE

On the heights of Killiecrankie
   Yester-morn our army lay :
Slowly rose the mist in columns
   From the river's broken way ;
Hoarsely roared the swollen torrent,
   And the pass was wrapped in gloom,
When the clansmen rose together
   From their lair amidst the broom.
Then we belted on our tartans,
   And our bonnets down we drew,
And we felt our broadswords' edges,

And we proved them keen and true;
And we prayed the prayer of soldiers,
    And we yelled the gathering-cry,
And we clasped the hands of kinsmen,
    And we swore to do or die!
Then our leader rose before us
    On his war-horse black as night—
Well the Cameronian rebels
    Knew that charger in the fight!—
And a cry of exultation
    From the bearded warriors rose;
For we loved the house of Claver'se,
    And we thought of good Montrose.
But he raised his hand for silence:
    'Soldiers! I have sworn a vow—
Ere the evening star shall glisten
    On Schehallion's lofty brow,
Either we shall rest in triumph,
    Or another of the Graemes
Shall have died in battle-harness
    For his Country and King James!
Strike this day as if the anvil
    Lay beneath your blows the while,
Be they covenanting traitors,
    Or the brood of false Argyle!
Strike! and drive the trembling rebels
    Backwards o'er the stormy Forth;
Let them tell their pale Convention
    How they fared within the North.
Let them tell! that Highland honour
    Is not to be bought nor sold,

That we scorn their prince's anger
  As we loathe his foreign gold.
Strike ! and when the fight is over,
  If ye look in vain for me,
Where the dead are lying thickest,
  Search for him that was Dundee !'

.   .   .   .

Through the scattered wood of birches,
  O'er the broken ground and heath,
Wound the long battalion slowly,
  Till they gained the field beneath;
Then we bounded from our covert :
  Judge how looked the Saxons then,
When they saw the rugged mountain
  Start to life with armèd men !
Like a tempest down the ridges
  Swept the hurricane of steel,
Rose the slogan of MacDonald—
  Flashed the broadsword of Lochiel !
Vainly sped the withering volley
  'Mongst the foremost of our band—
On we poured until we met them,
  Foot to foot, and hand to hand.
Horse and man went down like drift-wood
  When the floods are black at Yule,
And their carcasses were whirling
  In the Garry's deepest pool,
Horse and man went down before us—
  Living foe there tarried none
On the field of Killiecrankie,
  When that stubborn fight was done !

And the evening star was shining
  On Schehallion's distant head,
When we wiped our bloody broadswords,
  And returned to count the dead.
There we found him gashed and gory,
  Stretched upon the cumbered plain,
As he told us where to seek him,
  In the thickest of the slain.
And a smile was on his visage,
  For within his dying ear
Pealed the joyful note of triumph,
  And the clansmen's clamorous cheer:
So, amidst the battle's thunder,
  Shot, and steel, and scorching flame,
In the glory of his manhood
  Passed the spirit of the Graeme!

Open wide the vaults of Atholl,
  Where the bones of heroes rest—
Open wide the hallowed portals
  To receive another guest!
Last of Scots, and last of freemen—
  Last of all that dauntless race
Who would rather die unsullied
  Than outlive the land's disgrace!
         William Edmondston Aytoun.

FLODDEN FIELD

The English shafts in volleys hailed,
In headlong charge their horse assailed:
Front, flank, and rear, the squadrons sweep
To break the Scottish circle deep,
    That fought around their king.
But yet, though thick the shafts as snow,
Though charging knights like whirlwinds go,
Though bill-men ply the ghastly blow,
    Unbroken was the ring;
The stubborn spearmen still made good
Their dark impenetrable wood,
Each stepping where his comrade stood,
    The instant that he fell.
No thought was there of dastard flight ;
Linked in the serried phalanx tight,
Groom fought like noble, squire like knight,
    As fearlessly and well;
Till utter darkness closed her wing
O'er their thin host and wounded king.
Then skilful Surrey's sage commands
Led back from strife his shattered bands ;
    And from the charge they drew,
As mountain-waves from wasted lands
    Sweep back to ocean blue.
Then did their loss his foemen know :
Their king, their lords, their mightiest low,
They melted from the field as snow,
When streams are swoln and south winds blow,
    Dissolves in silent dew.

Tweed's echoes heard the ceaseless plash,
  While many a broken band,
Disordered, through her currents dash
  To gain the Scottish land;
To town and tower, to down and dale,
To tell red Flodden's dismal tale,
And raise the universal wail.
Tradition, legend, tune, and song
Shall many an age that wail prolong :
Still from the sire the son shall hear
Of the stern strife and carnage drear
  Of Flodden's fatal field,
Where shivered was fair Scotland's spear,
  And broken was her shield !

MARMION, *Scott*.

Scott

THE FLOWERS OF THE FOREST

I've heard the liltin' at our yowe-milkin',
  Lasses a-liltin' before the dawn o' day;
But now they are moanin' in ilka green loanin'.—
  The Flowers o' the Forest are a' wede away.

At buchts in the mornin', nae blythe lads are scornin',
  The lasses are lonely, and dowie, and wae;
Nae daffin', nae gabbin', but sighin' and sabbin',
  Ilk ane lifts her leglen and hies her away.

In hairst, at the shearin', nae youths now are jeerin',
   The bandsters are lyart, and runkled, and grey;
At fair, or at preachin', nae wooin', nae fleechin'—
   The Flowers o' the Forest are a' wede away.

At e'en, at the gloamin', nae swankies are roamin',
   'Bout stacks wi' the lasses at bogle to play;
But ilk ane sits drearie, lamentin' her dearie—
   The Flowers o' the Forest are a' wede away.

Dule and wae for the order sent our lads to the Border!
   The English, for ance, by guile wan the day;
The Flowers o' the Forest, that focht aye the foremaist,
   The prime o' our land, are cauld in the clay.

We'll hear nae mair liltin' at our yowe-milkin',
   Women and bairns are heartless and wae;
Sighin' and moanin' on ilka green loanin'—
   The Flowers o' the Forest are a' wede away.

Jean Elliot.

THE WIDOW'S LAMENT

   Ma lüve built me a bonnie boo'er,
   An' cled it a' wi' lily floo'er;
   A brawer boo'er ye ne'er did see—
   Than ma true lüve he built for me.

   There cam a man by middle-day,
   He spied his sport an' went away;
   An' brocht the king at deid o' nicht,
   Wha brak ma boo'er an' slew ma knicht.

He slew ma knicht tae me sae dear,
He slew ma knicht an' poined his gear ;
Ma servants a' for life did flee,
An' left me in extremitie.

I sewed his sheet, makin' ma mane,
I watched the corpse masel alane ;
I watched beside it nicht an' day ;
Nae livin' cratur cam that way.

I took his bodie on ma back,
An' whiles I gaed and whiles I sat ;
I delved a grave an' laid him in,
An' happed him wi' the turf sae green.

But think na ye ma hert was sair,
When I laid the mools on his yellow hair ?
O think na ye ma hert was wae,
When I turned aboot awa tae gae ?

Nae livin' man I'll lo'e again,
Syne that ma bonnie knicht is slain !
Wi' ae lock o' his yellow hair
I'll chain ma hert for evermair !

Old Border Ballad.

THE TOOM SADDLE

Hie upon Hielands
    And low upon Tay,
Braw Geordie Campbell
    Rade oot on a day.

Saddled and bridled
    And gallant rade he ;

Hame cam his guid horse,
    But never cam he!

Oot cam his auld mither
    Greetin fu' sair,
An' oot cam his bride
    Rivin' her hair.

Saddled and bridled
    An' buited rade he;
Toom hame cam the saddle,
    But never cam he!

Saddled and bridled
    An' buited rade he,
A plume in his bonnet,
    A sword at his knee.

But toom cam his saddle
   A' bluidie to see;
Oh, hame cam his guid horse,
   But never cam he!

Anonymous.

THE TWA CORBIES

As I was walkin' a' ma lane,
I heard twa corbies makin' mane;
The tane until th' other did say:
'Where sall we gang and dine th' day?'

'In ahint yon auld fail dyke,
I wot there lies a new-slain knight;
And naebody kens that he lies there,
But his hawk, his hound, and his lady fair.

'His hound is to the hunting gane,
His hawk to fetch the wild-fowl hame,
His lady's taen another mate,
So we may mak our dinner sweet.

'Ye'll sit on his white hause-bane,
And I'll pike out his bonnie blue een:
Wi' ae lock o' his gowden hair,
We'll theek our nest when it grows bare.

'Mony a ane for him maks mane,
But nane sall ken where he is gane:
Ower his white banes when they are bare,
The wind sall blaw for evermair.'

Traditional.

FLORA MACDONALD'S LAMENT

Far over yon hills of the heather sae green,
  And doun by the corrie that sings to the sea,
The bonnie young Flora sat sighing her lane—
  The dew on her plaid, and the tear in her ee.
She looked at a boat, wi' the breezes that swung
  Away on the wave, like a bird of the main;
And aye as it lessened, she sighed and she sung:
  ' Fareweel to the lad I shall ne'er see again,
Fareweel to my hero, the gallant and young,
  Fareweel to the lad I shall ne'er see again ! '

The muir-cock that craws on the brow o' Ben Connal,
  He kens o' his bed in a sweet mossy hame;
The eagle that soars o'er the cliffs o' Clan Ronal',
  Unawed and unhunted, his eyrie can claim.
The solan can sleep on his shelf o' the shore,
  The cormorant roost on his rock o' the sea;
But ah ! there is one whose hard fate I deplore,
  Nor house, ha', nor hame, in this country has he.
The conflict is past, and our name is no more;
  There's nought left but sorrow for Scotland and me.

The target is torn from the arm of the just,
  The helmet is cleft on the brow of the brave,
The claymore for ever in darkness must rust;
  But red is the sword of the stranger and slave.
The hoof of the horse, and the foot of the proud
  Have trod o'er the plumes on the bonnets of blue:
Why slept the red bolt in the breast of the cloud,
  When tyranny revelled in blood of the true ?
Fareweel, my young hero, the gallant and good !
  The crown of thy fathers is torn from thy brow.

James Hogg.

JAMIE TELFER OF THE FAIR DODHEAD

It fell about the Martinmastide,
   When our Border steeds get corn and hay,
The Captain of Bewcastle hath bound him to ride,
   And he's owre to Tividale to drive a prey.

The first ae guide that they met wi',
   It was high up in Hardhaughswire;
The second guide that they met wi',
   It was laigh down in Borthwick water.

'What tidings, what tidings, my trusty guide?'
   'Nae tidings, nae tidings, I hae to thee;
But gin ye'll gae to the fair Dodhead,
   Mony a cow's calf I'll let thee see.'

And when they cam to the fair Dodhead,
   Right hastily they clam' the peel;
They loosed the kye out, ane and a',
   And ranshackled the house right weel.

Now Jamie Telfer's heart was sair,
   The tear aye rowing in his e'e;
He pled wi' the Captain to hae his gear,
   Or else revenged he wad be.

The Captain turned him round and leuch;
   Said, 'Man, there's naething in thy house
But ae auld sword without a sheath,
   That hardly now would fell a mouse.'

The sun wasna up, but the moon was down,
   It was the gryming of a new-fa'en snaw,
Jamie Telfer has run ten miles a-foot,
   Between the Dodhead and the Stob's Ha',

And when he cam to the fair tower yett,
   He shouted loud, and cried weel hie,
Till out bespak auld Gibby Elliot,
   ' Wha's this that brings the fray to me ? '

' It's I, Jamie Telfer o' the fair Dodhead,
   And a harried man I think I be !
There 's naething left at the fair Dodhead
   But a waefu' wife and bairnies three.'

' Gae seek your succour at Branksome Ha',
   For succour ye'se get nane frae me !
Gae seek you succour where ye paid black-mail,
   For, man, ye ne'er paid money to me.'

Jamie has turned him round about,
   I wat the tear blinded his ee,
' I'll ne'er pay mail to Elliot again,
   And the fair Dodhead I'll never see ! '

He has turned him to the Tiviot side,
   E'en as fast as he could drie,
Till he cam to the Coultart Cleugh,
   And there he shouted baith loud and hie.

Then up bespak him auld Jock Grieve,
   ' Wha's this that brings the fray to me ? '
' It's I, Jamie Telfer o' the fair Dodhead,
   A harried man I trow I be.

' There 's naething left in the fair Dodhead,
   But a greeting wife and bairnies three,
And sax poor ca's stand in the sta',
   A' routing loud for their minnie.'

' Alack a wae ! ' quo' auld Jock Grieve,
  ' Alack ! my heart is sair for thee !
For I was married on the elder sister,
  And you on the youngest of a' the three.'

Then he has ta'en out a bonnie black,
  Was right weel fed with corn and hay,
And he's set Jamie Telfer on his back,
  To the Catslockhill to tak the fray.

And when he cam to the Catslockhill,
  He shouted loud, and cried weel hie,
Till out and spak him William's Wat,
  ' O wha's this brings the fray to me ? '

' It's I, Jamie Telfer o' the fair Dodhead,
  A harried man I think I be !
The Captain of Bewcastle has driven my gear ;
  For God's sake rise, and succour me ! '

' Alas for wae ! ' quoth William's Wat,
  ' Alack, for thee my hear is sair !
I never cam by the fair Dodhead
  That ever I fand thy basket bare.'

He's set his twa sons on coal-black steeds,
  Himsel' upon a freckled grey,
And they are on wi' Jamie Telfer
  To Branksome Ha' to tak the fray.

And when they cam to Branksome Ha',
  They shouted a' baith loud and hie,
Till up and spak him auld Buccleuch,
  Said, ' Wha's this brings the fray to me ? '

' It's I, Jamie Telfer o' the fair Dodhead,
    And a harried man I think I be !
There's naught left in the fair Dodhead,
    But a greeting wife and bairnies three.'

' Alack for wae ! ' quoth the gude auld lord,
    ' And ever my heart is wae for thee !
But fye gar cry on Willie, my son,
    And see that he come to me speedilie !

' Gar warn the water, braid and wide,
    Gar warn it sune and hastilie !
They that winna ride for Telfer's kye,
    Let them never look in the face o' me !

' Warn Wat o' Harden, and his sons,
    Wi' them will Borthwick Water ride ;
Warn Gaudilands, and Allanhaugh,
    And Gilmanscleugh, and Commonside.

' Ride by the gate at Priesthaughswire,
    And warn the Currors o' the Lea ;
As ye come down the Hermitage Slack,
    Warn doughty Willie o' Gorrinberry.'

The Scotts they rade, the Scotts they ran,
    Sae starkly and sae steadily !
And aye the owre-word o' the thrang
    Was, ' Rise for Branksome readily ! '

The gear was driven the Frostylea up,
    Frae the Frostylea unto the plain,
When Willie has looked his men before,
    And saw the kye right fast drivand.

'Wha drives thir kye?' 'gan Willie say,
  'To make an outspeckle o' me?'
'It's I, the Captain o' Bewcastle, Willie;
  I winna layne my name for thee.'

'O will ye let Telfer's kye gae back?
  Or will ye do aught for regard o' me?
Or by the faith of my body,' quo' Willie Scott,
  'I 'se ware my dame's calfskin on thee!'

'I winna let the kye gae back,
  Neither for thy love, nor yet thy fear;
But I will drive Jamie Telfer's kye,
  In spite of every Scott that 's here.'

'Set on them, lads!' quo' Willie then;
  'Fye, lads, set on them cruellie!
For ere they win to the Ritterford,
  Mony a toom saddle there sall be!'

Then til't they gaed, wi' heart and hand,
  The blows fell thick as bickering hail;
And mony a horse ran masterless,
  And mony a comely cheek was pale.

But Willie was stricken owre the head,
  And through the knapscap the sword has gane;
And Harden grat for very rage
  When Willie on the grund lay slain.

But he 's ta'en aff his gude steel cap,
  And thrice he 's waved it in the air;
The Dinlay snaw was ne'er mair white
  Nor the lyart locks of Harden's hair.

'THE SCOTTS HAD GOTTEN THE VICTORY'

'Revenge! revenge!' auld Wat 'gan cry;
　'Fye, lads, lay on them cruellie!
We'll ne'er see Tiviotside again,
　Or Willie's death revenged sall be.'

O mony a horse ran masterless,
　The splintered lances flew on hie;
But or they wan to the Kershope ford,
　The Scotts had gotten the victory.

John o' Brigham there was slain,
　And John o' Barlow, as I hear say;
And thirty mae o' the Captain's men
　Lay bleeding on the grund that day.

The Captain was run through the thick of the thigh
　And broken was his right leg bane;
If he had lived this hundred years,
　He had never been loved by woman again.

'Ha'e back the kye!' the Captain said;
　'Dear kye, I trow, to some they be!
For gin I suld live a hundred years,
　There will ne'er fair lady smile on me.'

Then word is gane to the Captain's bride,
　Even in the bower where that she lay,
That her lord was prisoner in enemy's land,
　Since into Tividale he had led the way.

'I wad lourd have had a winding-sheet,
　And helped to put it owre his head,
Ere he had been disgraced by the Border Scott,
　When he owre Liddel his men did lead!'

There was a wild gallant amang us a',
　His name was Watty wi' the Wudspurs,
Cried, ' On for his house in Stanegirthside,
　If ony man will ride with us ! '

When they cam to the Stanegirthside,
　They dang wi' trees, and burst the door;
They loosed out a' the Captain's kye,
　And set them forth our lads before.

There was an auld wife ayont the fire,
　A wee bit o' the Captain's kin :
' Wha dare loose out the Captain's kye,
　Or answer to him and his men ? '

' It 's I, Watty Wudspurs, loose the kye,
　I winna layne my name frae thee !
And I will loose out the Captain's kye,
　In scorn of a' his men and he.'

When they cam to the fair Dodhead,
　They were a welcome sight to see !
For instead of his ain ten milk kye,
　Jamie Telfer has gotten thirty and three.

And he has paid the rescue shot,
　Baith wi' gowd and white monie ;
And at the burial o' Willie Scott,
　I wat was mony a weeping ee.

Old Border Ballad.

IT IS NOT YOURS, O MOTHER, TO COMPLAIN

It is not yours, O mother, to complain,
　Not, mother, yours to weep,
Though nevermore your son again
　Shall to your bosom creep,
　Though nevermore again you watch your baby sleep.

Though in the greener paths of earth,
　Mother and child no more
We wander; and no more the birth
　Of me whom once you bore
　Seems still the brave reward that once it seemed of yore ;

Though as all passes, day and night,
　The seasons and the years,
From you, O mother, this delight,
　This also disappears—
　Some profit yet survives of all your pangs and tears.

The child, the seed, the grain of corn,
　The acorn on the hill,
Each for some separate end is born
　In season fit, and still
　Each must in strength arise to work the almighty will.

So from the hearth the children flee
　By that almighty hand
Austerely led ; so one by sea
　Goes forth, and one by land ;
　Nor aught of all man's sons escapes from that command.

So from the sally each obeys
  The unseen almighty nod;
So till the ending all their ways
  Blindfolded loth have trod:
  Nor knew their task at all, but were the tools of God.

And as the fervent smith of yore
  Beat out the glowing blade,
Nor wielded in the front of war
  The weapons that he made,
  But in the tower at home still plied his ringing trade;

So like a sword the son shall roam
  On nobler missions sent;
And as the smith remained at home
  In peaceful turret pent,
  So sits the while at home the mother well content.

Robert Louis Stevenson.

PROUD MARGARET

'Twas on a night, an evening bright,
  When the dew began to fa',
Lady Margaret was walking up and down,
  Looking o'er her castle wa'.

She looked east, and she looked west,
  To see what she could spy,
When a gallant knight came in her sight,
  And to the gate drew nigh.

' You seem to be no gentleman,
  ' You wear your boots so wide;
' But you seem to be some cunning hunter,
  ' You wear the horn so syde.'

' I am no cunning hunter,' he said,
  ' Nor ne'er intend to be ;
' But I am come to this castle
  ' To seek the love of thee ;
' And if you do not grant me love,
  ' This night for thee I'll die.'

' If you should die for me, sir knight,
  ' There's few for you will mane,
' For mony a better has died for me,
  ' Whose graves are growing green.

' But ye maun read my riddle,' she said,
  ' And answer my questions three ;
' And but ye read them right,' she said,
  ' Gae stretch ye out and die.—

' Now what is the flower, the ae first flower,
  ' Springs either on moor or dale ?
' And what is the bird, the bonnie bonnie bird,
  ' Sings on the evening gale ? '

' The primrose is the ae first flower,
  ' Springs either on moor or dale ;
' And the thistlecock is the bonniest bird,
  ' Sings on the evening gale.'

' But what's the little coin,' she said,
  ' Wald buy my castle bound ?
' And what's the little boat,' she said,
  ' Can sail the world all round ? '

' O hey, how mony small pennies
  ' Make thrice three thousand pound ?

'Or hey, how mony small fishes
    'Swim a' the salt sea round?'

'I think ye maun be my match,' she said,
    'My match, and something mair;
'You are the first e'er got the grant
    'Of love frae my father's heir.

'My father was lord of nine castles,
    'My mother lady of three;
'My father was lord of nine castles,
    'And there's nane to heir but me.

'And round about a' thae castles,
    'You may baith plow and saw,
'And on the fifteenth day of May,
    'The meadows they will maw.'

'O hald your tongue, lady Margaret,' he said,
    'For loud I hear you lie!
'Your father was lord of nine castles,
    'Your mother was lady of three;
'Your father was lord of nine castles,
    'But ye fa' heir to but three.

'And round about a' thae castles,
    'You may baith plow and saw,
'But on the fifteenth day of May
    'The meadows will not maw.

'I am your brother Willie,' he said,
    'I trow ye ken na me;
'I came to humble your haughty heart,
    'Has gar'd sae mony die.'

'If ye be my brother Willie,' she said,
  'As I trow weel ye be,
'This night I'll neither eat nor drink,
  'But gae alang wi' thee.'

'O hald your tongue, lady Margaret,' he said,
  'Again I hear you lie;
'For ye've unwashen hands, and ye've unwashen feet,
  'To gae to clay wi' me.

'For the wee worms are my bedfellows,
  'And cauld clay is my sheets;
'And when the stormy winds do blow,
  'My body lies and sleeps.' *Old Ballad.*

EPISTLE TO A YOUNG FRIEND

I lang hae thought, my youthfu' friend,
  A something to have sent you,
Tho' it should serve nae ither end
  Than just a kind memento :
But how the subject-theme may gang,
  Let time and chance determine ;
Perhaps it may turn out a sang ;
  Perhaps, turn out a sermon.

Ye'll try the world soon, my lad ;
  And, Andrew dear, believe me,
Ye'll find mankind an unco squad,
  And muckle they may grieve ye :
For care and trouble set your thought
  Ev'n when your end's attained ;
And a' your views may come to nought,
  Where ev'ry nerve is strained.

I'll no say men are villains a';
 The real, harden'd wicked,
Wha hae nae check but human law,
 Are to a few restricked;
But, och! mankind are unco weak,
 An' little to be trusted;
If *self* the wavering balance shake,
 It's rarely right adjusted!

Yet they wha fa' in fortune's strife,
 Their fate we shouldna censure;
For still, th' important end o' life
 They equally may answer;
A man may hae an honest heart,
 Tho' poortith hourly stare him;
A man may tak a neibor's part,
 Yet hae nae cash to spare him.

Ay free, aff han', your story tell,
 When wi' a bosom crony;
But still keep something to yoursel
 Ye scarcely tell to ony:
Conceal yoursel as weel's ye can
 Frae critical dissection;
But keek thro' ev'ry other man,
 Wi' sharpen'd sly inspection.

The sacred lowe o' weel-placed love,
 Luxuriantly indulge it;
But never tempt th' illicit rove
 Tho' naething should divulge it:

I wave the quantum o' the sin,
   The hazard of concealing;
But, och! it hardens a' within,
   And petrifies the feeling!

To catch Dame Fortune's golden smile,
   Assiduous wait upon her;
And gather gear by ev'ry wile
   That's justify'd by honor;
Not for to hide it in a hedge,
   Nor for a train attendant;
But for the glorious privilege
   Of being independent.

The fear o' Hell's a hangman's whip,
   To haud the wretch in order;
But where ye feel your honour grip,
   Let that ay be your border:
Its slightest touches, instant pause—
   Debar a' side-pretences;
And resolutely keeps its laws
   Uncaring consequences.

The great Creator to revere,
   Must sure become the creature;
But still the preaching cant forbear,
   And ev'n the rigid feature:
Yet ne'er with wits profane to range,
   Be complaisance extended;
An atheist laugh's a poor exchange
   For Deity offended!

When ranting round in pleasure's ring,
   Religion may be blinded;
Or if she gie a random sting,
   It may be little minded;
But when on life we're tempest-driv'n—
   A conscience but a canker—
A correspondence fixed wi' Heav'n,
   Is sure a noble anchor!

Adieu, dear, amiable youth!
   Your heart can ne'er be wanting!
May prudence, fortitude, and truth,
   Erect your brow undaunting!
In ploughman phrase, 'God send ye speed,'
   Still daily to grow wiser;
And may ye better reck the rede
   Than ever did th' adviser!

Burns.

THE NICHT IS NEIR GONE

Hay! nou the day dauis;
The jolie Cok crauis.
Nou shroudis the shauis,
   Throu Natur anone.
The thissell-cok cryis
On lovers wha lyis:
Nou skaillis the skyis;
   The nicht is neir gone.

The feildis ou'rflouis
With gouans that grouis;
Quhair lilies lyk lou is,
   Als rid as the rone.

The turtill that treu is,
With nots that reneuis
Hir pairtie perseuis.
   The nicht is neir gone.

The sesone excellis
Thrugh sueetness that smellis.
Nou Cupid compellis
   Our hairtis ech one
On Venus wha waikis,
To muse on our maikis,
Syn sing, for thair saikis,
   The nicht is neir gone.

The freikis on feildis
That wight wapins weildis
With shyning bright shieldis
   As Titan in trone;
Stiff speirs in reistis,
Ouer cursoris cristis,
Ar brok on thair breistis:
   The nicht is neir gone.

So hard ar thair hittis,
Some sueyis, some sittis,
And some perforce flittis
   On grund whill they grone.
Syn groomis that gay is,
On blonkis that brayis
With suordis assayis:
   The nicht is neir gone.

Alexander Montgomery.

FREEDOM

Ah ! Freedom is a noble thing !
Freedom makes man to have liking !
Freedom all solace to man gives :
He lives at ease that freely lives !
A noble heart may have none ease,
Nor ellys nought that may him please,
If freedom fail : for free liking
Is yearned o'er all other thing.
Nor he, that aye has lived free,
May not know well the property,
The anger, nor the wretched doom,
That is coupled to foul thraldom.
But, if he had essayed it,
Then all perquer he should it wit ;
And should think freedom more to prize
Than all the gold in world that is.

Barbour.

TIBBIE FOWLER

Tibbie Fowler o' the glen,
   There's owre mony wooin' at her ;
Tibbie Fowler o' the glen,
   There's owre mony wooin' at her.
Wooin' at her, puin' at her,
   Courtin' at her, canna get her ;
Silly elf ! it's for her pelf
   That a' the lads are wooin' at her.

Ten cam' east, an' ten cam' west,
   Ten cam' rowin' o'er the water:
Ten cam' down the lang dike side,
   There's two-an'-thirty wooin' at her.
There's seven but, there's seven ben,
   Seven in the pantry wi' her;
Twenty head about the door,
   There's ane-an'-forty wooin' at her.

She's got pendles in her lugs,
   Cockle-shells wad set her better;
High-heel'd shoon an siller tags;
   An' a' the lads are wooin' at her.
Be a lassie e'er sae black,
   Gin she ha'e the name o' siller,
Set her upon Tintock tap,
   The wind will blaw a man intill her.

Be a lassie e'er sae fair,
   Gin she want the penny siller
A flee may fell her in the air,
   Before a man be even'd till her.
Wooin' at her, puin' at her,
   Courtin' at her, canna get her;
Silly elf! it's for her pelf
   That a' the lads are wooin' at her.
                           Anonymous.

TIBBIE FOWLER

THE SPAEWIFE

O, I wad like to ken—to the beggar-wife says I—
Why chops are guid to brander and nane sae guid to fry.
An' siller, that's sae braw to keep, is brawer still to gie.
—*It's gey an' easy speirin'*, says the beggar-wife to me.

O, I wad like to ken—to the beggar-wife says I—
Hoo a' things come to be whaur we find them when we try,
The lasses in their claes an' the fishes in the sea.
—*It's gey an' easy speirin'*, says the beggar-wife to me.

O, I wad like to ken—to the beggar-wife says I—
Why lads are a' to sell an' lasses a' to buy;
An' naebody for dacency but barely twa or three.
—*It's gey an' easy speirin'*, says the beggar-wife to me.

O, I wad like to ken—to the beggar-wife says I—
Gin death's as shüre to men as killin' is to kye,
Why God has filled the yearth sae fu' o' tasty things to pree.
—*It's gey an' easy speirin'*, says the beggar-wife to me.

O, I wad like to ken—to the beggar-wife says I—
The reason o' the cause an' the wherefore o' the why,
Wi' mony anither riddle brings the tear into my e'e.
—*It's gey an' easy speirin'*, says the beggar-wife to me.

Robert Louis Stevenson.

A BARD'S EPITAPH

Is there a whim-inspirèd fool,
Owre fast for thought, owre hot for rule,
Owre blate to seek, owre proud to snool,
    Let him draw near;
And owre this grassy heap sing dool,
    And drap a tear.

Is there a bard of rustic song,
Who, noteless, steals the crowds among,
That weekly this area throng,
          O, pass not by !
But, with a frater-feeling strong,
          Here, heave a sigh.

Is there a man, whose judgement clear
Can others teach the course to steer,
Yet runs, himself, life's mad career,
          Wild as the wave,
Here, pause—and, thro' the starting tear,
          Survey this grave.

The poor inhabitant below
Was quick to learn and wise to know,
And keenly felt the friendly glow,
          And softer flame ;
But thoughtless follies laid him low,
          And stained his name !

Reader, attend ! whether thy soul
Soars fancy's flights beyond the pole,
Or darkling grubs this earthly hole,
          In low pursuit ;
Know, prudent, cautious, self-control
          Is wisdom's root.

                                        Burns.

THE PACKMAN

There was a couthy Packman, I kent him weel aneuch,
The simmer he was quartered within the Howe o' Tough ;
He sleepit in the barn end amo' the barley strae
But lang afore the milkers he was up at skreek o' day,
An furth upon the cheese stane set his reekin' brose to
    queel
While in the caller strype he gied his barkit face a sweel ;
Syne wi' the ell-wan' in his neive to haud the tykes awa'
He humpit roon' the country side to clachan, craft an' ha'.

Upon the flaggit kitchen fleer he dumpit doon his pack,
Fu' keen to turn the penny ower, but itchin' aye to crack ;
The ploomen gaithered fae the fur', the millert fae the
    mill,
The herd just gied his kye a turn an' skirtit doon the
    hill,
The smith cam' sweatin' fae the fire, the weaver left his
    leem,
The lass forgot her comin' kirn an' connached a' the ream,
The cauper left his turnin' lay, the sooter wasna slaw
To fling his lapstane in the neuk, the elshin, birse an' a'.

The Packman spread his ferlies oot, an' ilka maid an'
    man
Cam' soon on something sairly nott, but never missed till
    than ;
He'd specs for peer auld granny when her sicht begood to
    fail,
An' thummles, needles, preens an' tape for whip-the-cat to
    wale,

THE PACKMAN

He'd chanter reeds an' fiddle strings, an' trumps wi' double
    stang,
A dream beuk 'at the weeda wife had hankered after lang;
He'd worsit for the samplers, an' the bonniest valentines,
An' brooches were in great request wi' a' kirk-gangin'
    queyns.

He'd sheafs o' rare auld ballants, an' an antrin swatch he sang
Fae ' Mill o' Tiftie's Annie,' or o' ' Johnnie More the
    Lang,'
He would lilt you ' Hielan' Hairry ' till the tears ran doon
    his nose,
Syne dicht them wi' a doonward sleeve an' into ' James the
    Rose ' ;
The birn that rowed his shou'ders tho' sae panged wi'
    things to sell
Held little to the claik he kent, an' wasna laith to tell,—
A waucht o' ale to slock his drooth, a pinch to clear his head,
An' the news cam' fae the Packman like the water doon the
    lade.

He kent wha got the bledder when the sooter killed his soo,
An' wha it was 'at threw the stane 'at crippled Geordie's coo,
He kent afore the term cam' roon' what flittin's we would
    see,
An' wha'd be cried on Sunday neist, an' wha would like to be,
He kent wha kissed the sweetie wife the nicht o' Dancie's
    ball,
An' what ill-trickit nickum catched the troot in Betty's wall,
He was at the feein' market, an' he kent a' wha were fou,
An' he never spoiled a story by consid'rin' gin 'twas true.

Nae plisky ever yet was played but he could place the
    blame,
An' tell you a' the story o't, wi' chapter, verse an' name,
He'd redd you up your kith an' kin atween the Dee an'
    Don,
Your forbears wha were hanged or jiled fae auld Culloden
    on,
Altho he saw your face get red he wouldna haud his tongue,
An' only leuch when threatened wi' a reemish fae a rung ;
But a' the time the trade gaed on, an' notes were rankit oot
Had lang been hod in lockit kists aneth the Sunday suit.

An' faith the ablach threeve upon't, he never cried a halt
Until he bocht fae Shou'der-win' a hardy cleekit shalt,
An' syne a spring-cart at tha roup when cadger Willie
    broke,
That held aneth the cannas a' that he could sell or troke ;
He bocht your eggs an' butter, an awat he wasna sweer
To lift the poacher's birds an' bawds when keepers werna
    near ;
Twa sizzens wi' the cairt an' then—his boolie rowed sae
    fine—
He took a roadside shoppie an' put ' Merchant ' on the sign.

An' still he threeve an' better threeve, sae fast his trade it
    grew
That he thirled a cripple tailor an' took in a queyn to
    shue,
An' when he got a stout guidwife he didna get her bare,
She brocht him siller o' her ain 'at made his puckle
    mair,

An' he lent it oot sae wisely—deil kens at what per cent—
That farmers fan' the int'rest near as ill to pay's the rent ;
An' when the bank set up a branch, the wily boddies saw
They beet to mak' him Agent to hae ony chance ava'.

Tho' noo he wore a grauvit an' a dicky thro' the week
There never was a bargain gaun 'at he was far to seek,
He bocht the crafter's stirks an' caur, an' when the girse
    was set
He aye took on a park or twa, an' never rued it yet ;
Till when a handy tack ran oot his offer was the best
An' he dreeve his gig to kirk an' fair as canty as the rest,
An' when they made him Elder, wi' the ladle it was gran'
To see him work the waster laft an' never miss a man.

He sent his sons to college, an' the auldest o' the three—
Tho' wi' a tyauve—got Greek aneuch to warsle thro's
    degree,
An' noo aneth the soundin' box he wags a godly pow ;
The second loon took up the law, an' better fit there's fyou
At chargin' sax an' auchtpence, or at keepin' on a plea,
An' stirrin' strife 'mang decent fouk wha left alane would
    'gree ;
The youngest ane's a doctor wi' a practice in the sooth,
A clever couthy cowshus chiel some hampered wi' a drooth.

The dother—he had only ane—gaed hine awa' to France
To learn to sing an' thoom the harp, to parley-voo an'
    dance ;
It cost a protty penny but t'was siller wisely wared
For the lass made oot to marry on a strappin' Deeside laird ;

She wasna just a beauty, but he didna swither lang,
For he had to get her tocher or his timmer had to gang :
Sae noo she sits ' My Lady ' an' nae langer than the streen
I saw her wi' her carriage comin' postin' ower Culblean.

But tho' his bairns are sattled noo, he still can cast the coat
An' work as hard as ever to mak' saxpence o' a groat ;
He plans as keen for years to come as when he first began,
Forgettin' he's on borrowed days an' past the Bible span.
See, yon's his hoose, an' there he sits ; supposin' we cry in,
It's cheaper drinkin' toddy there than payin' at the Inn,
You'll find we'll hae a shortsome nicht an' baith be bidden
    back,
But—in your lug—ye maunna say a word aboot the Pack.
Charles Murray.

CHA TILL MACCRUIMEIN

(Departure of the 4th Camerons)

The pipes in the streets were playing bravely,
  The marching lads went by,
With merry hearts and voices singing
  My friends marched out to die;
But I was hearing a lonely pibroch
  Out of an older war:
Farewell, farewell, farewell, MacCrimmon,
  MacCrimmon comes no more.

And every lad in his heart was dreaming
  Of honour and wealth to come,
And honour and noble pride were calling
  To the tune of the pipes and drum;
But I was hearing a woman singing
  On dark Dunvegan shore:
In battle or peace, with wealth or honour,
  MacCrimmon comes no more.

And there in front of the men were marching,
  With feet that made no mark,
The grey old ghosts of the ancient fighters
  Come back again from the dark;
And in front of them all MacCrimmon piping
  A weary tune and sore:
On the gathering day, for ever and ever,
  MacCrimmon comes no more.

A HIGHLAND REGIMENT, *Ewart Alan Mackintosh.*

MARIE HAMILTON

' Yestreen the queen had four Maries,
   The night she'll hae but three;
There was Marie Seaton, and Marie Beaton,
   And Marie Carmichael, and me.

' O often have I dress'd my queen,
   And put gold upon her hair;
But now I've gotten for my reward
   The gallows to be my share.

' Often have I dress'd my queen,
   And often made her bed;
But now I've gotten for my reward
   The gallows-tree to tread.

' I charge ye all, ye mariners,
   When ye sail owre the faem,
Let neither my father nor mother get wit
   But that I'm coming hame!

' I charge ye all, ye mariners,
   That sail upon the sea,
Let neither my father nor mother get wit
   This dog's death I'm to die!

' For if my father and mother get wit,
   And my bold brethren three,
O meikle wad be the gude red blude
   This day wad be spilt for me!

' O little did my mother ken,
   That day she cradled me,
The lands I was to travel in,
   Or the death I was to die!'

Anonymous.

CORONACH

He is gone on the mountain,
  He is lost to the forest,
Like a summer-dried fountain,
  When our need was the sorest.
The font, reappearing,
  From the rain-drops shall borrow,
But to us comes no cheering,
  To Duncan no morrow!

The hand of the reaper
  Takes the ears that are hoary,
But the voice of the weeper
  Wails manhood in glory.
The autumn winds rushing
  Waft the leaves that are searest,
But our flower was in flushing,
  When blighting was nearest.

Fleet foot on the correi,
  Sage counsel in cumber,
Red hand in the foray,
  How sound is thy slumber!
Like the dew on the mountain,
  Like the foam on the river,
Like the bubble on the fountain,
  Thou art gone, and for ever!

                              Scott.

SHON CAMPBELL

Shon Campbell went to college
  Because he wanted to,
He left the croft in Gairloch
  To dive in Bain and Drew ;
Shon Campbell died at college
  When the sky of spring was blue.

Shon Campbell went to college—
  The pulpit was his aim.
By day and night he ground; for
  He was Hielant, dour and game.
The session was a hard one;
  Shon flickered like a flame.

Shon Campbell went to college
  And gave the ghost up there,
Attempting six men's cramming
  On a mean and scanty fare.
Three days the Tertians mourned for him—
  'Twas all that they could spare.

Shon Campbell lies in Gairloch
  Unhooded and ungowned,
The green quadrangle of the hills
  To watch his sleep profound,
And the Gaudeamus of the burns
  Making a homely sound.

But when the last great Roll is called
  And adsums thunder loud,
And when the quad is cumbered
  With an eager jostling crowd,

The Principal who rules us all
    Will say : ' Shon Campbell, come,
Your Alma Mater hails you
    Magister Artium.'

                    W. A. Mackenzie.

AND YOU SHALL DEAL . . .

And you shall deal the funeral dole ;
    Ay, deal it, mother mine,
To weary body, and to heavy soul,
    The white bread and the wine.

And you shall deal my horses of pride ;
    Ay, deal them, mother mine ;
And you shall deal my lands so wide,
    And deal my castles nine.

But deal not vengeance for the deed,
    And deal not for the crime ;
The body to its place, and the soul to Heaven's grace,
    And the rest in God's own time.

                    THE PIRATE, *Scott.*

TO MARY IN HEAVEN

Thou ling'ring star, with less'ning ray,
    That lov'st to greet the early morn,
Again thou usher'st in the day
    My Mary from my soul was torn.
O Mary ! dear departed shade !
    Where is thy place of blissful rest ?
See'st thou thy lover lowly laid ?
    Hear'st thou the groans that rend his breast ?

That sacred hour can I forget?
  Can I forget the hallow'd grove,
Where, by the winding Ayr, we met,
  To live one day of parting love?
Eternity can not efface
  Those records dear of transports past,
Thy image at our last embrace,
  Ah! little thought we 'twas our last!

Ayr, gurgling, kiss'd his pebbled shore,
  O'erhung with wild-woods, thickening green;
The fragrant birch and hawthorn hoar,
  Twined amorous round the raptured scene:
The flowers sprang wanton to be prest,
  The birds sang love on every spray;
Till too, too soon, the glowing west
  Proclaim'd the speed of wingèd day.

Still o'er these scenes my mem'ry wakes,
  And fondly broods with miser-care;
Time but th' impression stronger makes,
  As streams their channels deeper wear.
My Mary! dear departed shade!
  Where is thy place of blissful rest?
See'st thou thy lover lowly laid?
  Hear'st thou the groans that rend his breast?

Burns.

REQUIEM

My wound is deep : I fain would sleep ;
  Take thou the vanguard of the three,
And hide me by the braken bush,
  That grows on yonder lilye lee.

O bury me by the braken bush,
  Beneath the blooming brier,
Let never living mortal ken
  That e'er a kindly Scot lies here.

From ' The Battle of Otterbourne.'

The Shields of Bruce and Douglas

PART II

FOLKLORE

PART II

FOLKLORE

Underneath all our veneers we Scots are a metaphysical people—a race of mystics and dreamers. Scratch the most 'practical' Scot and you find a poet. We are, in the truest sense, a deeply religious people; and we have been sneered at on occasions for our 'religiousness,' but those who have sneered have not understood—any more than we have understood, ourselves, very often—that our sense of the religious is a much more profound thing than it appears to be on the surface. Fundamentally, our sense of the religious is not a thing of warring creeds—it goes far beyond that—it goes back into the far dim and distant ages, long before John Knox and the coming of the Reformation; long before even St Ninian and St Columba brought to our shores the message of The Christ. Our Folklore Heritage proves it. Every race has its Folklore, its Superstitions, and its Mysteries in some degree; but amongst the Celts the degree is greater than almost anywhere else on earth. And it is from our Celtic forebears that we get most of our superstitions and our ancient beliefs, our tales of bogles and warlocks, kelpies and monsters, our second-sight, and our glamourie —our daft streak, and our love of the macabre and the awesome.

But many of our beliefs are not entirely of Celtic origin, and many of them have their counterparts, in variations, among other peoples as far-flung from us as the North American Indians and the Chinese. That the Indians and the

Chinese should hold beliefs in common is not altogether strange, since both races are of Mongoloid origin ; but that we should have beliefs in common with either, that are not known to any extent in, say, Central Europe, does appear amazing until we recall to mind the fact that there is in us, mingled with the Celtic, a fairly strong Scandinavian strain ; and we know that the ancient Norse landed and had settlements in what is now Canada, long before Columbus ' discovered' the American continent. And there would be for long, comings and goings between the Canadian and Canadian-Arctic settlements and the home country ; and between the home country and the Scandinavian colonies in Celtic Ireland and Celtic Scotland.

Be that as it may, it is a most significant fact that many of the beliefs we hold in common with the other Celtic peoples, and many of the beliefs we hold in common with the Scandinavians—and with the North American Indians—were, until quite recent times, entirely unknown in England other than in parts of her two northern counties—in that region of England that has been named, not without cause, SCOZIA IRREDENTA.

In the following pages, under different headings, an attempt is made to give an insight to some of the more popular beliefs and superstitions of Scotland, together with a few old rhymes and an old folk-tale, or two.

All that goes to make up what we call Folklore, must not be treated as something quite as puerile as much of it appears to be on the surface. Folklore is nowadays accepted as an important branch of antiquarian research, giving, as it does, an insight to the psychology of our forebears.

BIRTH

Among Scottish beliefs concerning birth, the best known is one that appears to be peculiarly our own—the conviction that the seventh child of a seventh child will always grow up to be ' fay,' or, at least, to turn out to be ' no canny.'

A child born at midnight is, also, regarded as being one who will live to be ' different '—either for good or for ill. Usually, the child born at midnight, or in the ' wee sma' oors,' is expected to manifest in later life some peculiar brilliance of intellect, even though such brilliance should be allied to a little wildness. Our National Poet's birth gives an excellent example of this particular belief's coming true on at least one occasion : was not Burns born in the early hours ?

When a child is first taken from the room in which it was born, it must be taken upwards, and never down. If the child is born in a ground-floor room it must be carried upstairs ; if born upstairs, it must be taken still higher—to an attic, or even to the roof; but if neither of these movements is possible, there is a subterfuge that will suffice : a chair or a box, or some other raised obstacle must be placed in the doorway of the room, and whoever carries the child on its first short journey must make the necessary ascent.

The newly-born child, in the first few days of its life, is exposed to the great danger of being stolen by the fairies, who are for ever on the look out for innocent babies, that they may take them in exchange for some of their evil ones. Something of this belief in the ' Changeling ' is known all over Scotland, and, in an oblique fashion even to those modern mothers who may never have heard of the actual superstition itself. How often do we hear a mother saying of a wayward son or daughter : ' That ane's nane o' mine ' ?

meaning, though she may not recognise the significance of what she says, that the youngster though of her body is not of her spirit. Certain fathers, of course, may make use of the expression, with a much more practical implication behind it ! But we are not concerned with such ' beliefs ' as that !

To avoid the possibility of the child being stolen by the fairies, there are, fortunately, a number of simple precautions that can be taken—any one of which is a sure safeguard : a barrier may be erected round the house, which the fairies are powerless to pass : someone, preferably the father, must walk seven times round the building sunwise, or *deiseil*. Obviously, this cannot be done to safeguard a child born in a tenement flat, high up and surrounded by hundreds of other flats ; but, no doubt, in such cases no precaution is necessary : I cannot see fairies in Gorgie, or in the Gorbals ; nor even in certain parts of, say, Dundee, or Aberdeen !

However, there are other means of circumventing the *sìthichean* than by building an invisible barrier. A knife placed in the cradle will do the trick ; and care must be taken not to carry fire nor light out of the house until the child is at least a week old. And the newly-born child must on no account be placed in anything but a borrowed cradle at first. After its first sleep in the borrowed cradle a new one may be got.

To ensure that a child will never know poverty, its right hand must be left severely alone at its first washing. And all visitors, seeing the child for the first time, should place a silver coin in its hand. If the child looses the coin it will grow up to be open-handed and generous, but if it grabs tightly it will be a ' grippy ' man or woman.

It is unlucky to weigh or measure an infant newly-born. And a cat, being an emissary of the Powers of Evil, must never be left alone in a room with the child. Nor should the cradle ever be rocked empty—either before or after the child is born.

The name that the child is to be given must never be spoken aloud until the minister speaks it at the christening ceremony. If anyone asks, they must not be told; nor must the minister be told by word of mouth—he must be handed a slip of paper with the name written on it when he asks for the name, or names, that the child is to have. If the minister objects to being made party to such a superstitious practice, there is not, apparently, any means of dodging him. Presumably, the risk must be taken.

When on the way to its christening, the child must be carried, at least some part of the way, by a young unmarried woman, who must have with her something to eat—usually a piece of bread and cheese—which she must present to the first man she meets, no matter who or what he may be.

The mother of a newly-born child must never leave the house after sunset until such time as she is ' kirkit.' If she does, she runs the risk of being carried off by the fairies to nurse one of their weaklings, for an ailing fairy child can only be restored to health by being fed on human milk.

Getting away a little from birth: when a child ' casts ' its first tooth, the tooth must be put in salt, wrapped in paper or a ' bit cloot,' and secreted in a mouse-hole.

DEATH

From Birth to Death seems a natural enough sequence of events—at least to the Scot; for, to us, death has never held the fears that it holds for some of the world's peoples. For centuries, to us as a more or less composite people, and for centuries before that to the two main constituent races from which we are descended, death has never meant the end. Far more than most occidental peoples we have always thought of death as another beginning, as a re-birth, and as a re-birth to something better. And this faith we held long before the Christian doctrine of the Immortality of the Soul was brought to us to lighten our Pagan hearts ! Although there is nothing to prove that our Pagan hearts were not light, and our souls free, at a time when some of our near neighbours were wandering in an extremely sordid spiritual darkness, somewhere on the dreary salt-marsh wastes of the Baltic. Indeed, there is much to prove that our distant ancestors held very decided views on spiritual re-birth, and the notion of another and a brighter world beyond.

Far down the centuries, there has come to us from the Scandinavian fringe, the story of *Valhalla*, the heaven of the warriors ; and from our Celtic forebears there has come the beautiful legend of *Tir-nan-Og*, the Land of Eternal Youth ; and other legends, too, of invisible other worlds—and, with each other-world, there goes a name of sheer poetic beauty : *Magh Meala*, the Plain of Honey ; and, too, Silver Cloud Plain, and the Country of Promise. In these Pagan heavens there were to be found all the noblest, and all the fairest : brave men and lovely women; and palaces ringing with music and laughter ; and wines there were, and wonderful foods. But the old Pagan Gaelic heavens were not places of effeminate luxuriousness, nor places of sensual orgies : the great pastime was in heaven, as on earth, warfare and bloodshedding, for the Gael was never at any time a pacifist, and a heaven without a fight in it would have been no heaven at all.

Through the ages, that conception of a heaven, naturally, changed ; and with the coming of Christianity it faded out to linger only as a tale that is told. Strangely enough, it needed the coming of Christianity to give us even the few terrors of death we possess ; and most of our beliefs to do with death are of comparatively recent origin.

Death is near at hand when a cock persists in crowing between midnight and three o'clock in the morning. The foundation of that superstition is easily accounted for. and it is common to most Christian peoples.

The howling of a dog in the night is always supposed to herald the approach of death, and if the dog is watched it will ' point ' the direction of where the death will take place. Dogs see wraiths where human eyes see nothing ; and horses, too, will shy and bolt, and whinny and neigh, in ways inexplicable to the material-minded.

A bird tapping at a window is a sign of death ; so, too, is a gull sitting on one leg on the top of a house. Death will come soon to the man or woman who sees a raven flying straight before him, or her, on the road he, or she, is taking. The laughter of an owl is a sure portent of death to someone in the neighbourhood. Strange and unaccountable rappings in a house are a sign of death's coming to someone living under the roof.

When anyone dies suddenly, he, or she, is supposed to have fallen a victim to the ' Evil Eye.'

To touch the corpse of a friend or an acquaintance is an indication that one had done nothing in any way to contribute to the death ; and touching, too, gives immunity from dreams about the dead.

There may be places where the old dead-rites are still observed : after the ' laying-out ' of the corpse, a wooden platter is placed on the breast of the dead, and on to the platter, separate and unmixed, is piled a little earth and a little salt—the earth symbolical of the corruptible body, and the salt symbolical of the immortal spirit. No fire must be lit in the room where the body lies ; and if a dog or a cat passes over the body it must at once be killed. Friends and neighbours, to prevent any supernatural interference with the body, take it in turns to ' sit up ' with the corpse. They are provided with a Bible, a candle, food, and a bottle of whisky. The clock is stopped, and if there is a mirror in the room it must be taken down or covered. Those who ' sit-up ' will wait for the coming of the dawn to be relieved of their duty, for there must be no coming or going in the dark for fear of what might be seen. This ' sitting-up ' is known as the ' wake,' or the ' lykewake.' There are tales of 'wakes' being carried through with singing and dancing : such a procedure being, obviously, a long-lingering remnant of some ancient Pagan rite of speeding the dead to the happier land beyond, and of rejoicing with him at his good fortune.

The Devil

The Devil in Scotland is rarely regarded with the same sort of awe and fear that he excites in most other countries. He is, more often than not, treated with a certain amount of humour ; for, despite some of his towering rages amongst the witches, he seems to be a bit of a humourous devil him-

TRYSTING THE DEVIL

self ; and, even when he feels like it, he rarely seems to be capable of doing much damage. He is a devil who likes to enjoy himself : he pipes, and fiddles, and drinks ; and he is a devil among the women ! No witch, for instance, need ever complain of his lack of attention, and he distributes his favours to the witch-women with commendable impartiality : young girls and octogenarians are all alike to the Devil.

Some pages further on, under the heading of *Witches and Witchcraft*, there will be further reference to the Devil, since the Devil and witches go together ; for, just as every witch is a mistress of the Devil, so is the Devil the Master of all witches ; and no witches' coven could be complete without his presence.

Some of the names given to the Devil in Scotland indicate the spirit of humour with which he is regarded. He is rarely referred to directly as ' The Devil,' or even by such names as ' The Evil One,' for that would indeed be asking for trouble.

But this ' tricky rascal,' as Professor MacLean calls him, may be called, with impunity, by any one of a score of by-names. *Dòmhnull Dubh*, or Black Donald is his usual name in the Gaelic. Other names given to him are no more serious than ' Auld Clootie,' ' Nick,' or ' Hornie ' ; and there are occasions when he is elevated to the peerage as ' The Earl o' Hell,' or is sent to swell the ranks of the un-titled landowners with the designation of ' The Laird o' Yon Place.' And quite recently I heard him spoken of as ' The Queer Fella ' ; but, as that was a war-time soldiers' name for the sergeant-major, there is no reason to suppose that that is other than quite a modern appellation for *Dòmhnull*.

Whether the Devil has been seen recently, or not, is not known ; but it is not so very long ago since he made quite regular appearances.

In Scotland, the Devil rarely turns up as he does in most countries, in the shape upon which Goethe based his character of the tempter, Mephistopheles. In Scotland, the Devil, Proteus-like, assumes any shape that takes his fancy for the time being : sometimes he does approach the popular conception of what a real devilish devil should be, as when he manifests himself as a beast-man, complete with horns, fire-flaming hair, black-spotted red face, and body encased in scales. That, no doubt, is his regulation uniform for commanding in flaming hell, where the scales will act as some sort of armour against the scorching of the fiery furnaces.

But usually Black Donald rolls up in some much less fantastic shape—out of respect, perhaps, for the Scottish post-Reformation loathing of such fripperies as fancy dress. Sometimes he appears as quite a handsome young man, sometimes in the nude, but generally clothed. There is, however, no record of his ever having turned up in the kilt. Perhaps, after all, our Scottish Devil is not a Scot ; most likely he is only an incomer, and his domicile only a temporary one. There is, for that matter, nothing to prove that he is not a migrating *Sasunnach*, with his permanent home on the other side of the Border. Or he may be an Ulster Irishman. In which case, probably, his domain lies somewhere beneath the bomb-proof vaults of Stormont.

Sometimes, in Scotland, the Devil comes in the shape of a black man, clothed or unclothed ; sometimes he is quite a respectable elderly gentleman in a discreet dark suit that would not disgrace an Elder ; sometimes he is a workman or a fisherman ; at other times a tradesman, for he is an expert at all trades but one—he was never permitted to learn the tailoring. For, whenever the deil's amang the tailors, the craftsmen bolt, so that he has never even learned how to baste.

But, whatever disguise he assumes, the Devil can always be discovered by one thing : the cloven hoof is ever in evidence : the Pan-like goats'-feet of him cannot be covered.

It is related that the Devil once kept a school in Scotland for the teaching of devilry to the principal chiefs and lairds. Among the aptest of his pupils was the Lord Reay of that period, who, like a good Mackay, turned rebellious as soon as he had learned all the devilment the Devil could teach him. Being reprimanded one day by his Master for taking too much upon himself, Lord Reay turned round, and, in a stand-up fight, gave the Devil such a licking, that, in order to get away, the Devil promised the peer that he would leave him alone in future, and that he would provide him with a legion of workers who would do his bidding, unquestioningly and without wages. The legion of workers, however, became a curse instead of a blessing, for they could work so quickly—building a farm-steading, for instance, in half a night was as nothing to them—that in a few days there was no work left for them to do ; but they howled for more, and made such a nuisance of themselves, that, in the end, Lord Reay, nearly out of his wits, drove them all down to the sea-shore and set them to the weaving of ropes of sand. They are still at it !

FAIRIES AND MERMAIDS

From the Devil and his Imps to the Fairies is not such a very far cry ; for our Scottish fairies are mostly an impish crew, and their women-folk a wanton lot. Our Scottish fairies bear little resemblance to the kindly fairy-folk of Ireland. And that is easily explained : the Irish fairy-folk the *leipreacháin*, and the *leannán sidhe*, for instance, are all Gaels—the kindliest and the most hospitable race in all the world. But the Scottish fairies are Picts—known in the Gaelic as *Cruithneach*, and in the southern vernacular as *Pechs*. And it is scarcely to be expected that they could be anything but devilish, or, at least, mischievous, descended, as they are, from that cruel, barbaric, and bloodthirsty race, who behaved so abominably to the Romans when they came north offering the benefits of their culture and their civilization.

One of the Pictish leaders was even rude enough—the Romans tell it themselves—to say of the Romans : ' To robbery, murder, and outrage, they give the lying name of government, and where they make a desert they call it peace.'

From such an ungrateful and ungracious race, then, are sprung our Scottish fairies.

Not all of them are bad, of course. On the contrary, some of them are quite good-natured, and quite prepared to be helpful. But their offers of help should be politely refused ; or, if accepted, accepted with great caution.

In those limited areas where once the Scandinavian element predominated, the fairies are sometimes known as *Trolls*, or *Trows*. In the Gaelic they are spoken of as *Daoine Sithe*, which may be translated, strangely enough, as

' Men of Peace.' And in certain parts of the south, they are often called *Guid Nichbouris*, or ' Good Neighbours.'

But it is more than probable that these friendly, and rather flattering, names were first given to them in a propitiatory sense. After all, why be rude to them when they possess such almighty powers, as they undoubtedly do ? The fairies can do almost anything, and it is well to keep in with them. They can do anything from destroying cattle and crops to running away with a good wife—flying away with her up the *lum* right before her husband's face. The fairy men are very fond of taking a good-looking human woman to mate with ; and as for the fairy women—! there is not a handsome lad in all the land who is really safe from their attentions. But, women-like, they are not as crude in carrying out their operations with human men as are their men-folk with human women. Not by force do they take their human lovers, but by guile and cunning : by sweet enticements and by silver words do the fairy women lure their victims from their homes, from their sweethearts and from their wives. And the Queen of the Fairies is the worst of all. A bad *bizzem* is she !

In the Shetlands and in the Hebrides, the fairies will often go to great lengths to secure a human mate : from island to island they will swim for days on end looking for the right lad or lass ; and, for this purpose, it is usual for them to change themselves into seals. Carefully they will watch by the shore ; and, by singing some enchanting song, or by some other means, they will entice their victim to the water's edge. Then they will send, floating in on the tide, something that the intended victim is sure to admire. And when the victim steps into the water to grasp the prize, he, or she, is immediately pulled below the waves, to know nothing more till the grand awakening in fairyland.

Although it is not usual for there to be any fruits of a human and a fairy union, it is well-known, of course, that all the MacCodrums, for one clan at least, are descended of a seal.

Shetlanders, without knowing it, often take fairy-seal-women for their wives. And sometimes very good wives they are, until the day comes when they have to return to the sea, and so to fairyland. And this is how a Shetlander may take a seal-woman for his wife, and know nothing about it until the day she vanishes ; and even then he may not understand—he may only think that his wife has run away with a foreign sailor, or something of the kind. When a seal-woman comes ashore, perhaps having failed to entice the man she wants into the waters, she puts off her seal skin and becomes to all outward appearances a normal-looking woman—but always a very beautiful one. As a beautiful woman she has little difficulty in courting the man of her choice, and eventually becoming his wife. But the day is sure to come—and it may be after years—when her own doffed seal skin is put before her by some mysterious means. Then is she powerless. She can do no other than put on the skin, and when she has done that she must make for the sea, and plunge into the waves, to be seen on earth no more.

And yet it has been known for a fairy-seal-woman, or a fairy-seal-man, to come and go between land and sea time and time again. There is, for instance, the story of the man who lost his sister for years, until one day he was driven ashore on an island far from his own, where he found her settled in a nice little house, a married woman. Her husband

was out, and she was waiting for his return ; and, not unnaturally, she insisted that her brother should wait to meet
him. After a while, there came in at the door, a large seal
with a fine-looking cod-fish in its mouth. It dropped the
fish on the table, and then went through to another room.
In a few minutes, there came from the room, a well-dressed
and handsome young man—the husband of the other man's
sister.

For supper they had the cod, and the best cod it was the
brother had ever tasted ; and the husband explained how
he had caught it—such a cod as no ordinary fisher could ever
hope to catch.

' I fell in with it,' he said, ' this morning, north of Foula.
A grand fish I could see it was, and I made up my mind to
bring it home ; but it was a good swimmer, and a hard two
hours' chasing it gave me. But at last I caught it, and when
I came up for breath, there before me, after my long chase,
was my own island and my own home ; and here I am.'

Mermaids are, of course, very well known in Scotland.
Our northern shores seem to be a particularly favourite
haunt of theirs ; and sometimes, for hours, they may be
seen, by those who have the eyes to see, sitting on a rock, or
even lolling on the sands or the shingle, combing their long
and luxuriant hair. The *Maighdean Chuain*, like the seal-
woman, and the ordinary land fairy-woman, is very fond of
taking a handsome lad as a lover ; and sometimes she will
heap all sorts of riches on him : gold, and silver, and pre-
cious jewels, taken from the deep vaults of the sea. But,
sometimes, too, she will lure her lover away beneath the
waves, to keep him a prisoner bound by long, slender,
chains of gold. Out beyond Duncansby Head there is a

great storehouse of jewels, where the Mermaid in charge for the Sea-god, has a whole host of once-human lovers.

There is danger in the love of a mermaid, for no matter how beautiful she may be, or how kindly, the affair always ends in disaster. That is why sensible fishermen, whenever they haul up a mermaid in their nets, always let her go. But, of course, there are fools among fishermen, as there are fools among other men, and sometimes silly and inexperienced lads will pull a mermaid aboard and keep her for their pleasure, only to rue it later—maybe even within an hour or two.

But sometimes it is the mermaid who suffers for her love and desire towards a human man; as, for instance, the mermaid of Iona, who left behind her on the shore what are known as ' The Mermaid's Tears.' It was a saint of ancient Iona that this mermaid fell in love with; and daily and nightly she would land on the holy shores of *I-Chaluim Chille* to pray that she might be given a human heart, and a human soul that her saintly lover might save for Christ; but unavailing were her prayers, for her love of the sea and of her sea life was greater than her love of the saint; and always, after meeting him, she was compelled to return to the waves. Great were the tears she shed, and, as each tear fell, it became a pebble. And there are the pebbles, that were once a mermaid's tears, strewn about the shores of Iona to this day.

And now to leave the sea, and to return to the fairies of the land—the fairies of the glens, and the hills, and the moors—the Brownies, the Goblins, the Spunkies, the May Moulachs; and the Kelpies that live in the lochs and the deep pools of our rivers.

The Kelpie, in particular, is much in evidence to-day : are there not people, of all kinds, flocking from the ends of the earth to the shores of Loch Ness ? Strange names are being given to the denizen—or denizens it may be—of Loch Ness. Some there are who maintain that the disturber of Loch Ness is a shark, or a whale, or a seal, that came up the Ness River on a flood and then found that it could not get back to the sea. What nonsense ! Shark, whale, or seal ! That is merely the matter-of-fact attempt at an explanation made by ignorant scientists, and other people who know no better. The ordinary folk, who call it the Loch Ness Monster, get much nearer to the truth, for a monster it certainly is, but what kind of a monster only the witches, and the poets, and other fay-like folk know. The Loch Ness Monster is, of course, no more and no less than an old-fashioned Kelpie—a beastie of a kind that has been known all over Scotland for ages.

For there is not a stretch of water in all the land that has not had, at some time or another, its Kelpie, or Water Horse, or *each uisge*, as it is in the Gaelic. But it is not every kelpie that has the conceit of the kelpie of Loch Ness —entertaining press-photographers, and almost giving interviews like a film-star. And it is just by such methods as that, that the whole of the fairy business is likely to be ruined ; so the less said about the impudent fellow in Loch Ness the better. And, after all, and for all that can be definitely known, maybe he is being well paid for it by some of the people in Inverness. In these hard times, even a kelpie might do a lot for an old railway horse, or a braxie sheep or two !

But the others—the unbribable kelpies—are dreaded

beasts, indeed. The real kelpie, like his Master, the Devil, can assume almost any shape he likes ; preferring, however, the shape of a beautiful horse, carefully groomed and exquisitely harnessed. In this shape, the kelpie will stroll casually along beside its intended victim. The victim, not unnaturally, admiringly strokes the lovely and lonely creature, only to find that the hand that has touched the horse cannot be removed, and so the poor victim is dragged into the kelpie's loch, there to be devoured.

In Sutherland, not so very long ago, there was a number of children playing beside a loch, when into their midst there came a beautiful and, apparently, owner-less horse. One of the boys, calling to his playmates to follow his example, mounted the creature's back. Before long there was a string of lads mounted—as many as ever the horse's back would hold, from its mane to its tail—and other boys there were hanging on to the beast in every lad-like way. But one boy there was, who had heard about kelpies and their ways ; and, as soon as he remembered, he tried to take his hand away ; but, strive as he might, the hand of him clung. Fortunately, the boy had sense enough to recognise that the loss of a hand was as nothing compared with the loss of his life. So, out came his knife, and off came his hand. And no sooner was he free, than up rose the kelpie, with fire and brimstone snorting from its nostrils, and high into the air it went, right over the loch, and down into the waters, carrying its human load and the amputated hand with it. And never more were those boys seen again.

It is a relief to know that the clever boy was able to cauterize his poor bleeding stump on some of the fiery brimstone left behind by the kelpie ; and it is good to know, too, that it was his left hand that he lost, and not his right, so that he is still of some use about his father's croft.

It is not always, however, that the kelpie comes as a horse. Like the fairy-seals, sometimes it comes in the shape of a handsome young man, or a beautiful young woman.

There was a lad in Badenoch courted by a beautiful, strange, young woman, who permitted him all sorts of liberties. But one night she forgot, and, instead of laughing in her ecstasy, she neighed like a horse. Then did the lad know who and what his sweetheart was. Fortunately for him he was in the kilt, and had his *sgian dubh* in his stocking-top. And when the lad had finished his work with the *sgian*, it was not a stabbed beauty that lay at his feet, but a grey kelpie covered in green loch slime !

And that, I think, is quite enough about kelpies.

Of the true fairies, ' the wee folk,' there are other kinds of tales—some of them quite pleasant, some of them even amusing. The quite recent story of Tomnahurich, for instance.

Tomnahurich is a hill at Inverness, and it was once prophesied that Tomnahurich would be put under lock and key, and the fairies secured within it. This surely came to pass when Tomnahurich was laid out as a cemetery—the most beautiful cemetery in Scotland, so it is said.

Well, not long ago there strode one morning through the streets of Inverness, two wild-looking piper-lads. Now, the kilt is not an uncommon sight in the streets of Inverness ; and, for that matter, a piper without a kilt, is a more uncommon sight than a piper in breeks. So that no notice was taken of these two fellows until they began to curse and swear in the Gaelic at all the cars that threatened to run them down in the narrow streets. Then, of course, they were taken in charge—for Inverness doesn't put up with that sort of thing, any more than it puts up with parking a car for more than thirty seconds anywhere within the burgh bounds.

Eventually, the pipers appeared before the sheriff, and in the Gaelic they told their tale.

Neither the one nor the other of them had ever seen a car before ! and they had imagined each car to be some sort of a queer beast that was bearing down on them. They said, that, one night, having come from Strathspey to pipe in Inverness they had been accosted by an old man who had offered them a guinea each, and as much whisky as ever they cared to drink, if they would go and pipe for him and a few of his friends. That had seemed to them to be a far better arrangement than piping for coppers in the street ; so speedily they had agreed, and had followed the old man.

Up Tomnahurich they had gone ; and half-way up they had come to a door, which the old man had opened. There, before them, there had been a beautiful ball-room filled with hundreds of handsome men and beautiful women all waiting for some music so that they might dance. The pipers had been given a dram, or two, and then they had begun to play. And so, the dance had gone on all through the night. And all through the night the pipers had been given all the whisky they had wanted. Then at last the dance had come to an end : the pipers had been given their guinea each, and had been turned out into the morning.

To the sheriff each showed his guinea—*a gold spade guinea*, which each had concealed from the police, but as soon as each coin was taken to be handed up to the sheriff it fell to dust. So the men were put back for inquiries to be made ; for there was something, indeed, very strange about two pipers who had never seen a car, and who had in their possession two obsolete coins that vanished at the touch of another's hand. In the police cells, a minister went to visit the men, each one of whom swore he had not long come from the battle of Sheriffmuir ; and they wanted to know what had happened to Inverness, for the police had refused to tell them anything ; and who and what were the police, they wanted to know. The minister thought he had better offer up a prayer ; but, at the first mention of the name of God, both pipers, together with their pipes, crumbled up, to lie at the minister's feet a heap of ancient dust.

It had been a long, long night in Tomnahurich !

On the Borders, and in Galloway, the favourite type of fairy is the Brownie, who, for all his English kind of name, is maybe of Gaelic or of Cymric origin. Somehow, he doesn't seem to be a Pict—although, of course, he may be. A useful sort of fellow is the brownie, but terrible is the pride that is on him at times.

For centuries the brownies have been quite good friends to the southern farmers, and other country folk. Every farmhouse on the Borders and in Galloway has its brownie —although, of course, the people will not admit it nowadays for fear of being ridiculed.

During the day-time the brownie vanishes ; and it is utterly useless calling him, or trying to tempt him to come from his hiding—wherever that may be. It is at night-time, when all the household is asleep, that the brownie comes out to do his work ; and it is customary for the mistress of the house to leave him some work to do—washing the supper dishes, or darning a pile of stockings, or any little thing like that—and never once does he fail to have his work all done and neatly put away for the morning.

And all that the brownie asks in return for his work is a little meal, or, maybe, a bit of cheese and a drink of milk. To offer any more, or to offer money, is to make an enemy of him for ever after. And many a brownie leaves his ' place ' in high dudgeon if his pride be offended in any such way.

And there is another curious thing about the brownie, that distinguishes him from all the other fairy-folk. The brownie is highly moral ! Not for him the wanton creed of Elfhame, and Elfhame's amoral queen. And woe betide the plough-lad or the dairy-maid whose conduct is not utterly circumspect ; and woe betide, too, the amorous housekeeper who sets her cap at the brownie's farmer-master. The day will not be far distant when she will be looking for another place.

GHOSTS

In this article on *Ghosts*, I have to apologise for thrusting in the personal element, and for getting away, to a certain extent, from my headline subject of *Folklore*. But there are ghost stories by the thousand in Scotland—as, indeed, there are everywhere—and even the most ' hard-headed '

and the most ' canny ' Scot has to admit at times that there
may be something in at least some of the ghost stories with
which our Scottish history and our Folklore is packed.

It may, therefore, be of greater interest for me to tell one
recent, personal, experience than to retail a dozen old
stories that may possibly have been heard before.

Without further apology for bringing myself into the
matter, it is necessary for me to explain that I am not an
old man living in dreams of the past, nor a particularly
young one with callow and comic visions of the future.   I
have lived an active and an interesting life.   I am inclined to
be a bit bitter about certain things, but I try to preserve a
sane and balanced outlook on most subjects.

As a preliminary to my story, I must explain that the
croft-house in which I live is situated on a heathery piece of
bogland moor, eight hundred feet above the sea, and miles
from anywhere.   A couple of hundred yards, or so, in front
of my door there is a heavily-wooded deep gully—a sort of
miniature glen—down which there tumbles, and sometimes
roars, a narrow mountain river, known as *An Allt Mòr*, or
' The Big Burn.'

On the other side of the water there is a high ridge, with,
at its northern end, a couple of small rounded hills of the
type known in the Gaelic as *màman* (in the singular, *màm*).

On many an occasion, since coming to live in this house,
I have heard the sound of pipes being played—and far and
away, and distant was their tone—and strange, too, was
something else about them.   At first, the strange tone
baffled me—there was something missing—but, at last, I
discovered what it was.   The pipes I was hearing had the
tone of the pipes I had often heard played in Ireland—the

kind of pipes that were played, as far as I can gather, in Scotland two or three centuries ago—the pipes with the two drones instead of the usual modern Scottish three—the pipes with the big bass drone missing.

But the fact that the heavy droning was not to be heard might, I thought, have been accounted for by distance. There was, I knew, no possibility of there being anyone playing within at least a couple of miles. Making inquiries, I discovered that, as a matter of fact, there was not a piper within six or seven miles ; and, more than that, I found that there could not possibly be anyone piping for far more miles than that in the direction from which I was always hearing the sounds of the music coming ; and, still more than that, I discovered that the man who had occupied this croft for years before I came to it, *had heard the piping regularly*, but no one had believed him.

Anyhow, the piping came to me at irregular intervals— and not always after dark—for that matter, I heard it as recently as two days ago. At first, I tried to find some other reason for the sounds : was it the wind in the trees ? was it the wind playing over and through the cairns with which the moor is dotted ? was it, even, the wind rippling over the iron roof of the barn, or playing in and around the broken timbers at the end of the steading ?

It was not any one of these things, for the sounds came from a far greater distance. Was it, then, the waters of the burn tumbling over stones and boulders ? was the sound occasioned by any one, or all, of the half-dozen, or so, waterfalls that go tumbling down to join the waters of the burn ?

I tramped all over the moor, and up and down the burn

sides I went, day after day, listening carefully in a score of different places. But in the end I had to admit that the sounds were not made by either winds or waters ; and that neither cairns nor trees were acting as Aeolian harps, or anything of the kind. I had to admit that there was something I could not discover, nor even hope to understand. I gave up the notion of trying to find anything out, and was content only to listen whenever my unseen piper-friend cared to come with his music to enliven my solitude.

And now comes the real story, for the tale of the phantom piper is no more than a preliminary to the big affair.

One brilliantly moonlit night at the beginning of this year—and several weeks after this book had been begun—I had sat writing until after midnight. Then, before going to bed, I went for a stroll over the moor. There was not a cloud in the sky, nor even a drift of mist about the hill-tops. The night was almost as bright as day, and over to the north-west, beyond *Tòrr a' Chluaine*, the great bulk of Ben Wyvis stood out black and clear. Nearer to me, and to the north-east a bit, I could see the two *màman* as clearly as at noon. Every tree on the moor stood out—each like a black silhouette—and clearly there came to me the sounds of the burn waters thrashing down the gully.

When suddenly, from the ridge on the other side, there came to me, high and clear, the sounds of the *pìobaireachd*. But I had grown so accustomed to hearing the strange pipes, that I no more than listened for a few minutes and then went in to bed.

I lay awake for a long time, and then I must have dozed. But, suddenly, I sat up. The moonlight was streaming in across my bed ; and outside, but distantly, there was going

on the most infernal and unearthly din I have ever heard :
there was the clash of metal on metal, and the hoarse yellings
of men—and, over all the din there was repeated time and
time again some particular phrase that I could not dis-
tinguish ; and, over and above everything—over all the
clashing and all the yelling—there was the wild high skirl of
the pipes, and not the pipes of one lone piper, but the pipes
of surely no less than a dozen.

Now, I have done my share of fighting—in brawls and
in battle—and I am still always ready for a scrap if circumstances warrant it—but, never in all my life, have I known
such ghastly fear as was on me that night, lying there in my
own bed, with four good thick stone walls around me.
Waiting in ambush on a dark road wasn't in it ; and
waiting to go ' over the top ' was no worse a horror. But,
for all that, I was forced from my bed. I had to go. And
there was no heroism in it. I was scared stiff. I called
myself every kind of damned fool that ever there was.

And then I flung my kilt about me—and the queer looking object I must have looked, with a kilt buckled on me
over a suit of green pyjamas !

As I went down the stairs, it was a great soldier that went
down—hair on end and trembling in every limb !

Then the sounds stopped. And then began again—but
with a difference : there was still the clatter of metals, but
the clatter was the clatter of hanging accoutrements, and
not the clash of arms in action. And the sounds were
coming nearer : down one side of the burn they came, and
up the other, and over the moor across the heather and bog
—the sounds of marching men—but all unreal—something
like the sounds of surf beating on a distant shore were the

sounds that the feet of the host appeared to be making. And the strange yelling had changed from the yells of men in fight to the triumphant and derisive yells of men who had been victorious. And, over it all, was the ranting skirling of the pipers.

By this time I could hear the dogs whining in the part of the steading where they sleep. I managed to run round to let them out : there are three of them—an extremely sagacious young bitch, and her two sons, a couple of hefty young lads about five months old. They dashed out of the steading, all three of them, in the direction from which the sounds were coming, barking and howling for all they were worth. Then they came tearing back. The bitch lay down at my feet, whining in a way I had never heard before, but the two pups, her sons, streaked away across the moor in the opposite direction like a couple of greyhounds ; and, incidentally, it was nine o'clock in the morning before they came back.

Nearer and nearer came the marching ghost-army : I could hear everything, but I could see nothing : the moor, to the eyes, appeared as deserted as ever. I stood petrified by the barn door.

The cohort passed within a few yards of me—first the pipers, and then a long straggle of talking, yelling men— and amongst it all there was the occasional screaming of a woman !

Then the army—or whatever it was—with the pipers leading, *passed clean through the house*, and went off south-westerly. I heard the passing. I waited, and gradually the sounds grew fainter. The ghost-army faded away into the night.

There is no more to tell, except that the hill on the other side of the burn, the hill from which the sounds of the fighting had first come, is known as *Mam a' Chatha*—the Hill of the Battle.

And there is the story for what it is worth ; although I suppose the answer to it is : ' Now, will someone else tell another ? ' Which, although it is a query, is the classic, and, perhaps, the only answer to every ghost-story.

MAGIC

And now, returning to Folklore as Folklore, we come to such things as can only be called by the oriental name of magic—charms ; magical, or holy, wells ; and such-like.

There are all kinds of charms, or amulets : certain kinds of pebbles ; specially treated birds' eggs ; twigs, or bits of wood, from particular trees—the rowan tree above all—and small pieces of leather, or even paper on which may be written certain directions, either in rhyme or prose. There is, for instance, the simple charm against rats and mice—a sort of writ of ejectment, which, of course, the vermin may, or may not, obey. A piece of paper is stuck up on the wall, not more than a few inches from the ground, so that the rats and mice may read as they run. On the paper is written :

> *Ratton and moose,*
> *Awa frae this hoose ;*
> *Awa ower to the mill,*
> *And there tak your fill !*

What the miller may say, when the vermin obey this order, is not recorded.

Invisibility is easily attained in Scotland ; and if Wells's Invisible Man had only been a Scot he need not have gone to half the trouble he did, nor need he have suffered the fate that overtook him.

To become invisible is a very easy matter ; and easy it is, too, to obtain the necessary magic stone. Take the eggs from a raven's nest, and boil them ; then return them to the nest. The birds realise that something has happened, and they fly away ; but, after three days, the male bird returns carrying a small piece of crystal in his beak. The only difficulty in the whole affair—and that is not a great one—is to get possession of this stone. The possessor of the stone can make himself invisible at will. All he has to do is to put the stone in his mouth. To become visible again he has only to take the stone from his mouth and put it into his pocket. Surely nothing could be simpler! Unless it be the other method—of catching fern seeds as they fall at midnight—and it must be exactly at midnight—on St John's Eve.

Everyone knows that there are certain magical powers about a horse-shoe ; and nearly everyone believes that the shoe must be affixed ends uppermost—to 'keep in the luck'—but that is only another silly English tale. In Scotland, the horse-shoe can be hung any way, for it is not so much a bringer of luck as a keeper-away of evil. And this is how it obtained the power to keep off witches and bogles and all other imps of the Devil : The Devil once upon a time at midnight pulled from his bed a smith in Lochaber, for badly his hooves needed shoeing. The smith, annoyed and frightened, but having the Devil in his power, not only burned the horn of the hoof he was shoeing, but the fleshy part, too. Then, in driving in the first nail, the smith deliberately hammered it into the flesh. The Devil screamed in agony, and hopped round the smithy on one unshod foot. He howled for the man to tear out the nail and to shoe him properly, but the smith refused until the Devil was ready to promise him anything. And the promise the man exacted was, that wherever a horse-shoe lay or hung no evil thing could pass. And the Devil, perforce, had to agree.

But there is something stronger against the Devil, and all evil, than all the horse-shoes in the world : there is the Rowan tree. No bogle, no imp, no witch, nothing of evil, dare ever come near the Rowan ; and even the tiniest twig of it will keep off all the legions of Hell that ever there are.

A growing Rowan, close by a house, will ensure perfect safety for the house and all in it—and there is scarcely a dwelling of any kind, bothy or castle—and particularly in the Highlands—that has not its Rowan tree somewhere close by.

But even no more than a simple cross of the Rowan's wood, placed over the door, will suffice to keep from the house all evil attentions.

No boat should ever venture on a loch without having at least a thole-pin of Rowan wood ; and no larger vessel should ever be launched without there being, somewhere among its timbers, a bit of the Rowan to safeguard it against the storms and the tempests that the sea-devils raise.

Cattle should never be driven with anything but a stick cut from the Rowan.

David Ritchie, the deformed pauper who was the original of Scott's Black Dwarf, was never without a piece of Rowan in his pocket, and his garden was filled with the magic trees.

Beside almost every Holy Well, or Magical Spring, there is a Rowan tree—planted there, no doubt, by the guardian good spirit of the well or spring to save the waters from any likelihood of evil contamination.

All over Scotland there are Holy Wells, and Healing Wells, and Wishing Wells.

There is the ' Fiddler's Well ' at Cromarty, the waters of which, taken in the early hours of the morning, will cure consumption ; there was a well on an island in Loch Maree that had the power to cure insanity, until it dried up under the great insult put on it by a shepherd who tried to cure his mad dog with its waters. Another magical well, drinking the waters of which was a cure for all ailments of the skin, gave up its virtues a few years ago after a woman bathed her scrofulous child in it.

The waters of a well at Bunchrew will cure whooping-cough ; and the waters of a well at Clachnaharry will wash away all diseases of the eyes. But Bunchrew and Clachnaharry are not the only places near Inverness with magical wells—there are over a dozen within a mile or two's radius of the burgh ; and the county as a whole is full of them.

There is a well in Lewis, the waters of which cannot be brought to the boil ; but they have all sorts of magical powers.

All over the south, too, there are Magic Wells : the county of Roxburgh, in particular, has any number.

The waters of many burns, and many waterfalls, have

healing powers. Almost any waterfall will cure toothache, for instance. All that the sufferer has to do, is to rise early, go to the waterfall ' dumb '—that is without speaking to anyone—strip naked, and stand under the icy cascade.

Having the tooth extracted seems an easier method.

SECOND SIGHT

The gift of Second Sight appears to have been ' written-up ' from every possible angle at some time or another, so that it seems almost futile to tackle the subject here. It may be even an impertinence to do so; in view of the fact that the subject has interested some of the greatest brains the world has known.

Hegel devoted much time and thought to the matter, and much space in his *Philosophie der Gheistes*, and scores of eminent men have gone deeply into it; but it still remains one of those mysterious things that lie beyond the understanding of man.

The gift of second sight, or prophecy by visions is, of course, not peculiar to Scotland; but it seems to have flourished more—and still does flourish more—in the mystic Celtic atmosphere of Scotland than almost anywhere else on earth.

As is usual in the case of Spiritualistic ' Mediums,' the ' Seer ' is invariably a person of no particular pretensions : in Scotland, more often than not, a simple fisherman or crofter; although there are records of the gift having been possessed by people of outstanding powers of intellect; but the possession of education, or super-intelligence, seems to get in the way of receptiveness; and that, of course, is a strong argument for the opinions of the sceptics, who main-

tain that the seers are no more than poor ' dafties ' imposing
on still greater ' dafties.'

But, as far as imposition is concerned, the gift is rarely,
if ever, ' professionalized ' ; and, indeed, many a man or
woman has had no more than one vision in a lifetime ; and
the majority of seers would rather be without the gift than
have it.

The vision may come in any place, and at any time of the
day or night, and it comes unbidden. There is no posing
about the Scottish seer—there is nothing of the fortune-
teller in him—simply he ' sees,' and simply he tells ; and
if he gains a reputation for his gift the reputation comes,
like the vision, unsought.

On the island of Eriskay there is, to-day, a *clachan*, every
inhabitant of which is reputed to have the ' sight.'

The most famous seer of the last two or three centuries
was Coinneach Odhar, usually referred to as The Brahan
Seer from the fact that he worked as a labourer, or in some
such other humble capacity, on the Brahan Estate.

Coinneach Odhar, or Kenneth the Sallow, was born at
Baile na Cille in the Lews about three hundred years ago,
but such an impression did his prophecies make that he is
still discussed in the Highlands as though he died no more
than a year or two ago.

The Brahan Seer prophesied the linking up of the chain
of lochs in the Great Glen about a hundred and fifty years
before Telford's Caledonian Canal came into being. The
sceptics put that down to natural shrewdness ; but natural
shrewdness does not explain away Kenneth's prophecy of
the battle of Culloden—delivered actually at Culloden,
where his words were taken down and preserved. Passing

over what later became the battlefield, he stopped, and said: 'This bleak moor, ere many generations have passed, shall be stained with the best blood of Scotland. Glad am I that I will not see that day.'

It must be remembered that there was scarcely a road at all in the Highlands when Kenneth truly prophesied that 'the day will come when there will be a road through the hills of Ross, and a bridge upon every stream.' And there was certainly no thought in the minds of men of such a tragedy to come as what was later to be known as the Highland Clearances; but long before the rapacity of alien land-owners drove out men that sheep might feed on the hills, Kenneth said: 'The clans will become so effeminate as to allow themselves to be driven from their native land by an army of sheep.'

But Kenneth's greatest prophecy—his best known, and, incidentally, his last—was the one that foretold the doom of the great House of Seaforth.

Kenneth Mackenzie, the third Earl of Seaforth, chief of his clan, and controller of vast tracts of land, visited Paris on some business for the king a year or two after the Restoration of Charles II. His jealous countess he left behind at Brahan Castle. Seaforth's stay in Paris was too prolonged for the lady's peace of mind; and, strange rumours of his conduct among the Parisiennes coming to her ears, she sent for Kenneth.

At first Kenneth would tell her nothing but that her lord was safe. 'Be satisfied,' he said, in answer to all her queries, 'ask no questions, let it suffice you to know that your lord is well and merry.'

But the countess wanted more than that; and with

entreaties, bribes, and threats, she managed at last to get at the truth. Kenneth's long harangue ended with his telling her that the earl was ' in a gay gilded room,' and that he was ' grandly decked out in velvets, with silks and cloth of gold,' and, more than that, that he could see the chief ' on his knees before a fair lady, his arm round her waist, and her hand pressed to his lips.'

At this, we are told ' the rage of the lady knew no bounds.' Poor Kenneth, unfortunately, came in for the rage that she should have waited to vent on her husband. Illogically, she blamed him for his insolence in daring to speak slightingly of the great Seaforth, and, immediately, before all who were assembled there, she denounced him for a slandering charlatan, and demanded his life as the penalty for speaking evil of her lord.

This was scarcely the reward that Kenneth had expected. At first he refused to believe the countess was serious ; but, to cut a long story short, within a few hours the unfortunate seer was conducted to Chanonry Point, and there burned to death in a tar-barrel on a charge of witchcraft.

But before his death he uttered the doom of Seaforth.

' I see into the far future,' he said ; ' and I read the doom of the race of my oppressor. The long-descended line of Seaforth will, ere many generations have passed, end in extinction and in sorrow. I see a chief, the last of his house, both deaf and dumb. He will be the father of four fair sons, all of whom he will follow to the tomb. He will live careworn, and die mourning, knowing that the honours of his line are to be extinguished for ever, and that no future chief of the Mackenzies shall bear rule at Brahan or in Kintail. After lamenting over the last and most promising of his sons, he himself shall sink into the grave, and the remnant of his possessions shall be inherited by a white-hooded lass from the east, and she is to kill her sister. And as a sign by which it may be known that these things are coming to pass, there shall be four great lairds in the days of the last Seaforth—the deaf and dumb chief; and these lairds shall be : Gairloch, Chisholm, Grant, and Raasay. And one shall be buck-toothed, another hare-lipped, another half-witted, and the fourth a stammerer. Chiefs like these shall be the allies and the neighbours of the last of the Seaforths ; and when he looks around him and sees them, he may know that his sons are doomed to death, that his broad lands shall pass away to the stranger, and that his race shall come to an end.'

And, in time, all that the seer predicted came to pass.

In 1794 there was born Francis Humberston Mackenzie, who became deaf, and latterly dumb ; and, when four sons were born to him, he looked around to find his neighbours and allies all as Kenneth had foretold over a hundred years before. One after another the sons of Seaforth died—the most promising of them last of all. And, on January the 11th, 1815, Lord Seaforth himself died—the last of his race. His title became extinct, and the chiefship of the Mackenzies, for what it was worth, passed to a remote collateral who succeeded to none of the lands : the Seaforth estates were inherited by Lord Seaforth's daughter—the white-hooded lass from the east. She was the widow of Sir Samuel Hood, who had had command of the Indian seas. She returned to Scotland in white weeds, and doubly ' Hooded ' by name.

Some years later she married again. She married a

grandson of the Earl of Galloway, who was a Stewart. One day, driving out with her younger sister in a pony carriage, the ponies took fright, and both women were flung from the carriage. The younger one was so severely injured that, after a lingering illness, she died. As the ' white-hooded lass from the east ' had been driving the carriage, and had failed to control the ponies, she was considered to have caused her sister's death.

And in such a way was the greatest prophecy of Coinneach Odhar fulfilled.

But if Kenneth is the most famous of seers, he is not, by many hundreds, the only one.

No more than a few years ago a man crossing a lonely and desolate moor saw a house where no house had ever been, or was ever likely to be ; and from the house, which was all lighted up, there came the sounds of music and dancing. Not long ago, on the very spot, an Englishman built a house as a shooting-box ; and every year the place is filled with his guests who dance and play into the early hours of every morning.

In the south, the rhyming prophecies of Thomas of Ercildoune, who lived in the thirteenth century, are still coming true.

The materialists may snort and scoff, but it is impossible to dismiss lightly the testimony of thousands who have actually seen age-old, or month-old, prophecies come true.

WITCHES AND WITCHCRAFT

For centuries witches occupied such an important place in the life of Scotland that Act after Act was passed for dealing with them. But the great day of the witch-tormentors did not come until just after the Reformation, when the biblical injunction to the effect that ' Thou shalt not suffer a witch to live,' was obeyed to such an extent that thousands of poor old women, and thousands of young ones, too, were done to death by the most ghastly methods that man's ingenuity could devise. Every possible type of torture and indignity was inflicted upon these poor wretches in the name of religion and righteousness. Following days, and sometimes weeks, of hideous torture, release from suffering usually came in the shape of death by burning alive.

The last witch to be killed in Scotland was burnt in a tar-barrel because she is said to have had her daughter shod with iron, and to have ridden the girl as one might ride a horse. To-day such a thing would, no doubt, be dismissed by a half-column in the papers, following a prosecution by the Scottish Society for the Prevention of Cruelty to Children. After which, the old dame would be tightly, and rightly, locked up in a Lunatic Asylum.

It was not until 1563 that Witchcraft became a capital offence, and from then onwards, for nearly a couple of centuries, a witch-panic seems to have raged throughout the land.

It is only fair to our forefathers to say that, at the same time, a similar state of affairs existed in every other Protestant land. And it is only fair to the Protestants in general, to say that the Catholics had their little burnings for equally senseless reasons.

The death penalty was exacted, not only from those reputed to be witches, but, too, from those who in any way associated with suspects.

No one appears to have been safe at the time when the witch fires were blazing at their height. A man, or more generally, a woman, had only to be what we should call to-day a ' little temperamental ' and that was enough to ensure a speedy and devilish death. An outbreak of cattle disease was a sure sign that the cattle had been ' bewitched,' and some old woman, who may have been seen a few days earlier looking at the beasts, would go to her ' trial ' and later to the tar-barrel. Should anyone fall ill, with even the most minor complaint, following the visit of some obnoxious relative, or unwanted acquaintance, the relative or acquaintance was responsible, and denouncement and death immediately followed.

To the reforming zealots, no action was too puerile but it could be made to form the basis of a charge. And those who hesitated to condemn, were in their turn condemned : either they were themselves witches, or worse—Catholics or Atheists.

But, leaving historical realities for Folklore, we find that witches, endowed with marvellous powers, existed in Scotland far back in the dim and distant ages. The story of MacBeth and the witches may, or may not, be true ; but Dumbarton Rock still stands to testify to the power of the witches who hurled the huge boulder at St Patrick. And did not the Wizard Michael Scott split the Eildon Hills in three ?

In Sutherland, on either side of the Kyle of Durness there is a huge boulder. The one on the west side of the kyle lies a few feet from the shore, the one on the east well above high-water mark. And this is how they come to be there : There were two witches of prodigious physical strength, who quarrelled incessantly with each other as to which was the stronger of the two. At last they decided to settle the matter. Each one was to fling, from her own side of the kyle, a great stone. The great stones were raised, balanced, and flung ; and there they are to this day.

English witches, so we are told, always travelled on broomsticks ; but the broomstick was rarely used in Scotland. For crossing lochs and rivers, and even for going from island to island in the sea, an eggshell served as a boat. That is why the majority of Scots boys and girls are taught to turn their eggshells upside down in the egg-cup, and to break them up with the spoon. They are then, of course, useless to the witches.

Sometimes witches transformed themselves into animals, the better to go about their business. Usually it was some small animal, generally a hare ; but often it was as a cat that the witch went on her errands. There was once an old man who was sorely tormented by cats, until one day he took down his sword and wounded several of them. That day a number of the women in the district were found to have sword cuts.

Isobel Gowdie, who was burned in 1662, gave the following rigmarole as the charm by which she, and other witches of her acquaintance, lost human shape and took on that of a hare :

> *I sall gang intill a hare,*
> *Wi' sorrow, sigh, and muckle care ;*
> *And I sall gang in the devil's name,*
> *Ay while I come back again.*

To regain human shape another charm was chanted :

Hare, hare, God send thee care ;
I am in a hare's likeness now,
But I shall be ane woman e'en now,
Hare, hare, God send thee care.

Isobel Gowdie also explained that not only did she and her associates at times become hares and cats, but also that there were occasions when they became crows ; and that ' When we will be in the shape of crows we will be larger than ordinary crows, and will sit upon branches of trees.'

Witches banded themselves together in ' covens.' A coven consisting of thirteen : The Devil, and an ' officer,' or ' Devil's Registrar,' a ' maiden,' and ten others—either witches or warlocks. The ' maiden ' was usually the Devil's favourite, and was invariably a comely, good-looking lass. No doubt the ' ae winsome wench ' in the ' cutty sark o' Paisley harn,' who took Tam o' Shanter's fancy at Kirk-Alloway, was the ' maiden ' of that particular meeting.

A witch could be detected by any one of several tests. Every witch had a certain mark on her body, known as the ' Devil's Claw.' This mark was supposed to be made by the Devil at the time he made the witch his own. It was an insensitive spot into which a pin could be driven without drawing blood ; and a large pin was the witch-finder's tool. The witch would be stripped before a number of the godly, and the pin jabbed into her body until the ' Devil's Claw ' mark was found.

Ducking was another method of detection. The witch would be flung into a pool or a loch. If she drowned, she

was innocent ; if she floated, she was guilty ; and she
would be fished out of the water to be burned.

BAIRNS' RHYMES

*Most of the Bairns' Rhymes of Scotland are of consider-
able antiquity. Some of those set out on the following pages
are still in use. Many of them will, no doubt, stir a pleas-
urable chord in the memories of older readers ; and particularly in the memories of those exiles who left the Old
Country at an early age—those whose recollections of
Scotland are inextricably bound up with their childish
years, and with the games they once played at home.*

*Here is the Scottish equivalent of the English ' I'm the
king of the castle' :*

I, Wullie Wastle,
Stand here on ma Castle ;
An' a' the dogs o' your toon,
Will never drive Wullie Wastle doon !

*And here is a rather precocious little thing, sung by little
girls when playing with a ball :*

Stottie ba', hinnie ba', tell to me,
How mony bairns am I to hae ?—
Yin to leeve, and yin to dee,
And yin to sit on the nurse's knee !

*The use of the next rhyme is explained by the rhyme
itself :*

Nieve-nievie nick-nack,
Whit haun wull ye tak ?
Tak the richt, tak the wrang,
I'll beguile ye gin I can.

With arms linked behind their backs, little girls will walk up and down singing :

Jeanie Mac, Jeanie Mac, Bonnie Jeanie MacGee,
Turn your back aboot to me ;
An' gin ye fin' ony bawbee,
Pick it up an' gie't to me.

Here is a rhyme for ' Kiss-in-the-Ring,' or some other similar game :

Och, here a puir widow frae Babylon,
Wi' six puir bairns a' alane ;
Yin can bake, an' yin can brew,
Yin can shape, an' yin can sew,
Yin can sit at the fire an' spin,
An' yin can bake a cake for the king ;
Come pick ye east, come pick ye west,
An' pick the yin that ye loe best.

And this to yell at a liar :

Liar, liar, lick-spit,
In ahint the caunlestick !
Whit's guid for awfu' liars ?—
Brimstane an' muckle fires !

This to secure a fair start at a race :

Are ye saddled ?—*Aye.*
Are ye bridled ?—*Aye.*
Are ye ready for the ca' ?—*Aye ! Aye ! ! Aye ! ! !*
Aff then, an' awa !

*On giving a bairn pick-a-back ; or when one boy is about
to be a ' horse,' and the other a ' rider ' :*

Matthew, Mark, Luke, an' John,
Haud the cuddy till I loup on ;
Haud it fast, an' haud it shüre,
Till I win ower the misty muir.

In imitation of a toast :

Here's to you and yours,
No forgettin' us an' oors ;
An' whenever you an' yours
Comes to see us an' oors,
Us an' oors'll be as guid
To you and yours,
As ever you an' yours
Was to us an' oors,
Whenever us an' oors
Cam to see you an' yours.

*The following little bit of business philosophy comes,
naturally enough, from Glasgow :*

Oh, the bonnie wee barra's mines,
It disna belong tae MacHara ;
The fly wee bloke,
He stuck tae ma rock,
So I'm gaunna stick tae his barra !

*And the next, which cannot be more than a hundred years
old, or so, also comes from Clydeside :*

I saw the Forty-second,
I saw them gang awa.

I saw the Forty-second
Mairchin' tae the Broomielaw.
Some o' them had white kirseckies,
Some o' them had nane ava.
I saw the Forty-second,
I saw them gang awa.
I saw the Forty-second
Mairchin' tae the Broomielaw.

*That is usually sung to the tune of ' Wha wadna fecht
for Charlie ? ' The ' kirseckie ' was the short white coat at
one time worn by kilted troops. The word being derived,
undoubtedly, from the Gaelic ; perhaps from CAORA, a
sheep, and SEICHE, a hide, or skin.*

*And from the Glasgow district, too, comes ' Babbity
Bowster ' :*

Wha learnt ye to dance, Babbity Bowster, Babbity Bowster,
Wha learnt ye to dance, Babbity Bowster brawly ?

Ma mither learnt me to dance, Babbity Bowster, Babbity
  Bowster,
Ma mither learnt me to dance, Babbity Bowster brawly.

Wha gied ye the keys to keep, Babbity Bowster, Babbity
  Bowster,
Wha gied ye the keys to keep, Babbity Bowster brawly ?

Ma mither gied me the keys to keep, Babbity Bowster,
  Babbity Bowster,
Ma mither gied me the keys to keep, Babbity Bowster
  brawly.

*The air of ' Tam o' the Linn,' the words of which follow, is
mentioned in ' The Complaynt of Scotland,' 1548. The
words have, no doubt, undergone much change since then :*

Tam o' the Linn cam up the gait,
Wi' twenty puddens on a plate,
An' ilka pudden had a preen.
We'll eat them a', quo' Tam o' the Linn.

Tam o' the Linn had nae breeks to wear,
So he coft him a sheep's-skin to make him a pair,
The skinny side oot, the woolly side in,
It's grand simmer cleedin', quo' Tam o' the Linn.

Tam o' the Linn, he had three bairns,
They fell in the fire in ilk ither's airms ;
Oh, quo' the bunemaist, *I've got a het skin ;*
Jings ! It's hetter below, quo' Tam o' the Linn.

Tam o' the Linn gaed ower the moss,
To seek a stable till his horse ;
The moss was open, an' Tam fell in,
Dod ! I've stabled masel, quo' Tam o' the Linn.

*The cloker, or broody hen, commemorated in this little
Border rhyme must have been a gey teuch yin :*

There was a cloker dabbit at a man,
He dee'd for fear, he dee'd for fear.
There was a cloker dabbit at a man,
An' that's no sae queer, no sae queer !

An appeal to the rain to go away :

Rainy, rainy, rattlestanes,
  Dinna rain on me ;

Rain on Johnny Groats's hoose,
　Far ayont the sea !

Or the following :

Rain, rain, gang away,
Come ye back on weshin' day.

In the north, on a snowy day, the children chant :

The wise men o' the Eas'
Are pluckin' their geese,
　And flingin' the feathers away, away,
　Flingin' the feathers away.

*The following is sung as an insult to the people of Bowden
in the county of Roxburgh, by the children of neighbouring
villages :*

Tillieloot, Tillieloot, Tillieloot o' Bowden !
Oor cat's kittled in Airchie's wig ;
Tillieloot, Tillieloot, Tillieloot o' Bowden,
Three o' them naked, an' three o' them cled !

*And this couplet, for some hidden reason, is regarded as
insulting by the Soutars of Selkirk :*

Soutars yin, soutars twa,
Soutars in the Back Raw !

*And, passing from Soutars to Weavers, there is the
following from Edinburgh :*

As I gaed up the Canongate,
　And through the Netherbow,
Four-and-twenty wabsters
　Were swingin' in a tow ;

The tow gied a crack,
  The wabsters gied a girn,
Fie, let me doun again,
  I'll never steal a pirn ;
I'll never steal a pirn,
  I'll never steal a pow ;
Fie, let me doun again,
  I'll steal nae mair frae yow.

  *Scott has a version of the following as a chapter-heading
in ' Rob Roy' :*

Baron o' Buchlyvie,
May the foul fiend drive ye,
And a' to wee bits rive ye,
For buildin' sic a toon,
Where there's nae horse's meat,
Nor naethin' for a man to eat,
Nor even a chair to sit doon.

  *The Baron o' Buchlyvie was one of the Buchanans of
Kippen, who styled himself ' King of Kippen,' from which
elevation of Kippen to the dignity of a kingdom, the following
saying arose :*

Oot o' Scotland and into Kippen !

A FEW OLD RHYMES AND SAWS ON PLACES

Annan, Tweed, and Clyde,
Rise a' oot o' ae hillside ;
Tweed ran, Annan wan,
Clyde fell, an' brak its neck ower Corra Linn.

Ye'll be kissed, an' I'll be kissed,
  We'll a' be kissed th' morn :
The braw, braw lads o' Jethart toun
  Will kiss us a' th' morn.

Cairnsmuir o' Fleet,
  Cairnsmuir o' Dee,
An' Cairnsmuir o' Carsphairn—
  The biggest o' the three.

Carrick for a man,
  Kyle for a coo,
Cunningham for corn an' bere,
  An' Galloway for ' oo.'

Edinburgh's big,
But Biggar's Biggar.

Ae crook o' the Forth
Is worth an earldom in the north.

'Tween the Isle o' May
An' the links o' Tay,
Mony a ship's been cast away.

When Finhaven Castle rins to sand,
The warld's end is near at hand.

Aberdeen shall be a green,
  An' Dundee be dung doon ;
But Forfar will be forfar still,
  An' Brechin a braw burgh-toon.

Ae mile o' Don's worth twa o' Dee,
Except for salmon, stane, an' tree.

Glasgow for bells,
Lithgow for wells,
Falkirk for beans and peas.

Jethart justice—first hang your man, and judge him efter.

Teri buss an' Teri Odin,
Hawick lads that feil at Flodden :
Imitatin' Border bowmen
Aye defend your richts and common.

Dunse dings a'.

A FEW RHYMES ABOUT THE WEATHER

Gin the gress should grow in Janiveer,
It'll be the worst for't a' the year.

Mony hawes,
Mony snaws.

Gin Candlemas-day be dry and fair,
The half o' winter's to come and mair ;
Gin Candlemas-day be wet and foul,
The half o' winter's gane at Youl.

Mist in May, and heat in Jüne,
Gars the harvest come richt süne.

Mairch water an' May sun,
Maks claes clean, an' maidens dun.

Whene'er the mune is on her back,
Mend your shoon, an' sort your thack.

East wind and wast
Foretells a blast ;
An' north an' sooth,
Foretells a drooth.

Nae weather's ill,
Gin the wind bide still.

Mist on the hills
Brings water to the mills ;
Mist in the hollows—
Fine weather follows.

To talk o' the weather's the folly o' men,
For when rain's on the hill, there'll be sun in the glen.

THE LOW ROAD

An old Celtic belief—current still in Scotland, and not
only in Scotland, but in Ireland, too, and in Wales and
Brittany—has it that when a man meets with death in a
foreign land, his spirit returns to the place of his birth by
an underground fairy way—The Low Road.

In 1745, during the retreat of the Scottish army following
its invasion of England, several of the wounded had, unfortunately, to be left behind in Carlisle as they could not
struggle further.   Many of them fell into the hands of the
English and were flung into Carlisle gaol.   The song *The
Bonnie Banks o' Loch Lomond*, which was undoubtedly
written at the period, tells of two of the Scottish prisoners
—one of whom was to be released, and who would take
The High Road home to Scotland, whilst the other, who

was to be executed, would take The Low Road. As the release of one and the execution of the other were timed for the same hour, the Dead, travelling by The Low Road with the speed of a spirit, would, naturally—or supernaturally—be in Scotland before the Living, who would have to tramp several weary miles of The High Road before he could hope to cross the Border.

If this little story were better known we might have *The Bonnie Banks o' Loch Lomond* sung more in the spirit in which it should be sung, and less in the entirely wrong, but more customary, spirit of vainglorious ranting.

THE KING O' THE CATS

This amusing little folk-tale hails from Badenoch. Whether or not there is any written version of it I do not know. I have only heard it told, and must re-tell it in my own words.

Once upon a time, on a frosty moonlit night, a man was struggling along a mountainy road, when, suddenly, he saw before him three cats. And that was strange enough, as the man was miles from any house—and cats, as surely everyone knows, never stray far from the shelter of a house and the warmth of a fire—but stranger still was the fact that each of the three cats was weeping bitterly.

A bit further along the road, the three cats were joined by another three. And then, by threes and fours, and by half-dozens, the road became packed with cats—grey cats and black cats, big cats and little cats, she-cats and Toms. Never was seen such a sight so strange ; and surely all the cats in Badenoch, and far beyond, must have been gathered there on that road, that night.   And never a blink at the man did they give—not one of them—he might not have been there at all.

And then, suddenly, from over a hill, and on to the road there came four big pole-cats bearing a small, cat-sized coffin.

' And what, in the name of heaven, will this be ? ' thought the man, but never a word did he say.

After a while the cats—the whole concourse—following the coffin-bearers, mounted a bit of a hill, and there they spread themselves in a mighty, weeping, circle.

Then the four pole-cats began to scratch the earth, digging a grave for all they were worth.

And, what with the digging, and what with the weeping and wailing that was going on, the man was able to creep quite close to the coffin and take a good peep at it.   After all that he had seen, there was nothing could amaze him ; so that he was not a bit put out, or surprised, when he looked at the coffin, and saw that it was draped with a purple cloth that had worked on it, in threads of gold, a cypher and a royal crown.

Having seen that, the man stepped back, for he was no more than a poor and simple man who knew his place, and it was not for him to be too near a royal funeral ; but, for all that, he thought no harm might be done by his waiting in the background to see what happened.

After a while, when the grave was dug to the satisfaction of the four pole-cats, a big black Tom rose up to deliver an impassioned oration in very good Cat-Gaelic, which is not unlike Irish ; but as the man only had the Gaelic of Badenoch devil a word could he understand , except the one ever-repeated word *righ*, and that meaning ' king.'

After the burial, and after all the cats had gone, the man went on his way.

But as the funeral had kept him late, he thought it best to seek for shelter. In the distance he could see a twinkling light, and at last he came to a cottage. He knocked at the door and walked in.

'Hail to the house!' said he; and 'Hail to the Stranger!' was the welcome answer he got; for that was always the way in Badenoch before the people took to keeping English tourists as the principal industry of the district.

Whilst the woman of the house prepared some supper, the *fear-an-tighe* brought out the bottle, and he and the traveller sat each one on either side the fire; and the traveller telling the tale of his strange adventure on the road.

And he finished the story with a fine description of the gold-worked royal crown and cypher on the purple cloth that had been over the coffin.

When—suddenly—the cat of the house, and it no more than a bit of a kitten, leapt to its feet from the rug where it had been dozing. Out came its claws, up went its back, and into the burning peats it spat.

And '*A Dhè!*' it yelled; 'then me father's dead! *Ochòin! Ochòin!* Treason and treachery! But I'll yet be king o' the cats!'

And up the chimney he vanished.

THE STORY OF THE HEATHER ALE

The story of the heather ale is well-known. There are several good tales based on the old folk-story ; and Robert Louis Stevenson made use of the theme for one of his poems.

The story is told here in Anglo-Scots, or Scotticized English, as a tale for bairns.

Once upon a time, lang syne, there were folk in this country called Pechs—or, as some say, Picts. Queer wee folk they were with red hair ; and wild they were—wilder far even than the wild Heilanders, and that's saying a lot. And the Pechs didna even wear a kilt—they wore nothing at all except a bit of paint, and that's how they got their name, so some folks say, frae the Romans who tried to beat them and to get the country. But the Romans couldna frighten the Pechs—not they ! and the Pechs were the only people in all the world that the Romans couldna beat. As a matter o' fact, the Pechs beat the Romans—and such licks they gave them that the Romans were frightened out of their wits and built a great wall across the north of England to keep out the Pechs ! And that just shows !

Well now, if the Romans could beat everybody in the world except the Pechs, and the Pechs could beat the Romans, the Pechs must have been the greatest fighters and the bravest men in all the world. That stands to reason. And it must have been a wonderful lot of people who did beat the Pechs in the end, for they were beaten— they were beaten by the Scots.

Well, after a while these two wonderful races mixed and mingled—just think o' that !—the two bravest races in the world, the Picts and the Scots. And those are the people that we're descended frae. And that just shows a lot more ! The only trouble is, we are still kind o' fond of quarrelling amongst ourselves—just like the Picts and Scots lang syne —and that's where we're done. Silly ! but there it is.

And we're a stubborn lot—and thrawn—just like the king o' the Pechs.

Now, the Pechs were very fond of drinking ale. Oh, but wonderful ale it was—not a bit like the stuff you smell outside public houses to-day. Not a bit ! Heather ale it was, and so wonderful that folk all over the world heard about it, and wanted some. No doubt that was what the Romans were after ! And the Scots !

But the secret of this wonderful ale was only kenned by the king of the Pechs and his eldest son. The king had to tell his son, for fear of being killed in battle ; so that if he were killed, his son, when he became king, would know all about it and could tell his son, and so on. And that's how the secret was kept, and passed on, from father to son.

But when the Scots came they didna ken this exactly. And, as they wanted the secret, they sent for the old king to come and tell them all about it ; and, as he had been beaten, he had to do as he was told.

Well, the king o' the Scots looked at the old beaten king o' the Pechs, and demanded to know the secret of the heather ale. But do you think the old Pech king would tell ? Not he !

So the king o' the Scots said, all right, he would have to torture him. Well, of course, the king o' the Pechs didna fancy that ; so in the end he said he would tell ; but he meant to jouk the king o' the Scots for all that.

He said he would tell on one condition. He said he

would only tell if first they killed his son. You see what he was driving at? For he meant that the secret should never be known.

Said he:

> *My son ye maun kill,*
> *Before you I will tell*
> *How we brew the yill*
> *Frae the heather bell!*

Well, the king o' the Scots sent for the Pech prince, and had him killed on the spot right before his own father.

'And now,' said the king o' the Scots, 'what aboot it?'

'What aboot what?' asked the king o' the Pechs.

'Aboot this heather yill, of course,' said the king o' the Scots.

'Awa!' said the auld Pech king; 'd'ye think I'm tellin' you?'

'Well,' said the Scots king, 'ye promised, if I had your son killed; and there he is as deid as a log.'

'Aye,' said the Pech king, 'juist so. And now ye may kill me, for I'll never tell!'

And then he recited:

> *And though me ye may kill,*
> *I winna you tell*
> *How we brew the yill*
> *Frae the heather bell!*

So they just cracked him ower the heid! And serve him right—the thrawn auld deil!

And that's how the secret died. And that's why any ale made to-day is just poor stuff in comparison, for the heather ale o' the Pechs must have been a grand drink all right to have had all that bother and stramash made about it.

But that Pech king was a daft auld fool with all his stubbornness. And, if he was the last king o' the Picts, he certainly wasna the last thrawn auld fool, for there's still a lot like him left in Scotland.

THOMAS THE RHYMER

Thomas the Rhymer, True Thomas, or Thomas of Ercildoune, as he is variously called, flourished in the thirteenth century. It is supposed that his real name was Thomas Learmont.

True Thomas is mentioned by Barbour in his LIFE OF BRUCE *; and Fordun, a few years later, also refers to him. From Fordun, the following story is derived :*

On the day before the death of Alexander III (1285), he did foretell the same to the Earl of March, saying, ' before the next day at noon, such a tempest shall blow as Scotland has not felt for many years before.' The next morning, the day being clear, and no change appearing in the air, the nobleman did challenge Thomas of his saying, calling him an impostor. He replied that noon was not yet past ; about which time a post came to advertise the earl of the king his sudden death. ' Then,' said Thomas, ' this is the tempest I foretold ; and so it shall prove to Scotland.' Whence or how he had this knowledge can hardly be affirmed ; but sure it is that he did divine and answer truly of many things to come.

Tradition ascribes to Thomas many rhyming prophecies : whether or no he was the author of all, or any, of those with which he is credited, can only be a matter of conjecture. Be that as it may, the ' Rhymes of True Thomas ' occupy a not unimportant part in our folklore.

Here is one :

> At Eildon Tree, if you should be,
> A brig owre Tweed you there may see.

Of this rhyme, Scott says :

This rhyme seems to have been founded in that insight into futurity possessed by most men of a sound and combining judgment. The spot in question commands an extensive prospect of the course of the river ; and it was easy to see that, when the country became in the least degree improved, a bridge would be somewhere thrown over the stream. In fact you now see no fewer than three bridges from the same elevated situation.

Thomas is supposed to have prophesied the battle of Pinkie (1547) in a rhyme ending :

> Between Seton and the sea,
> Mony a man that day shall dee.

The rhymes of Thomas were as well known in the Highlands and the Isles as they were in his native county of Berwick. In the Highlands it is firmly believed that Thomas was foretelling the Highland Clearances of the eighteenth and nineteenth centuries when he said :

The teeth of the sheep shall lay the plough on the shelf.

The following prophecy is considered to have been fulfilled when the last Earl Marischal was banished in 1746, *and his lands of Inverugie forfeited :*

Inverugie by the sea,
Lordless shall thy landis be ;
And underneath thy hearthstane
The tod shall bring her broodis hame.

The tod (the fox) seems to have been very fond of bringing ' her broodis hame ' to the hearthstanes of Scots castles. There are several historical references to this having actually happened. Dunottar is one castle where this is supposed to have happened, and Dunvegan in Skye is another. In the rhyme given above, Dunottar is sometimes substituted for Inverugie.

One of the most famous of the rhymes attributed to Thomas is :

York was, London is, but Edinburgh shall be
The greatest o' the three.

York was, of course, the principal city of the Romans during their occupation of what is now England. London's position we are forced to recognise. Apparently Edinburgh's great day (and Scotland's !) has yet to come.

Thomas is supposed to have given the following rhyme on his own infallibility :

When the saut gaes abüne the meal,
Believe nae mair o' Tammie's tale.

Chambers, commenting on this rhyme, says :

This seems to mean . . . that it is just as impossible for the price of the small quantity of salt used in the preparation of porridge to exceed the value of the larger quantity of meal required for the same purpose, as for his prophecies to become untrue.

One of the rhymes—a great favourite on the Borders—runs :

Tide, tide, whate'er betide,
There'll aye be Haigs at Bemersyde.

And there certainly always had been Haigs in possession of Bemersyde, since the time of Petrus de Haga, who obtained his charter to the lands in the reign of Malcolm IV, until close on a hundred years ago, when the main branch died out. Thomas, in consequence, lost a little prestige ; but the rhyme and Thomas were hailed again with great glee, when, just after the war, the nation presented Bemersyde to Earl Haig, a cadet of the ancient family.

THE WAITING WARRIORS

Thomas of Ercildowne, during his retirement, has been supposed, from time to time, to be levying forces to take the field in some crisis of his country's fate. The story has often been told, of a daring horse-jockey having sold a black horse to a man of venerable and antique appearance, who appointed the remarkable hillock upon Eildon hills, called the Lucken-hare, as the place where, at twelve o'clock at night, he should receive the price. He came, his money was paid in ancient coin, and he was invited by his customer to view his residence. The trader in horses followed his guide in the deepest astonishment through several long ranges of stalls, in each of which a horse stood motionless,

while an armed warrior lay equally still at the charger's feet.
' All these men,' said the wizard in a whisper, ' will awaken
at the battle of Sheriffmuir.' At the extremity of this extraordinary depot hung a sword and a horn, which the
prophet pointed out to the horse-dealer as containing the
means of dissolving the spell. The man in confusion took
the horn and attempted to wind it. The horses instantly
started in their stalls, stamped, and shook their bridles, the
men arose and clashed their armour, and the mortal,
terrified at the tumult he had excited, dropped the horn
from his hand. A voice like that of a giant, louder even
than the tumult around, pronounced these words :

Wo to the coward that ever he was born,
That did not draw the sword before he blew the horn.

A whirlwind expelled the horse-dealer from the cavern, the
entrance to which he could never again find.

Scott : LETTERS ON DEMONOLOGY AND WITCHCRAFT.

*Although Scott makes no mention of the fact, this story
of Thomas the Rhymer and the sleeping warriors is undoubtedly founded on the old Celtic tale—a tale told in
Ireland as well as in Scotland—of the Fian Warriors, who
are said to be waiting in a cavern until the day comes when
all Gaeldom shall rise against its oppressors. Beside the
entrance to the cavern there hangs a horn that must be
blown three times. In a crisis, hundreds of years ago, someone went to call the Fianna. He blew the horn once, and
the warriors awakened and rose on their elbows. They are
still in that position, waiting for the horn to be blown again,
and again ; for the man who went to call them dropped dead
with fright ; and no one now knows where the cavern is.*

PART III

.

FACTS

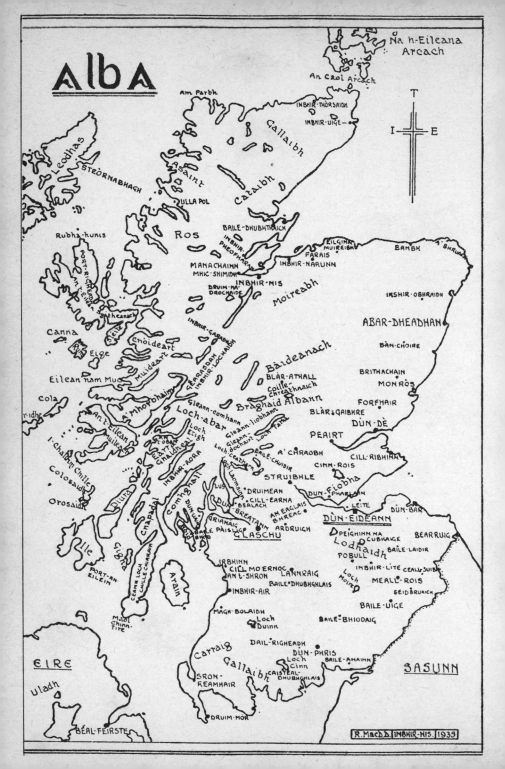

PART III

LANGUAGE—GAELIC AND SCOTS

It is extremely difficult to arrive at such figures, but a rough estimate based on recent computations suggests that there are not less than ten thousand persons in Scotland who have no English, and who speak nothing but the Gaelic. And it is estimated that there are over 170,000 of Scotland's population who are bi-lingual, speaking both English and Gaelic with, more or less, equal fluency. Despite the decrease of Gaelic speakers shown in official figures a few years ago, there is every reason to believe that the number of Gaelic speakers is now steadily, if very slowly, increasing. There are, of course, too, thousands of Scots Gaelic speakers outwith Scotland who are not subject to linguistic statistical returns.

Obviously, it is not possible to go very deeply into the language here ; but it may be of interest if certain rough explanations are given : in the first place, as a corollary to one or two other sections of this book ; and in the second place, because of the large number of Gaelic words that appear throughout Scottish life and literature in general.

There are eighteen letters in the Gaelic alphabet :
A, B, C, D, E, F, G, H, I, L, M, N, O, P, R, S, T, U.
Note the omission of J, K, Q, V, W, X, Y and Z.

And these eighteen letters serve most adequately all the requirements of an extremely complete language. In the Gaelic, with very few exceptions, each sound has its own definite symbol, either of one plain letter or accented letter, or of a collection of letters. There are few, if any, such anomalies as are to be found in English, as, for instance, the O in *for*, *ton*, and *hot* ; and the A in *far*, *war*, and *hat* ; or, to go still further, the classic example of OU in such words as *plough*, *through*, *cough*, *rough*, and *dough*.

It is impossible here to explain all the differences that there are in the Gaelic vowel sounds, or to explain how and where they differ from the vowel sounds of English : it will be sufficient here, to say that, for the most part, *I* has the sound of *ee* in English ; and *U* has the sound of the English *oo* (not *yew*). *E* in the Gaelic has sometimes the sound of *e* in the English word *get*, but mostly its sound approximates to the *a* in *say*. All these are, of course, not rules ; they are merely examples ; and there are many variations, but in the Gaelic the variations of sounds are definitely shown, either by the vowel letter being accented one way or the other, or by the vowel letter's position in conjunction with that of some other letter.

The consonants, roughly, have almost the same sounds as in English ; but with the following important exceptions : C and G are always hard ; L is usually liquid—something like the L sound in the English word *brilliant* ; CH is nearly always guttural as in *loch*. It never has the English sound as in *cheap*. And that applies equally to the beginning of a word as to the end. Thus : *Chat* is not sounded like *Tchat*, nor like *Kat* ; and if there is any difficulty in pronouncing it, say *Lochat*, and then knock the *lo* off it. *D* has a softer sound than in English : more like a *T* sound, and sometimes like the sound of *J* ; *B*, more often than not, softens almost to a *P* sound. *N* very often has the sound of

English *ng* as in *thing*. *S* before *e* or *i* is pronounced like *sh* as in English *sh*all.

But as this is not a Gaelic lesson, and as it cannot be any more than the giving of a few very rough hints to the general reader who has no Gaelic at all, it is not necessary, nor desirable, to go any further with pronunciations, other than to explain now what happens to certain letters under the process of what is known as aspiration.

It must be understood first that H is little more than an auxiliary letter in the Gaelic, but its position in the alphabet is an extremely important one. Certain consonants when followed by an H change their sounds entirely ; and certain others when followed by an H have their sounds considerably modified, or even nullified altogether. The aspirable consonants are : *b, c, d, f, g, m, p, s* and *t*. And the changes they undergo when aspirated are, roughly, as follow :

BH sounds like *V* in English.

MH like *V*, but pronounced more nasally.

CH guttural.

DH⎫ usually like *gh* in *ugh* ; but before *i* or *e* they are
GH⎭ equal to *y*.

FH silent, except in two or three words where the *h* only is heard.

PH like *F*.

SH like *H*.

TH like *H*.

There are, of course, definite rules governing aspiration ; but they cannot be gone into here. And one example will suffice to show how aspiration works. Thus : *mór* means ' big,' and *beinn* means ' mountain ' ; but when we wish to say ' big mountain ' we do not say *mór beinn*. The adjective follows the noun, and in this case the noun aspirates the adjective *mór* and turns it into *mhór*, which gives it the sound of ' vor.' So : *beinn mhór*.

And there is another little ' trick ' in the Gaelic, which, like aspiration, is governed by definitive rules, and which, like aspiration, operates in the language for the sake of greater euphony : in certain circumstances—and they are very few—certain letters are ' eclipsed ' by others : in this way : *Mac* means ' son,' *an* means ' the,' and *Sasunnach* means ' Englishman.' The three words together, using the genitive form *Sasunnaich*, would mean ' Son of the English-man,' but a *t* creeps in to ' eclipse ' the initial *S* of *Sasun-naich*, and so, instead of *Mac an Sasunnaich*, we get *Mac an t-Sasunnaich*, which sounds something like *Mac un Tasunnich*. The same thing occurs in the personal name *Mac an t-Saoir*, meaning ' Son of the Carpenter,' which sounds not unlike, and is usually anglicized as ' Macintyre.'

Sometimes an *'h*, which is sounded, is interpolated, as in *Òglaich na h-Alba*, ' Youth of Scotland.' And, again, this interpolation of the *h* is governed by a hard and fast rule.

To finish off this little rough explanation, here are just a few Gaelic words that the general reader is often likely to meet :

agus	and	*caraid*	friend
Alba	Scotland	*dubh*	dark, black
Albannach	Scotsman	*Eire*	Ireland
an, am	the	*Eireannach*	Irishman
beag	small	*Gaidheal*	Gael
bean	woman	*òg*	young
Ban-Albannach	Scotswoman	*pòg*	kiss

Sasunn	England	*slàinte*	health
siorramachd	county	*tigh*	house
sìth	fairy	*uisge-beatha*	whisky

SCOTS

Scots, as an expression referring to language, was originally spelled SCOTTIS, *and at one time meant the Gaelic. Modern Scots is a tongue richly spiced with words of Gaelic and French origin. The French words came into the country during the time of the ' Auld Alliance' ; and the Gaelic words are, of course, remnants left from the time when Gaelic was the language of all Scotland. Here are just a few Scots words together with their Gaelic correspondences :*

Scots	Gaelic	Scots	Gaelic
Airt	Àirde	Eizel	Éibhleag
Bannock	Bonnach	Fiere	Fear, Fir
Bard	Bàrd	Gab	Gab
Beck	Beic	Gillie, Keelie	Gille
Bothy	Bothan	Gloamin	Glòmanaich
Brae	Bràighe	Ingle	Aingeal
Braw	Brèagha	Kail	Càl
Breeks	Briogais	Kebbuck	Càbag
Brogue	Bròg	Loof	Làmh
Cairn	Càrn	Oxter	Achlais
Coup	Cop	Pig (jar, etc.)	Pigeadh
Cranreuch	Crann-reodhadh	Redd	Réidh
Ding	Dinn	Reel	Righil
Dowie	Dubhach	Scrog	Sgrog
Dule	Doilgheas	Skelp	Sgealb

Slaister	Sluaisdir	Trachle	Draghail
Sneeshan	Snaoisean	Trooshter	Trusdair
Spunk	Spong	Turkas	Turcais
Swap	Suaip	Wheesht	Uist
Toom	Taom	Winnock	Uinneag

The above list represents only a few out of hundreds. Below are a few of the many words that have come into Scots from French direct :

Scots	French or Old French	Scots	French or Old French
Ashet	Assiette	Grosset	Groseille
Aumrie	Armoire	Jalouse	Jalouser
Bonally	Bon aller	Kimmer	Commère
Boss	Boisson	Reeforts	Raifort
Calander	Calandre	Ruckle	Recueil
Caraff	Carafe	Spairge	Asperger
Fadge	Fouace	Spence	Despence
Fash	Facher	Stovie	Étuvé
Gardyloo	Gardez l'eau	Sybo	Cibo
Gigot	Gigot	Tassie	Tasse

NAMES—SURNAMES AND CHRISTIAN NAMES IN GAELIC

It has been computed that over ninety per cent of the names in use in Scotland are of Gaelic, or, at least, of Celtic, origin ; and, with the increasing interest that is being taken in the language movement, many people in Scotland are beginning to do what a number of the Irish have been doing for some time—make use of two names :

the true Gaelic name, and the anglicized form of it that came to them at birth. To many, this may seem to be a fantastic procedure, but to others it appears to have some not altogether strange depth in it.

In any case, to the Scot with his love of genealogy and things of a like nature, there is always something fascinating in the study of names.

Here are lists of Christian names and surnames in their anglicized form together with the Gaelic of them. Limitations of space prevent my being able to give derivations, pronunciations, or meanings ; but the interested individual will find little difficulty in discovering what his, or her, name means, and how it should be pronounced. Some names suggest their own meanings. It is to be hoped that every Scot understands that MAC means ' Son,' or ' Son of.' MAC should always be written in full. To write Mc or M' as, for example, McDonald or M'Donald is analogous to writing Donalsn or Donalds' for Donaldson. GIL in a name stands for GILLE, meaning ' Follower ' or ' Adherent.' Thus, GILCHRIST (GILLE CHRIOSD) means ' Follower of Christ ' ; and MACGILLANDERS (MAC GHILLE AINDREIS) means ' Son of the Follower of (St) Andrew '.

CHRISTIAN NAMES : MEN

Anglicized form, or English— *Gaelic—*
Adam | Adhamh
Alexander, Alec | Alasdair, Alai
Allan, Alan | Ailean
Andrew | Aindreas
Angus | Aonghus

Archibald	Gilleasbuig
Arthur	Artur, Art
Barry	Barra
Bartholomew	Parthalan
Bernard	Bearnard
Charles	Tearlach
Christopher	Crìostoir, Crìsdean
Colin	Cailean
David	Daibhidh
Dermott	Diarmid, Diarmad
Donald	Dòmhnull
Dugald	Dughall
Duncan	Donnchadh
Edmond	Eamonn
Edward	Eideard
Ernest	Earnan
Evan, Ewen	Eoghann
Farquhar	Fearchar
Fergus	Fearghus
Finlay	Fionnlagh
Francis, Frank	Próinsias, Frang, Frannsaidh
Gavin	Gabhan
George	Seòrus, Deòrsa
Gerald	Gearald
Gillian	Gille-Eathain
Godfrey	Goraidh
Hector	Eachann
Henry	Eanruig
Hugh	Uisdean
Iver	Iomhar
James	Seumas

John	Iain
Joseph	Seòsamh
Kenneth	Coinneach
Lachlan	Lachlann
Lawrence	Labhruinn
Louis, Lewis	Lùthais
Luke	Lùcas
Magnus	Mànus
Malcolm	Calum, Colm
Mark	Marcus
Martin	Màrtainn
Michael	Mìcheil
Morris	Muireach
Mungo	Mungan
Murdoch	Murchadh
Neil	Niall
Nicol, Nicholas	Neacal
Norman	Tormod
Patrick	Pàdruig
Paul	Pòl
Peter	Peadar
Pierce	Piaras
Richard	Risteard
Robert	Raibeart
Roderick	Ruairidh
Ronald	Raonull, Raghnall
Samuel, Somerled	Somhairle
Simon	Sìm
Stephen	Stìabhan
Thomas	Tómas
Walter	Bàtair
William	Uilleam, Liam

CHRISTIAN NAMES : WOMEN

Anglicized form, or English—	*Gaelic—*
Agnes	Una, Aigneis
Alice	Ailis
Amelia	Aimil
Angelica	Aingealag
Annabella	Anabal
Anne	Anna
Barbara	Barabal
Beatrice	Beitris
Bridget	Brìghde
Catherine	Catriona
Christina	Cairistìona
Dora	Doireann
Dorothy	Diorbhàll
Eileen	Eibhlin
Eleanor	Eilionoir
Elizabeth	Ealasaid
Evelyn	Eibhlin
Flora	Fionnghuala
Frances	Frangag
Grace	Gráinne
Grizel	Giorsal
Helen	Eilidh
Honora	Onóra
Isabel	Iseabal, Iosbail
Jane	Séana
Janet	Seònaid
Jean	Sìne
Joan, Johann	Siùbhan
Kate	Ceit

Kathleen	Caitlìn
Kirsty	Ciorstag, Ciorstan
Letitia	Leitis
Lily, Lilian	Lili
Louisa, Lucy	Liùsaidh
Mabel	Moibeal
Margaret	Mairearad, Mairghread
Marion	Mór
Marjory, Margery	Marsali
Martha	Marta
Mary	Màiri
Milly, Mildred	Milread
Molly	Màille
Muriel	Muireall
Nelly	Neilli
Norah	Nóra
Peg, Peggy	Peigi
Queenie	Cuìni
Rachel	Raonaid, Raonaild
Rose	Ròs, Róis
Sarah	Mór
Sheila	Sìlis, Sìle, Sìghle
Susan	Siùsan
Sybil	Sibeal
Winifred	Una

Many of the foregoing Christian names shown in the Gaelic column are, of course, not names of Gaelic origin, but are merely translations or transliterations of names brought into the country under foreign influences : Scandinavian, French, Norman-French and English. The same thing applies to many of the surnames following.

My authority for some of the translated names is the only printed work there is, as far as I know, dealing exclusively with Gaelic personal names : ' SLOINNTE GAEDHEAL IS GALL' LE PADRAIG DE BHULBH. And that is Irish ; but as the Scots-Gaelic and the Irish are fundamentally one language we cannot go very far wrong. Where I have taken translations from ' SLOINNTE GAEDHEAL IS GALL' I have Scotticized the spelling ; and where I have ventured to make translations myself, I have done so under the guidance of two well-known authorities on the subject : Mr John N. MacLeod of Knockbain School, Kirkhill, Inverness, and his son, Mr Calum Iain MacLeod, to both of whom I am most deeply indebted for much kindly help and advice.

But even then it is not to be expected that every Gaelic scholar will agree entirely with the spellings. That would be hoping for too much in dealing with a language that has, from the academic point of view, been sadly neglected until quite recently ; and that is, from a modern viewpoint, still in a state of flux to a certain extent. Even in Ireland— in SAORSTAT EIREANN—where Gaelic is now the national language—backed by the government, and taught in all the schools—there is still much argument over the spelling of certain words, and particularly over the spelling of personal names.

In any case, these lists are not offered for the criticism of the expert : they are offered for the interest of the general reader.

SURNAMES

Anglicized form, or English—	*Gaelic—*
Abbott	Mac an Aba
Adair	Mac Daraich
Adam, Adamson	Mac Adhaimh
Alexander	Mac Alasdair
Allan	Mac Ailean
Anderson	Mac Ghille Aindreis
Andrews	Mac Ghille Aindreis
Archibald	Mac Ghille-easpuig
Armstrong	Mac Ghille-làidir
Arthur, Arthurs	Mac Artuir
Askill	Mac Asgaill
Aspig	Mac Ghille-easpuig
Badger	Mac an Bhruic
Bailey, Baillie	Bàillidh, Mac an Bhàillidh
Bain, Bean	Mac Bheathain
Baker	Bacstair
Ballantine	Bealantin
Barron	Baran, Mac an Bharain
Beattie	Mac a' Bhìadhtaiche
Bell	Mac Ghille-chluig
Bishop	Mac Ghille-easpuig
Black	Mac Ghille-dhuibh
Brehon, Brain	Mac an Bhreitheimh
Brien	Mac Bhrìain
Britton	Mac an Bhreatannaich
Brown	Mac Ghille-dhuinn
Bruce	Brus
Buie, Bowes, Bowie	Mac Ghille-bhuidhe
Cairns	Mac a' Chùirn

Cameron	Camshron
Campbell	Caimbeul
Carmichael	Mac Ghille Mhicheil
Carpenter	Mac an t-Saoir
Carrick	Mac a' Charraigaich
Carter	Mac Artuir
Carthy	Mac Cardaidh
Cassie	Mac an Chasaig
Cattanach	Mac Ghille Chatain
Charles	Mac Thèarlaich
Chisholm	Siosal
Clark, Clerk	Mac a' Chléirich
Cochrane	Mac Còcaire
Colla, Coll	Mac Colla
Collins	Mac Cailean
Colquhoun	Mac a' Chombaich
Comyn, Cumming	Cuimean
Connell	Mac Conaill
Cormick	Mac Cormaic
Cowan	Mac a' Ghobhainn
Cowley	Mac Amhlaidh
Craig	Creag, Mac na Creige
Crichton	Mac Ghille Chriosd
Cross	Mac na Croise
David, Davidson, Davison	Mac Dhaibhidh
Dean	Mac Dhuibhne
Dermott	Mac Dhiarmaid
Dewar	Mac an Deòir
Doan	Mac Ghille-dhuinn
Dominie	Mac a' Mhaighstir
Donald, Donaldson	Mac Dhòmhnuill

Donlevy	Mac Dhuinn-shléibhe
Donogh	Mac Dhonnchaidh
Dougall, Dugald	Mac Dhùghaill
Douglas	Dubhghlas
Dowie	Mac Dhuibh
Doyle	Mac Dhùghaill
Drummond	Drummann
Duff, Duffson	Mac Dhuibh
Duffy	Mac Dhubh-shithe
Duncan, Duncanson	Mac Dhonnchaidh
Dweeney	Mac Dhuibhne
Edie	Mac Adhaimh
Edmonds, Edmondston	Mac Eamoinn
Edom, Edomson	Mac Adhaimh
Ellar	Mac Ealair
English	Mac an t-Sasunnaich
Ennis	Mac Aonghuis
Erskine	Arascain
Ervine	Irbhinn
Farmer	Mac an Tuathanaich
Farquhar, Farquharson	Mac Fhearchair
Fergus, Ferguson	Mac Fhearghuis
Field	Faithche
Fingan	Mac Fhionghuin
Finlay, Finlayson	Mac Fhionnlaigh
Finn	Mac Fhìnn
Fisher	Mac an Easgair
Fleming	Mac an Fhlanriseich
Fletcher	Mac an Fhleisteir
Forbes	Foirbéis
Forrester	Coilleach, Mac a' Choilleich

Forsyth	Foirseadh
Fox	Mac an t-Sionnaich
Francis	Mac Fhraing, Mac Fhrann-saidh
Frankin	Mac Fhraingein
Fraser, Frazer	Friseal
French	Mac an Fhraingich
Gall	Mac a' Ghoill
Gallach, Galway	Mac a' Ghallach
Garty	Mac Càrdaidh
Gavin	Mac Gabhain
Gibb, Gibbons, Gibson	Mac Gìobuin
Gilbert	Mac Ghille Brìghde
Gilbey	Mac Ghille-bhuidhe
Gilbride	Mac Ghille Brìghde
Gilchrist	Mac Ghille Chriosd
Gildea	Mac Ghille Dhè
Gilduff	Mac Ghille-dhuibh
Gilfillan	Mac Ghille Fhaolain
Gillean	Mac Ghille Eathain
Gillespie	Mac Ghille easpuig
Gillies	Mac Ghille Iosa
Gilmartin	Mac Ghille Mhàrtainn
Gilmore	Mac Ghille Mhoire, Mac Ghille-mhór
Gilroy	Mac Ghille-ruaidh
Glennon	Mac Ghille Fhionnain
Godfrey, Godfreyson	Mac Goraidh, Mac Guaidhre
Goodman	Mac Ghille-mhaith
Gordon	Gordon, Gordan

Gorey	Mac Guaidhre
Gow, Gowan	Mac a' Ghobhainn
Graham	Greumach
Grant	Grannd
Gray	Liath, Mac Ghille-léith
Gregor, Gregorson	Mac Griogair
Guinness	Mac Aonghuis
Gunn	Guinne
Haig	Mac Thaoig
Hall	Mac Càthail
Halpin	Mac Ailpein
Hardy	Mac Càrdaidh
Harold	Mac Araild
Harrison, Harris	Mac Eanruig
Hector	Mac Eachainn, Mac Eachairn
Henderson	Mac Eanruig
Hendry, Henryson	Mac Eanruig
Hughes	Mac Uisdein, Mac Aoidh
Huston	Mac Uisdein
Inglis	Mac an t-Sasunnaich
Innes	Mac Aonghuis
Irving, Irwin	Irbhinn
Jameson, Jamieson	Mac Sheumais
Johnson, Johnston	Mac Iain, Mac Eòghainn, Mac Eòin
Judge	Mac an Bhreitheimh
Kennedy	Ceannaideach, Mac Ualraig
Kenneth, Kenny	Mac Coinnich
Kerr	Cearr, Mac Ghille-chearr
Kilgallon	Mac Ghille Chailein

Kilroy	Mac Ghille-ruaidh
King, Kingston	Mac an Rìgh
Knight	Mac an Ridire
Lachlan	Mac Lachlainn
Lagan	Mac Lathagain
Lamont, Lamont, Lomond	Mac Laomainn
Lauder	Mac Ghille-làidir
Laverty	Mac Fhlaithbheartaich
Lawrence, Laurenson	Mac Labhruinn
Lee, Leigh	Mac an Léigh
Lennon	Mac Ghille Fhionnain
Lennox	Mac an Leamhanaich
Lewis	Mac Lùthais
Lindsay	Mac Ghille Fhionntaig
Little	Beag, Mac Ghille-bhige
Livingstone	Mac an Léigh, Mac Dhuinn-shléibhe
Lloyd	Mac Leòid
Lord	Mac an Thighearna
Lucas	Mac Lucais, Mac Ghille-dhubhghlais
Lundie	Lunndaidh
MacAdam	Mac Adhaimh
MacAffy	Mac Dhubh-shìthe
MacAleese	Mac Ghille Iosa
MacAlister	Mac Alasdair
MacAlpin	Mac Ailpein
MacAndrew	Mac Aindreis
Macantaggart	Mac an t-Sagairt
MacArdle	Mac Ardghail
MacArthur	Mac Artuir

MacAskill	Mac Asgaill
MacAulay	Mac Amhlaidh
Macaward	Mac a' Bhàird
MacBain, MacBean	Mac Bheathain
MacBeth	Mac Bheathain
MacBride	Mac Ghille Brìghde
MacCaig	Mac Thaoig
MacCallum	Mac Chaluim
MacCaw	Mac Adhaimh
MacCleary, Macleery	Mac a' Chléirich
MacColl	Mac Colla
MacConnachy	Mac Dhonnchaidh
MacConnell	Mac Dhòmhnuill
MacCormack	Mac Cormaic
MacCoy	Mac Aoidh
MacCullen	Mac Cuilinn, Mac Chailein
MacDermott	Mac Dhiarmaid
MacDonagh	Mac Dhonnchaidh
MacDonald	Mac Dhòmhnuill, Dòmh-nullach
MacDougall	Mac Dhùghaill
MacDuff	Mac Dhuibh
MacDuffy	Mac Dubh-shìthe
MacEchern, MacEchran	Mac Eachairn
MacElvy, MacElwee	Mac Ghille-bhuidhe
MacEndry	Mac Eanruig
MacEwen	Mac Eòghainn
MacFadden, MacFadyen	Mac Phaidein
MacFarlane	Mac Phàrlain
MacFate	Mac Pheadair
MacFedries, MacFetrish	Mac Pheadruis

MacGill	Mac Ghille
MacGilvray	Mac Ghille-bhràth
MacGowan, MacGown	Mac a' Ghobhainn
MacGraw	Mac Rath
MacGregor	Mac Griogair
MacHenry, MacHendrick	Mac Eanruig
MacInnes	Mac Aonghuis
Macintosh	Mac an Tòisich
Macintyre	Mac an t-Saoir
MacIver	Mac Iomhair
MacKay	Mac Aoidh
MacKechnie	Mac Eachainn
MacKellar	Mac Ealair
MacKenna	Mac Coinnich
MacKenzie	Mac Coinnich
MacKerchar	Mac Fhearchair
MacKillop	Mac Fhilib
MacKinley	Mac Fhionnlaigh
MacKinnon	Mac Fhionghuin
MacLachlan	Mac Lachlainn
MacLaren, MacLauren	Mac Labhruinn
MacLarty	Mac Fhlaithbheartaich
MacLean	Mac Ghille Eathain
MacLeay	Mac Dhuinn-shléibhe
MacLehose	Mac Ghille Iosa
MacLellan	Mac Ghille Fhaolain
MacLennan	Mac Ghille Fhionnain
MacLeod	Mac Leòid
Maclernon	Mac Ghille Earnain
MacManus	Mac Mhànuis
MacMaster	Mac a' Mhaighstir

MacMichael	Mac Mhìcheil
Macmillan	Mac Ghille-mhaoil
Macnab	Mac an Aba
MacNaughton	Mac Neachdainn
MacNeil	Mac Nèill
MacNicol	Mac Neacail
MacPatrick	Mac Phàdruig
MacPhee	Mac Dubh-shìthe
Macpherson	Mac a' Phearsoin, Mac Mhuirich
Macquarrie	Mac Guaidhre
MacQueen	Mac Shuibhne
Macquillan	Mac Cuilinn
Macrae	Mac Rath
MacRobb	Mac Rob
MacRobert	Mac Raibeirt
MacRonald	Mac Raonuill, Mac Raghnaill
MacRory	Mac Ruairidh
Mactaggart	Mac an t-Sagairt
MacTavish	Mac Thamhais
MacVeagh	Mac Bheatha
MacVean	Mac Bheathain
MacVicar	Mac a' Bhiocair
MacVitie	Mac a' Bhìadhtaiche
MacWalter	Mac Bhàtair
MacWard	Mac a' Bhàird
Malcolm	Mac Mhaol Chaluim, Mac Ghille Chaluim
Marquis, Mark	Mac Mharcuis
Martin	Mac Mhàrtainn

Master, Masterson	Mac a' Mhaighstir
Matheson, Matthews	Mac Mhathain
Melville	Mac Mhaol Mhìcheil
Menzies	Mèinn, Mèinnearach
Morison	Mac Ghille Mhoire, Mac Mhuirich
Munro	Mac an Rothaich
Murdoch	Mac Mhurchaidh
Murray	Mac Mhuirich, Moirreach
Nelson, Neilson	Mac Nèill
Nichol, Nicholson	Mac Neacail
Parlan, Partland	Mac Phàrlain
Paterson	Mac Pheadair
Paton	Mac Phaidein
Paul	Mac Phàil
Phillips	Mac Fhilib
Rankin	Mac Fhraingein
Robb, Robson	Mac Rob
Robertson	Mac Raibeirt, Mac Dhonnchaidh
Ronald, Ronaldson	Mac Raonuill, Mac Raghnaill
Rose, Ross	Ròs, Ròis
Rowan	Mac a' Chaorainn
Salmon	Mac Bhradain
Samuel	Mac Shomhairle
Scott	Scot, Scotach
Shaw	Mac Ghille-sheathanaich, Mac Shithich
Simson, Sims	Mac Shimidh
Sinclair	Mac na Ceardadh

Smith	Mac a' Ghobhainn
Somerled	Mac Shomhairle
Stevenson	Mac Stìbhein
Strachan	Struthain
Strong	Mac Ghille-làidir
Stuart, Stewart	Stiùbhard
Taylor	Mac an Tàilleir
Thomas, Thomson	Mac Thómais
Tosh	Mac an Tòisich
Turner	Mac an Tuairneir
Vaughan	Mac Mhathain
Walker	Mac an Fhùcadair
Wallace	Uallas
Walrick	Mac Ualraig
Walsh	Mac an Chuimrich
Walters, Waters	Mac Bhàtair
Ward	Mac a' Bhàird
White	Mac Ghille-bhàin
Williams, Williamson	Mac Uilleim
Workman	Mac an Oibriche
Young	Mac Ghille-òig

As MAC means ' Son,' a woman, obviously, cannot correctly use this prefix in the true Gaelic form of her name. A woman must prefix the genitive of her patronymic with NIC (which is an abbreviation of NIGHEAN MHIC). As, for example, MÀIRI NIC AILPEIN for the usual anglicized form Mary MacAlpin.

THE DAYS AND THE MONTHS IN GAELIC

Monday	Di-luain
Tuesday	Di-màirt
Wednesday	Di-ceudain
Thursday	Dior-daoin
Friday	Di-h-aoine
Saturday	Di-Sathuirne
Sunday	Di-dòmhnaich
January	Am Faoilteach
February	An Gearran
March	Am Màrt
April	An Giblin
May	An Céitean
June	An t-Og-mhios
July	An t-Iuchar
August	An Lùnasdal
September	An t-Sultùine
October	An Dàmhar
November	An t-Samhainn
December	An Dùdlachd
Christmas	Nollaig
Hogmanay	Oidhche Challain
New Year's Day	Là na bliadhna úire
May Day	Là Bealltuinn

CLANS

THE PRINCIPAL CLANS AND FAMILIES

Limitations of space preclude the possibility of this section being anything but sketchy and incomplete. It is to be hoped that anyone bearing an important name that is not represented will not take the omission amiss.

There are many books dealing with the subject at length : most of them good and reliable, and the majority of them extremely cheap.

CLAN CHATTAN

As a preliminary to the following pages of notes dealing with some of the clans, it is necessary to say something first of Clan Chattan, since reference is made to it so often. Indeed, many histories of Scotland, making innumerable references to Clan Chattan, fail to give any indication of what Clan Chattan really was ; with the result that many readers recognise the name without knowing anything of what it stands for.

Clan Chattan was not a clan in the accepted sense of the word. Clan Chattan was a federation of clans ; and what are usually referred to as Septs of Clan Chattan were in reality individual clans, each with its own Chief, the Chief of each ' sept ' recognising—more or less—the Captaincy, or generalship, of Mackintosh of Mackintosh as head of the whole confederation.

The Clan Chattan Bond of 1609 gives the components of the confederation as : the Macintoshes, the Macphersons, the MacQueens, the MacBeans, the Macleans of Dochgarroch, the MacGillivrays, the Farquharsons, the

MacPhails, the Shaws, and several of lesser importance—
some Clarks, some Gows, some Gillanders, and a few of the
Davidsons.

In early records the name of Cattanach (of the Cattans)
interchanges with the name Macintosh.

The name is derived from *Gille-Chatain*, meaning the
follower, or disciple of Cattan, or St Cattan, but history
does not record who the first *Gille-Chatain* was.

The name should be pronounced, not with the *tch* sound
of the English *ch*, as in *chapter*, but with the Gaelic light
guttural sound of the *ch* in *loch*.

BRODIE

This is a territorial name, derived from the lands of
Brodie in Moray, given to the progenitor of the family in
1160 by King Malcolm when he transplanted the Moray
rebels. The Chief is styled Brodie of Brodie. There is an
important cadet branch designated Brodie of Lethen.

BRUCE

A name of Norman origin, originally de Brus. David I
conferred the lordship of Annandale on Robert de Brus,
son of the Robert de Brus, who was a knight in the train
of William of Normandy. His great-great-grandson was
King Robert I, who, before establishing his right to the
throne, was Earl of Carrick.

BUCHANAN

A territorial name, taken from the lands of Buchanan in
the county of Stirling. Dr MacLauchlan says : ' The name
of the Buchanans, an ancient Celtic race, is ecclesiastical,

and it is likely that that of MacAuslan, by which they were anciently designated, passed into Buchanan on the lands and chiefship of the clan falling into the hands of an ecclesiastic. The family, at various times, has intermarried with their near neighbours, the Menteiths, the Grahams, and the Edmondstons of Duntreath. Patrick Buchanan, who fell at Flodden, was the grandfather of the ' King of Kippen.' The family lands in Menteith and the Lennox are now possessed by the Duke of Montrose.

CAMERON

The origin of this name is said to be *cam-shròn* (crooked nose), the appellative of some early chief. The first known chief was *Dòmhnull Dubh* (Dark Donald) c. 1400. There are Camerons of Fassifern, of Erracht, of Inverailort, and, the principal branch, the Camerons of Lochiel. The chief is Lochiel, and the lands of Lochiel are in Lochaber.

CAMPBELL

This name, like that of Cameron, is generally supposed to have originated in a physical peculiarity of some progenitor : *cam-beul* (crooked, or wry, mouth). The name first appears in 1216, as being of Menstrie in the county of Stirling. The leading family, of Argyll, was founded by *Cailean Mór*, from whom the Duke of Argyll takes his Gaelic patronymic, *MacChailean Mór*. There are many important branches of the clan, notably of Lochow, of Glenlyon, of Cawdor, of Loudon, and, of Breadalbane.

CHISHOLM

Originally a Border clan, with branches designated of Chisholme, of Stirches, of Dundorne. The name is now very common in the Beauly district of the county of Inverness, and on Loch Ness-side ; the founder of the northern branch being the Lord of Chisholm, who married into the family of The Constable of Urquhart Castle, and became possessed of the lands of Strathglass. The Chisholms, at one time a very important clan, have intermarried with the Scotts of Buccleuch, the Douglases of Drumlanrig, the Buchanans, and the Frasers. At one time a branch of this clan held the hereditary office of Bailie and Justiciar of the Ecciesiastical Lordship of Dunblane.

COLQUHOUN

A territorial name (pronounced Co-hoon), taken from lands in the Lennox. At an early date there were three important branches : of Kilpatrick, of Luss, and Colquhoun of Colquhoun.

CUMIN

All the Cumins in Scotland are said to descend from John Cumin, the son of a father who was slain at Alnwick with Malcolm III. The Cumins were Lords of Badenoch. The clan began to decline in the middle of the fourteenth century. Cumming and Comyn are other spellings of the same name.

DAVIDSON

A sept of Clan Chattan. The Davidsons of Invernahaven were related to the Cumins of Badenoch. The Davidsons (*Clann Daibhidh*) were almost annihilated at the famous clan battle of the North Inch in 1396. There are Davidsons of Davidston, and Davidsons of Cantray.

DOUGLAS

The origin of the Douglases is legendary. The name is from the Gaelic *Dubh ghlas*, and was so written, with the prefix ' de ' in the time of Bruce. At various times, the Douglases have intermarried with every powerful and important family in the country. Douglases are, or were, Dukes of Hamilton, Dukes of Queensberry, and, in the peerage of France, Dukes of Touraine ; Earls of Douglas, of Morton, of Angus, of Mar, of Avondale, of Moray, of Ormond, of Selkirk, of Orkney. There are Douglases of Lochleven, of Dornoch, of Muldearg (in Ross), of Carr, of Timpendean, of Bonjedward, and many others.

The name of Douglas, for good—and evil—runs like a red line through the chequered history of Scotland.

DRUMMOND

This family is said to have originated with a grandson of Andrew, King of Hungary. The name is a territorial one, from the lands of Drummond or Drymen in the county of Stirling. Certain lands in the county of Perth were conferred on Sir Malcolm Drummond by Bruce after Bannockburn. Annabella Drummond married Robert III, and so became Queen. A Drummond, James, fourth Earl of Perth, was Lord Chancellor, and was created Duke of Perth by James VII. There are Drummonds of Concraig, and of Hawthornden ; and there are Drummonds of Blair Drummond.

ELLIOTT

An important Border family with several branches, notably, of Larriston, Braidlie, Arkleton, and Stobs. The

Earl of Minto is descended of the Elliotts of Stobs. The first Elliotts were designated of Redheuch.

FARQUHARSON

A sept of Clan Chattan. The first of the clan was Farquhar, one of the Shaws of Rothiemurchus. The Mac-Kerrachers are of the same line. The Farquharsons are styled in the Gaelic *Clann Fhionnlaidh*, after *Fionnlaidh Mòr*, who fell at the battle of Pinkie, at which he was Standard Bearer. There are Farquharsons of Monaltrie, Haughton, and Finzean.

FERGUSON

An established clan in Athol before the time of Bruce, of whom they were amongst the most loyal supporters. The Fergusons hold, or have held lands at various times in the counties of Aberdeen, Banff, Kincardine, Argyll, Ayr, and Dumfries ; and in different places in Galloway. There are Fergusons of Kinmundy, and of Pitfour ; and, notably, of Craigdarroch.

FORBES

A territorial name from the parish of Forbes in the county of Aberdeen. The first on record was John of Forbes in the time of William the Lion. Lord Pitsligo was a Forbes. There are Forbeses of Culloden, of Moniemusk, of Tolquhoun, and of Craigievar.

FRASER

A name of Norman origin. At one time a powerful clan in the south, now they are mainly to be found about Beauly and Inverness, where the Chief, Lord Lovat, holds extensive lands. The Christian name of the Chief is invariably Simon, in any case he is always, in the Gaelic, *MacShimidh*, and from that fact, the Simsons, Simons, and MacSims claim descent of the Fraser chief. Some years ago the then Lord Lovat, wishing to increase the numerical strength of his clan, offered a boll of meal to a number of Livingstones as an inducement to change their name. Several accepted the offer, and their descendants are to this day referred to, around Beauly, as ' Boll of meal Frasers.'

GORDON

Another powerful clan of Border origin, taking their name from lands in The Merse. All the Gordons are said to descend from Sir Adam Gordon, who lived in the time of Alexander III. Adam or Edom has always been a popular name among the Gordons. From this, most Scottish Adams, Adamsons, MacAdams, and Edomsons claim to be descended of the Gordons. The clan for centuries has been settled in the county of Aberdeen. The Marquis of Aberdeen and the Marquis of Huntly are Gordons. There are Gordons of Gordonstoun, of Earlstoun, and of Lochinvar.

GRAHAM

The Duke of Montrose is the head of the most important branch of the Grahams. All the Grahams are reputed to descend from a famous warrior who breached the Roman wall in 420. Wallace's leading lieutenant was a Graham. As long ago as 1360 there were Grahams styled of Montrose. There are Border and Galloway Grahams as well as those of Menteith, Stirling, and Perth. Bonny Dundee was a Graham, and so, too, of course, was The Great Marquis of Montrose.

GRANT

The Grants are said to be of the same stock as the Mac-Gregors. The Grant territory is chiefly in Strathspey, where the clan has been numerous and powerful for centuries. A Grant was Sheriff of Inverness in the time of Alexander III. The most important cadet branches of the clan are designated of Monymusk, and of Glenmoriston.

GUNN

A clan reputedly of Norse origin, descended from Guin, the eldest son of one of the Norse Kings of Man. For centuries the Gunns have been settled in Caithness and Sutherland ; and according to Calder in his *History of Caithness* they descend from Gunn, a brother of the pirate Sweyne who settled at Ulbster. For centuries they carried on a bloody feud with the Mackays and the Keiths.

JOHNSTON

A famous family of Border reivers. There is also a northern branch of the family. The Johnstons were originally styled de Johnstoun. There are, or were, Johnstons of Gretna, of Newbie, of Annandale, and of Elphinstone. There were also Johnstons of Warriston, and of Galabank. At one time the title of Lord Ruthven was held by an illegitimate branch of the Gretna Johnstons.

KERR

A name reputedly of Gaelic origin (*Cearr*—meaning ' left-handed '). Carr and Ker are other spellings of the name. At one time a very powerful Border clan. Branches of the family have held many titles. The Duke of Roxburgh is a Ker (Innes-Ker) ; and the Marquis of Lothian, a Kerr. Sir Robert Kerr was created Earl of Ancrum in 1633. There are, notably, Kerrs of Ferniehirst, and Kerrs of Linton.

LAMONT

The name Lamont or Lamond is derived from the Norse *lagamadr*, a lawman, which was the title of a Norse official in charge of conquered or colonized territory. Despite the Norse derivation of the name, the founders of the clan are reputed to have come with the Gaelic-Irish invasion of Dalriada. In 1646 the Lamont country about Lochgilp was ravaged by the predatory Campbells, who massacred over two hundred of the clan. The Chiefs of the Lamonts were of Inveryne. Important cadet branches are : the Lamonts of Ardlamont, the Lamonts of Knockdow, and the Lamonts of Auchinshellich.

LESLIE

Four peerages have been held by members of this clan : the Earldom of Rôthes, the Earldom of Leven, and the Baronies of Newark and Lindores. And many Leslies distinguished themselves as soldiers of fortune, holding, at various times, high rank in the armies of France, Poland, Russia, Sweden, and Hungary. The name is of territorial origin. The first Leslie recorded was Bartholf of Leslie, who lived in the reign of William the Lion.

LINDSAY

Mainly an Angus clan, said to be descended from Ivar, Iarl of the Uplanders. The Earl of Crawford is Chief of the clan. There have been many important branches of the clan ; notably, the Lindsays of Edzell, the Lindsays of Balcarres, and the Lindsays of the Byres.

LOGAN (See Maclennan)

MACALISTER

This clan is descended from a MacDonald, *Alasdair Mór*, who lived in the thirteenth century. The clan for several hundred years has been settled, mainly, in Kintyre, but during the fifteenth and sixteenth centuries settlements were made in Bute and Arran.

MACALPIN

Alpin is a name of Cymric origin. The MacAlpins claim descent from Kenneth MacAlpin, the ancestor of a long line of kings. But the MacAlpins have never been a united clan under a chief. There is an old saying : *Cnuic is uillt is Ailpeinich*, meaning, 'Hills and Streams and MacAlpins.' The obvious inference being that the MacAlpins are as old as the mountains and the rivers !

MACARTHUR

The MacArthurs are a branch of the Campbells, tracing their descent from the original stock. In the time of

Alexander III, there were two main branches of the Campbells : those of *MacChailean Mór* (see under Campbell),
and those of *MacArtuir* ; the MacArthurs for long maintaining their right to the chiefship. The chief was appointed Captain of Dunstaffnage ; but in the time of
James I, the MacArthur lands were forfeited, and the chief
beheaded, after which the branch of *MacChailean Mór* came
into greater prominence. A family of MacArthurs were
for many generations hereditary pipers to the MacDonalds
of Sleat. The chiefship of the MacArthurs is now said to
rest in a branch that has been for several generations settled
in Islay. Some of these MacArthurs were pipers and
armourers to the MacDonalds of Islay.

MACBEAN

A sept of Clan Chattan. The MacBeans are said originally to have belonged to MacBeth's province of Moray ;
and the name, to a certain extent, is interchangeable with
MacBeth (Gaelic : *Mac Beathain*). MacVean is the same
name, from the Gaelic *Mac Bheathain* (Bh sounded like V).
The name is found near Inverness, in Strathdearn, and in
Badenoch. The story of how Gillies MacBean, who stood
six feet four inches in height, held the gap in a wall at
Culloden is famous. He accounted for a considerable
number of the enemy before he was overpowered and
killed.

MACDONALD

The oldest and the most famous of the clans, and at one
time a great power in the land. The MacDonalds are
descended from Donald, the grandson of Somerled of the

Isles ; but, beyond that, goes a much older descent from Conn of the Hundred Battles (c. 125 A.D.). The leading branches of Clan Donald are : the MacDonalds of Clan-Ranald, the MacDonalds of Glengarry, the MacDonalds of Sleat, and the MacDonalds of Keppoch. The princely title of Lord of the Isles belonged to the MacDonalds.

MacDougall

Descended from Dugall, a son of Somerled of the Isles. For centuries the MacDougalls held the lands of Lorn and the islands adjacent. An important branch of the clan were the MacDougalls of Dunolly.

MacDuff

The MacDuffs are descended from the ancient Celtic Lords of Fife, or Kings of Fife. At later periods there were MacDuffs of Banff, and MacDuffs of Strathbogie.

MacFarlane

'The wild MacFarlane's plaided clan.' The MacFarlanes are descended from the ancient Celtic Lords of Lennox. The name comes from *Phàrlain*, the aspirated form of *Pàrlan* in the genitive. For years the MacFarlanes held lands in the county of Dumbarton, but in 1624 many of them were driven out. These MacFarlanes went to the north-east, into the county of Aberdeen, and there assumed other names : MacCondy and MacInnes amongst them.

MacGregor

The MacGregors claim to be of royal descent. Their motto is *Is Rioghail mo dhream*, meaning 'Royal is my Race.' The earliest possessions of the clan were in Glenorchy. For centuries the MacGregors were persecuted. Sir Walter Scott says of the MacGregors : ' They were famous for their misfortunes and the indomitable courage with which they maintained themselves as a clan.' For over a century, the name was utterly proscribed, and it needed an Act of Parliament to annul the suppression of the name. During the period of proscription many of the MacGregors had, perforce, to change their names. It was in 1774 that the ban was removed. The famous Rob Roy was a Mac-Gregor of Glengyle. The name MacGregor means son of Gregor, in Gaelic *Griogair*. And, in connection with this, it is of interest to note the error in Gaelic that Scott made in his song ' The MacGregor's Gathering,' where he anglicizes *Griogairach*, meaning ' of the MacGregors,' as Grigalach.

MACINTOSH

This name is in Gaelic *Mac an Tòisich*, meaning Son of the Thane ; and since that part of the name that imme-diately follows the ' Mac ' is not a personal name, but merely an anglicized form of the article ' *an* ' it should never be ' Englished ' with a capital I, as MacIntosh, nor certainly should it ever be spelt MacKintosh. The same thing applies to Macintyre (Mac an t-Saoir), but not to MacInnes, the Innes being an anglicized form of the proper name *Aonghus*.

The Macintoshes were the leading sept of Clan Chattan ; their chief being ' Captain ' of Clan Chattan, although at times this honour was disputed by the chief of the Mac-phersons. The thane from whom the Macintoshes descend was most likely the Thane of Rothiemurchus. The Shaws are of the same descent. The Chief of the Macintoshes is Macintosh of Macintosh, who spells his name as Mac*k*intosh!

MACINTYRE

The Macintyres are said to be a sept of the MacDonalds of Sleat. The Macintyres occupied lands at Glenoe, Loch Etive for a period of five- or six-hundred years. There were also Macintyres in Badenoch attached to Clan Chattan; and a family of Macintyres in the county of Perth were hereditary pipers to the Menzies of Menzies.

MACKAY

This name, as spelt, is a badly anglicized form of *Mac Aoidh*, ' Son of Hugh.' In Gaelic the Mackays are known collectively as *Clann Mhorgain*, but this applies usually only to the Sutherland Mackays. The Argyle Mackays being, as a rule, *Clann Aoidh*. The first historic chief of the clan was called ' Angus the Absolute ' from the fact that he had under his command over 4,000 men.

MACKENZIE

The name MacKenzie is an anglicized form of *Mac Coinnich*, ' Son of Kenneth.' The Mackenzies or Mac-Kenzies are said to be of pure Scoto-Gaelic descent, and were at one time a very powerful clan, holding much land in Kintail.

MACLACHLAN

The MacLachlans are believed to have been in possession of Strath-Lachlan in Argyle as long ago as the tenth or eleventh centuries. The family from whom the Mac-Lachlans are descended are said to have given kings to Ireland for over a thousand years. The name is common in Ireland, usually as MacLoughlin. The MacLachlan of the '45 was an A.D.C. to the Prince, and was killed at Culloden. The Chief is known as MacLachlan of Mac-Lachlan.

Maclean

The Macleans are said to descend from a famous warrior known as Gillian of the Battle-axe. From a remote period the Macleans were a powerful clan, holding lands in Mull. From the Castle of Duart in Mull comes the designation : Maclean of Duart. There are other important branches of the clan in the Macleans (or Maclaines) of Lochbuie ; the Macleans of Ardgour and the Macleans of Brolas. Brolas is now united with Duart under the chiefship of Maclean of Duart and Brolas. The present chief, Sir Fitzroy D. Maclean, is the direct male representative of both branches.

Maclennan

The Maclennans and the Logans are of the same stock. It is traditionally understood that the first Maclennan was a Logan. Maclennan is the anglicized rendering of *Mac Ghille-Fhionnain*, meaning ' S n of the follower, or disciple, of Finnian.' At one time the Maclennans were a numerous and fairly powerful clan in Kintail, and elsewhere in Ross.

Macleod

The progenitor of this clan is said to be Leoid, the son of Olav, King of Man. There are two main branches of the clan : the MacLeods of Harris, and the MacLeods of the Lewes, but in the sixteenth century the chiefship of the Lewes MacLeods became extinct in the male line, and the lands passed to a Mackenzie of Kintail who had married a daughter of the Lewes MacLeod. Again the lands passed, but the history of this affair is too involved to be dealt with here. The principal cadet branches of the clan are, or were, the MacLeods of Raasay, the MacLeods of Cadboll, and the MacLeods of Bernera. There are also the Mac-Leods of Morven, of Talisker, of Glendale, and the Mac-Leods of Assynt. The Chief is MacLeod of MacLeod, of Dunvegan in Skye. In 1716 a peerage was conferred on the MacLeod of his day by James VIII.

The MacCrimmons, the most famous of pipers, were for centuries hereditary pipers to the MacLeods.

MACMILLAN

Records show that this clan, or a branch of the clan, was established' at an early period in Lochaber. They were loyal retainers of Lochiel. Tradition says that the clan was removed by Malcolm IV (1153-65) from Lochaber to the Crown Lands of Loch Tay in the county of Perth. At a later period Macmillans were found in Knapdale and Galloway. The Knapdale branch soon reached great power and influence. A boulder at Knap Head was said to have written on it a couplet that has been much quoted for centuries. A translation of it runs :

> While currents run and winds blow cold,
> Macmillan's right to Knap shall hold.

A representative of the Galloway Macmillans was a leader of the Cameronian Covenanters.

MACNAB

The Macnabs are of ecclesiastical origin. The name is derived from the Gaelic *Mac an Aba*, ' Son of the Abbot.' And the Macnabs are said to be descended from the abbots of Glendochart, although it is more than probable that the son of any abbot would be called *Mac an Aba*. As a clan, the Macnabs were powerful in the time of Alexander III.

MACNAUGHTON

The name *Neachdainn* is said to be Pictish. In the twelfth century the MacNaughtons are recorded as being in possession of Strathtay. A century later they are recorded as possessing extensive lands in Argyle.

MACNEILL

There are two main branches of this clan : the Mac-Neills of Barra, and the MacNeills of Gigha, both of which trace their descent back to a common ancestor *Niall Òg*, the son of another *Niall*, or Neil, who was the founder of the family, and who lived at the beginning of the twelfth century.

MACPHERSON

This name, meaning ' Son of the parson,' was common all over the north in the fifteenth century. As a clan, the Macphersons vied with the Macintoshes for the captaincy of Clan Chattan. They were centred in Badenoch. The Chief of the Macphersons is known as Cluny, from the estate of that name.

MACRAE

This name is in the Gaelic *Mac Rath*, which may mean ' Son of Fortune,' that is ' Son of the fortunate one ' ; or it may mean ' Son of Grace.' And if ' Son of Grace,' then they are probably of ecclesiastical origin. *Rath* appears as a personal, or Christian, name both in Scotland and in Ireland as early as in the fifth century. As a surname MacRae, in one or another of its variations, is common in Ireland to-day, and in Ayr and Galloway. There are also Macraes in the county of Perth, but the Macraes are principally found in Kintail, where, as a clan, they have flourished since the fourteenth century. The name is now spelt in many ways in different parts of the country, and in Ireland : MacCreath, MacGraw and Magrath being three of the spellings in which the name is found ; with, of course, the usual bastardized forms of Mac : Mc and M', found in so many names nowadays.

MACQUEEN

This name is in the Gaelic *Mac Shuibhne*—the *bh* is mute, as is the initial S when treated in this form. The sound in the Gaelic being something like Macwheen, the bastardized form MacQueen or Macqueen has arisen in English. *Suibhne* is the Gaelic form of the Norse Sweyn. So that the MacSweens, the Sweens, the Swains, and the Swans may have with the MacQueens, a common origin. The name is the same as the Irish Sweeney. The MacQueens entered the Clan Chattan in 1609, the bond being signed by a ' Sween MacQueen.'

MALCOLM

In the Gaelic *Maol Chaluim*, being the genitive of *Maol Calum*, meaning Bald Calum. The Malcolms were settled at a very early period in Argyle and the Lennox. The principal branch of the Malcolms are styled of Poltalloch.

OGILVIE

The Ogilvies are descended from a son of an Earl of Angus (*O Gille Bhuidhe*—Grandson of the Yellow-haired Lad?). There are, or were, many cadet branches of the clan, notably the Ogilvies of Inverquharity, of Strathearn, and of Dunlugus. The Earl of Airlie is head of the clan. There have, at different times, been several peerages and baronetcies among the Ogilvies.

ROBERTSON

The Robertsons are properly *Clann Donnchaidh*, that is, children, or descendants, of Duncan. The name Robertson derives from a Robert of this clan who lived in the fifteenth century, and who possessed extensive lands which were erected into the Barony of Struan. There are several cadet branches of the Robertsons of Struan, among them being, the Robertsons of Lude, of Inches, of Kindeace, of Blairfettie. There are many lairdships among the Robertsons in Atholl and other parts of the county of Perth. At an early period some of the clan settled in the county of Aberdeen and retained, or re-took, the original clan name. Other Robertsons reverted to the original name after the '45, and in various forms, as Donnachie, Mac-Connachie, Duncan, it is found in many different parts of the country. The Chief of the Robertsons is styled Struan.

Rose

The Roses of Kilravock have held their property through a descent of nineteen generations. Their recorded history begins in the reign of Alexander II. The Roses of Kilravock have, at various times, intermarried with all the important families in the north.

Ross

In the Gaelic the Rosses are known as *Clann Aindreis*, that is, children of Andrew. From this, many Andersons, Andrews, and MacAndrews, claim relationship. The name Ross seems to be of territorial origin. Apart from the descendants of the original Earls of Ross (if any), the most ancient line is that of Balnagown, descended from William, Earl of Ross in the time of Robert I. After the death of the last Earl of Ross, the lairds of Balnagown became chiefs of the clan, which at one time was one of the most powerful in the country. Ross of Pitcalnie is now supposed to represent the ancient line of Balnagown. Balnagown means ' the township of the smiths.'

Scott

At one time the Scotts were the most powerful of the Border clans. They are said to be of Norman origin ; but probably they were Gaelic Scots who were given that name in general by the Cymric inhabitants of the Borders long before Uchtredus filius Scoti came north after the Norman invasion of England. The Scotts of Buccleuch are said to descend from Richard, a son of Uchtredus filius Scoti, and the Scotts of Balwearie from another son, Michael. The principal branches of the Scotts in addition to those of Buccleuch and Balwearie, are, or were, the Scotts of Scotstarvit, of Harden, of Goldielands, of Thirlestane, of Dunninald, and of Ancrum.

STEWART

The history of the Royal House of Stewart is well known, but it may be of interest to note here that the first traced ancestor in Scotland was Walter, the son of a Breton noble, Alan of the ancient house of Dinan. Walter received from David I the office of Great Steward, or Grand Steward, of Scotland, an office that was made hereditary in his family. Walter was the founder of Paisley Abbey. Later, the name of the office was assumed as a surname by Walter's grandson. Another Walter married the Princess Marjorie Brus, by whom he had a son, Robert. The direct line failing, Robert ascended the throne as Robert II, and so brought the name of Stewart to the Royal House that, for five centuries, occupied the throne of Scotland.

Ross

THE CLAN SLOGANS

The word Slogan is derived from the Gaelic SLUAGH-GHAIRM—SLUAGH meaning a host or army, and GHAIRM a shout or yell. The word, therefore, originally described a battle-cry, and not the trade exhortation that it connotes to-day !

Here are a few of the old battle-cries :

Clan	Slogan	Meaning
Buchanan	Clàr Innis !	Name of an island in Loch Lomond.
Cameron	Chlanna nan con thigibh an so is gheibh sibh feòil !	' Sons of the hounds come hither for flesh ! '
Campbell	Cruachan !	Name of a mountain near Loch Awe.
Colquhoun	Cnoc Ealachainn !	Name of a hill.
Cranstoun	Henwoodie !	Name of gathering-place.
Douglas	A Douglas ! A Douglas !	——
Forbes	Lonachan !	Name of a hill.
Farquharson	Càrn na Cuimhne !	' The Cairn of Remembrance.'
Fraser	Caisteal Dùnaidh !	Castle Downie.
Gordon	A Gordon ! A Gordon !	——
Grant	Creag-Ealachaidh !	' Rock of Alarm.'
Hepburn	Bide me fair !	——
Home	A Home ! A Home !	——
MacAlpin	Cuimhnich bàs Ailpein !	Remember the death of Alpin !

MacDonald	Fraoch Eilean !	'Heather Isle.'
MacDougall	Buaidh no bàs !	'Victory or death !'
MacFarlane	Loch Sluaigh !	'Loch of the Host.'
MacGregor	Ard Coille !	'The wooded height.'
Macintosh	Loch Maigh !	Loch Moy.
MacKenzie	Tulach Àrd !	Name of a hill.
MacLaren	Creag an Tuirc !	'The Boar's Rock.'
Macpherson	Creag Dhubh !	'The Black Craig.'
Macrae	Sgùrr Urain !	Name of a mountain.
Maxwell	Wardlaw !	Name of a hill.
Menzies	Geal is Dearg suas !	'Up with the White and the Red !'
Munro	Caisteal Faolais 'n a theine !	'Castle Foulis ablaze !'
Scott	Bellendaine !	Name of gathering-place.
Seton	Set On ! Set On !	——

In addition to clan slogans there were also District, or Town, battle-cries ; of which, among many others, there were the following :

Dumfries	Loreburn !	Name of a burn.
Glenlivat	Buadhaich !	Conquer !
Hawick	Teri Buss !	——
Jedburgh	Jethart's Here !	——

And then there is the National Slogan :

Alba gu bràth !	——	Scotland for Ever !

APPELLATIONS TO CLANS AND FAMILIES AND TOWNS

Nearly every name in Scotland has some appellative tacked on to it. Some of the descriptions may be true— some undoubtedly are, or were ; some of them must have been bestowed by enemies ; others, obviously, came by ' alliteration's artful aid.' In any case they are all interesting.

Only a few of the many appellations can be quoted here —not so much from lack of space, as from the fact that many are utterly unprintable !

Armstrong :	The Sturdy Armstrongs
Boyd :	The Trusty Boyds
Cameron :	The Crooked Camerons
Campbell :	The Greedy Campbells
Dalrymple :	The Dirty Dalrymples
Douglas :	The Doughty Douglases
Duff :	The Lucky Duffs
Fraser :	The Bold Frasers
Gordon :	The Gay Gordons
Graham :	The Gallant Grahams
Hamilton :	The Haughty Hamiltons
Hay :	The Handsome Hays
Hume :	The Haughty Humes
Johnston :	The Gentle Johnstons (applied ironically)
Kerr :	The Crabbed Kerrs
Lindsay :	The Light Lindsays
MacDonald :	The Brave MacDonalds
Macintosh :	The Fiery Macintoshes

Maclean :	The Luckless Macleans
MacNeil :	The Proud MacNeils
Macrae :	The Wild Macraes
Menteith :	The False Menteiths
Morrison :	The Manly Morrisons
Murray :	The Muckle-mouthed Murrays
Rutherford :	The Bold Rutherfords
Scott :	The Saucy Scotts
Scott (Buccleuch) :	The Bold Buccleuchs
Seton :	The Lang Setons
Somerville :	The Pudden Somervilles

And here are a few rhymes associated with certain names :

Atholl : Duke o' Atholl—king in Man,
An' greatest man in a' Scotlan'.

Crauford : This spüne ye see, I leave in legacie
To the maist-moothed Crauford after me.
Whaever sells it, curst let him be !

Dalrymple and Dundas : First came the men o' mony wimples,
In common language ca'd Darimples ;
An' after them there came Dundases,
Wha rade oor lords an' lairds like asses !

Douglas : Sae mony guid as o' the Douglases have
been,
Of one surname was ne'er in Scotland seen.

Gordon : Ken ye the Gordons' Gramacie ?—
To curse and swear, and damn and lee !
And that's the Gordons' Gramacie.

Graham :   Wad the Gallant Grahams but stand by me,
        The dogs might douk in English bluid,
    Ere a foot's breadth I wad flinch or flee !

Haig :   Tide, tide, whate'er betide,
    There'll ay be Haigs in Bemersyde.

Kennedy :   'Tween Wigtoun and the toun o' Ayr,
        Portpatrick and the Cruives o' Cree,
    Nae man need think for ta bide there,
        Unless he court wi Kennedie.

Leslie :   Between the Less Lee and the Mair,
    Leslie slew a knicht, an' left him there.

Towns and districts, too, have their appellations :

Aberdeen :   The Brave Toun
Ayr :   Auld Ayr
Dunblane :   Drukken Dunblane
Edinburgh :   The Guid Toun
Forfar :   Brosie Forfar
Kirkcaldy :   The Lang Toun
Lauder :   Lousy Lauder
Linlithgow :   The Faithfu' Toun
Musselburgh :   The Honest Toun
Sleat :   Russet Sleat of beauteous women

CLAN BADGES

In the old days every clan had its badge, and a sprig of the appropriate plant was sported by every clansman in his bonnet. The modern habit of wearing a silver crest-brooch in the bonnet is strongly deprecated in some quarters as being an encroachment on the rights of the chief, but these are democratic days and the clans are scattered, and mostly chief-less; so that there is no real modern reason why the silver crest-brooch should not be worn.

Here is a list of some of the old clan-badges :

Buchanan	Oak, Bilberry
Cameron	Oak, Crowberry
Campbell	Wild Myrtle
Chisholm	Fern
Colquhoun	Dogberry, Hazel
Davidson	Red Whortleberry
Drummond	Wild Thyme, Holly
Farquharson	Little Sunflower, Foxglove
Forbes	Broom
Fraser	Yew
Grant	Pine
Gordon	Ivy
Graham	Laurel
Gunn	Juniper, Roseroot
Johnston	Red Hawthorn
Lamont	Crab Apple
MacAlpin	Pine
MacArthur	Wild Myrtle, Fir Club Moss
MacAulay	Cranberry
MacDonald	Heath

MacDougall	Bell Heath
MacFarlane	Cranberry
MacGregor	Pine
Mackay	Red Grass
Mackenzie	Holly
MacLachlan	Rowan
MacLean of Duart	Crowberry
MacLean of Ardgour	Holly
MacLaine of Lochbuie	Blaeberry
Maclennan	Furze
MacLeod	Juniper
Macnab	Roebuckberry
MacNaughton	Trailing Azalea
Macpherson	Boxwood, Red Whortleberry
Macrae	Club Moss
Menzies	Rowan
Munro	Club Moss
Murray	Butcher's Broom, Juniper
Ogilvie	Whitethorn, Hawthorn
Robertson	Bracken
Ross	Juniper
Sinclair	Gorse
Urquhart	Gillyflower

DYES

The brilliance and greater depth of colour seen in old tartans, as compared with those of modern manufacture, is due to the fact that the old tartans were woven from wools dyed with natural vegetable dyes. Vegetable-dyed tartans and tweeds are still obtainable.

Before dying takes place, the wool has to be treated with a mordant. The usual mordant employed in home-dying was, and is, alum—although others, too, are used.

Below is a list of colours with the names of the roots, barks, herbs, and berries used to obtain the dyes. Many of these dyes are still used in the Islands.

Black	Alder Tree Bark
Black	Dock root
Blue	Elderberry
Brown (Yellowish)	Lichen
Brown	Dulse
Brown (Dark)	Blueberry with Gall nuts
Crimson	White Lichen
Crimson (Dark)	Dark Lichen
Grey	Yellow Water-flag root
Green	Broom
Green	Whin Bark
Purple	Sundew
Red	Rue root
Yellow	Bog Myrtle
Yellow	Bracken root
Yellow	St John's Wort

PLACE-NAMES

There is in most of our Scottish place-names real meaning ; there is more than that even ; there is in some of them sheer poetry. Most of our place names are of definite Celtic origin—either Gaelic or Cymric. There are, too, a few names beginning in ' Pit,' mostly to be found in Fife and Angus, which are believed to be of Pictish derivation. On the other hand we have, of course, place-names that are manifestly Anglic—and they are usually the least euphonious ; we have, too, names of Gaelic origin that have been so brutally anglicized as almost to defy transliteration, or even understanding ; although, taken on the whole, we have not suffered half so badly in this way as have the Irish.

The study of place-names is a most fascinating subject ; but, here, I can do no more than give a list of words and their meanings that may help to explain the significance of some of our place-names to the general reader.

I must necessarily, for the most part, give these words in their anglicized form, as, for instance, ' Inver,' standing for the Gaelic INBHIR. This transliteration is not too bad, since it does, more or less, preserve the sound of the Gaelic word. On the other hand, ' Kin,' for CEANN, is a barbarous form, that is almost as far removed from the Gaelic pronunciation as it is from the original spelling.

Word	Meaning	Example
Aber	River mouth (generally)	Aberdeen
Auch or Ach	A field	Achnasheen

Word	Meaning	Example
Ard or Aird	An altitude, a height	Ardeer
Alt or Uilt	A burn, a stream	Taynuilt
An	The, or, of the	Annan, Lochanard
An	Diminutive	Lochan
Avon	A river	Avondhu
Bal or Bally	A town, or village	Balerno
Ban	White, or fair	Banchory
Barr	A projection, or point	Dunbar, Barassie
Bea, or Beith	A birch-tree, or birches	Altbea, Beith
Bealach	A pass	Balloch
Beg, or Beag	Little	Glenbeg
Ben, or Ven	A mountain	Ben Lui, Ardven
Blair	A plain, a battle-field	Blair Atholl
Breac, or Vreck	Brindled, or chequered	Benvracky
Bui	Yellow	Loch Buie
Cambus	A creek	Cambuslang
Cairn	A heap of stones	Cairngorm
Col, or Caol	A strait	Colintraive
Can	Head, or headland	Cantyre
Clach	A stone, or stones	Clachnaharry
Corrie	A hollow	Corrieyarrick
Craig	A rock	Craigellachie
Cruach	A stack, or pile	Cruachan
Dal	A field, a meadow	Dalnaspidal
Dearg	Red	Glendearg
Du, or Dhu	Black, or dark	Glendhu, Douglas

Word	Meaning	Example
Drochit	A bridge	Drumnadrochit
Drum	A ridge	Drummore
Dun, or Dum	A fort	Dunbar, Dumfries
Esk	Water	Eskdale
Eilan	An isle	Eilan Donan
Fionn, or Fin	White, shining	Findon, Lochfyne
Gair	Short	Gairloch
Gart	An enclosure	Gartmore
Garve	Rough	Garvamore
Glas	Grey, or Water	Glasven, Douglas
Glen	A narrow valley	Glenluce
Gorm	Blue	Cairngorm
Inver, or Inner	River mouth, confluence	Inverurie, Innerleithen
Kil, or Kill	A church, or monastic cell	Kilmarnock, Killearn
Kin, or Ken, or Can	Head, or headland	Kinlochleven, Cantyre
Knock	A hillock	Knockbain
Kyle, or Caol	A strait, narrows	Kyles of Bute
Learg	A sloping plain	Largs
Lon	A meadow	Loanhead
Long	A ship, or ships	Langside
Mam	A rounded hill	Mam Soul
Mal, or Mel	A cape, a bare patch	Melrose, Mull
Mona	An upland moor	Moniaive, Moness
Mor, Mhor, Vohr	Big, great	Morven
Rath	A fort	Ruthven
Righ, or Ry, or Ree	A king	Dalry, Portree

Word	*Meaning*	*Example*
Ros	A promontory	Rosneath, Montrose
Scurr, or Scar	Precipitous hill	Scurr Ouran
Strath	A broad valley	Strathmore
Stron	A nose, promontory	Stranraer, Troon
Tigh	A house	Tighnabruaich
Tom	A mound	Tomnahurich
Uisge	Water	Esk

BATTLES

The principal battles fought on Scottish soil have either been battles of Civil War, or battles against the invading English.

Clan battles, of which there must have been hundreds, are not noted in this list.

1263 : *LARGS*—The Scots under Alexander II defeated the Norwegians under King Haco, and effectively put an end to the predatory incursions of the Norse.

1296 : *DUNBAR*—The English under Edward I defeated an army under John Balliol.

1297 : *STIRLING BRIDGE*—The Scots under Wallace defeated the English.

1298 : *FALKIRK*—The English under Edward I defeated Wallace and a Scots army.

1314 : *BANNOCKBURN*—King Robert I (Bruce) and the Scots defeated the English, who began with an army of vastly superior numbers, but who ended in flight, leaving behind over thirty-thousand slain.

1333 : *HALIDON HILL*—An English army under Edward III defeated the Scots.

1411 : *HARLAW*—An army under the Earl of Mar defeated the army of Donald, Lord of the Isles.

1449 : *SARK*—A Scottish force under Douglas defeated an invading English army.

1488 : *SAUCHIEBURN*—The nobles defeated James III, who was afterwards slain.

1545 : *ANCRUM*—The Scots army under the Earl of Angus routed the English, who left their leaders dead on the field.

1547 : *PINKIE*—The English defeated the Scots.

1568 : *LANGSIDE*—Moray and his rebel army defeated the supporters of Queen Mary.

1645 : *INVERLOCHY*—Montrose defeated the forces of Argyle.

1645 : *KILSYTH*—Montrose defeated the Covenanters.

1645 : *PHILIPHAUGH*—The Covenanters under Leslie defeated the Marquis of Montrose.

1650 : *DUNBAR*—The English under Cromwell defeated an army of Covenanters under Leslie.

1679 : *DRUMCLOG*—An army of Covenanters defeated the Viscount Dundee (Claverhouse).

1679 : *BOTHWELL BRIDGE*—The Covenanters routed.

1689 : *KILLIECRANKIE*—A Highland army under Claverhouse defeated a rebel army who were supporting the claims of William of Orange.

1715 : *SHERIFFMUIR*—An army of rebels against the Scottish Royal House of Stuart defeated the Royalist Jacobites under the Earl of Mar.

1745 : *PRESTONPANS*—The Scottish Royalist army under Prince Charles Edward defeated the English under Sir John Cope.

1746 : *FALKIRK*—Prince Charles Edward and his Scottish Army defeated the English and a few Scots rebels and traitors who were supporting the usurping House of Hanover.

1746 : *CULLODEN*—Following the tribulations of a long winter retreat from the midlands of England, the Scottish Royalist army of Prince Charles Edward was defeated by the English under the ' Butcher ' Cumberland.

AREA

The total area of Scotland (Land and Water) is 31,510 square miles. The greatest length of the mainland (Cape Wrath to the Mull of Galloway) is 274 miles; and the greatest breadth (Applecross to Buchan Ness) is 154 miles. Below is the area of each of the Counties, given in Acres :

Aberdeen -	- 1,261,521	Kirkcudbright -	574,588
Angus -	- 560,186	Lanark -	- 562,821
Argyle -	- 1,990,472	Mid-Lothian -	231,724
Ayr - -	- 793,600	Moray -	- 304,606
Banff -	- 410,112	Nairn - -	- 124,968
Berwick -	- 294,805	Orkney -	- 240,476
Bute -	- 139,432	Peebles -	- 226,899
Caithness -	- 448,068	Perth - -	- 1,617,808
Clackmannan -	30,477	Renfrew -	- 156,785
Dumbarton -	157,289	Ross & Cromarty -	1,970,004
Dumfries -	- 680,217	Roxburgh -	- 425,656
East Lothian -	179,142	Selkirk -	- 172,549
Fife -	- 314,952	Shetland -	- 352,889
Inverness -	- 2,616,545	Stirling -	- 286,338
Kincardine -	245,347	Sutherland -	- 1,297,849
Kinross -	- 46,487	West Lothian -	76,807
	Wigtown -	- 310,747	

THE ISLANDS

There are over 500 islands and islets off the Western coast ; of these, only about a hundred are inhabited. The total area of the Western Isles is 2,812 square miles, with little over 300 *square miles under cultivation. The Western Islands are divided into two main groups : The Inner Hebrides, and The Outer Hebrides. The principal islands of The Outer Hebrides are :*

Lewis (with Harris) (770 square miles)
North Uist
South Uist
Barra

And the islands of The Inner Hebrides are, principally :

Skye (643 square miles)
Mull (367 square miles)
Jura (160 square miles)
Islay (235 square miles)
Rum, Coll, Tiree, Colonsay, Gigha, and Iona.

Of the two main groups of the Northern Islands, The Orkneys and The Shetlands, the Orkney group consists of over ninety islands and islets, of which about thirty are inhabited. The total area of the Orkney group is 376 *square miles.*

In the Shetland group there are over a hundred islands and islets, with a total area of 551 *square miles. Twenty-nine of the Shetland Isles are inhabited. One of the Shetland Isles, Foula, is noted for its healing waters. Foula is udal property—the owner holds not from Crown or Government, but from ' God and the Sun.'*

Fair Isle, which is linked with the Shetland group for administrative purposes, is about half-way between the Orkneys and the Shetlands, which are about fifty miles apart.

LOCHS

The height above sea-level of the principal Lochs : given in feet.

The names of the Lochs are given in the usual anglicized forms as found in the English maps.

Loch Muick -	- 1310	Loch Quoich - - 555
Loch Ossian -	- 1269	Loch Tummel - - 450
Loch Ericht -	- 1153	Loch Voil - - - 410
Loch Laidon -	- 924	Loch Lubnaig - - 395
Loch Lee -	- 880	Loch Loyal - - 369
Loch Cobbinshaw	- 870	Loch Katrine - - 364
Loch Eilan -	- 840	Loch Leven - - 350
Loch Laggan -	- 819	Loch Earn - - 305
St Mary's Loch	- 803	Loch Chon - - 291
Loch Treig -	- 784	Loch Achray - - 276
Loch Affric -	- 744	Loch Luichart - - 270
Loch Mullardoch	- 704	Loch Shin - - 270
Loch Rannoch -	- 667	Loch Vennachar - - 270
Loch Doon -	- 660	Loch Naver - - 247
Loch Clunie -	- 606	Loch Assynt - - 215

The largest lochs are : LOCH LOMOND (24 miles long. Height above sea-level : 23 feet), and LOCH NESS (24 miles long, 800 feet deep, and 50 feet above sea-level).

RIVERS

The Tay -	-	-	- 117 miles
The Spey -	-	-	- 110 miles
The Clyde	-	-	- 106 miles
The Tweed	-	-	- 96 miles
The Dee -	·	-	- 90 miles
The Forth	-	-	- 66 miles

MOUNTAINS

The heights of the principal Mountains : given in feet.
For the most part the usual anglicized names as given on
most English maps are used.

Ben Nevis	- -	4406
Ben Macdhui	- -	4296
Braeriach -	- -	4248
Cairntoul -	- -	4241
Cairngorm	- -	4084
Ben Lawers	- -	3984
Mam Soul	- -	3877
Ben Avon -	- -	3843
Ben Mòr (Perth)	-	3843
Stobinian	- -	3827
Lochnagar	- -	3786
Bidean nam Beann	-	3766
Ben Alder	- -	3757
Ben Lui -	- -	3708
Ben Cruachan	- -	3689
Ben-y-Gloe	- -	3671
Schiehallion	- -	3547
Ben Dorain	- -	3523
Scurr Ouran	- -	3505
Glasmeal -	- -	3502
Ben Wyvis	- -	3429
Ben Attow	- -	3383
Buchaile Etive	-	3345
Ben Ime -	- -	3318
Ben Eay -	- -	3309
Sguir Alasdair (Skye)		3309
Ben Mòr (Assynt)	-	3273

Cuchullin	-	- 3234
Ben Vorlich	-	- 3224
Ben Slioch	-	- 3217
Ben Screel	-	- 3196
Ben Lomond	-	- 3192
Ben Mòr (Mull)		- 3169
Sgòrr nan Gillean		- 3167
Ben Clibreck	-	- 3154
Monadhliath	-	- 3087
Mount Keen	-	- 3077
Ben Chonzie	-	- 3048
Blaven -	-	- 3042
Ben Hope	-	- 3040
Scurr Donald	-	- 2915
Ben Arthur	-	- 2891
Ben Ledi -	-	- 2875
Goat Fell	-	- 2866
Canisp -	-	- 2779
Ben Resipol	-	- 2774
Merrick -	-	- 2764
Ben Vrackie	-	- 2757
Cheviot -	-	- 2676
Paps of Jura	-	- 2569
Ben Loyal	-	- 2504
Culter Fell	-	- 2454
Tinto -	-	- 2335
Ettrick Pen	-	- 2269

THE BURGHS

There are sixty-six Royal Burghs, and four Ancient Royal Burghs. (See under Law—Burghs).

Many of the Royal Burghs are in area and in population quite small. Below is a list of the Royal Burghs with a population of 5,000 and over :

Aberdeen	Irvine
Arbroath	Kinghorn
Ayr	Kirkcaldy
Brechin	Kirkwall
Burntisland	Lanark
Campbeltown	Montrose
Dumbarton	Peebles
Dumfries	Perth
Dundee	Renfrew
Dunfermline	Rothesay
Edinburgh	Rutherglen
Elgin	St Andrews
Forfar	Selkirk
Glasgow	Stirling
Inverness	Stranraer
	Wick

EDINBURGH : The Capital of Scotland has a municipal area of 32,402 acres. The former Burgh of Leith is now included in Edinburgh.

GLASGOW : Scotland's great commercial centre, with a population of more than double that of the Capital, covers a municipal area of 30,046 acres—over 2,000 acres less than Edinburgh.

The twelve smallest Royal Burghs, giving their populations, are :

New Galloway (307)	Falkland (779)
Inveraray (445)	Fortrose (875)
Culross (495)	Whithorn (951)
Lauder (628)	Lochmaben (1014)
Dornoch (725)	Inverbervie (1032)
Kintore (756)	Crail (1058)

There are other small burghs with populations of only a few hundreds, but they are Police or Parliamentary Burghs. The smallest Police Burgh is Abernethy (595), and the smallest Parliamentary Burgh is Cromarty (837).

ROSS AND CROMARTY

The name of Ross and Cromarty, as applied to the northern administrative area of that name, is a puzzle to most people.

The first Earl of Cromarty, Sir George Mackenzie of Tarbat, who was created Earl in 1703, obtained the privilege of having his various estates throughout Ross erected into a separate and new county of Cromarty. So that the county of Cromarty consisted of a number of isolated ' islands ' surrounded by the ' sea ' of Ross. There were eight or nine of these detached areas, estimated to measure, in all, about 350 square miles. They lay all over Ross—north, south, east, and west. This inconvenient arrangement lasted for almost two hundred years, being ended by the Boundary Commissioners in 1891, when the area became the Administrative County of Ross and Cromarty with Dingwall as the administrative headquarters.

THE STEWARTRY

There are two Stewartries : that of Orkney and Shetland, and that of Kirkcudbright. But when ' The Stewartry ' is mentioned it is usually Kirkcudbright that is meant.

The Stewartry of Kirkcudbright, by which designation the administrative County of Kirkcudbright is still known, came into being because the Gaelic people of the district would not permit the introduction of a Sheriffdom until some time about 1295, or 1296. The people of the Stewartry for many years retained their own laws and customs. The Comyns introduced a justiciary, which, on their fall, came into the rights of the Crown. Douglas ' The Grim ' succeeded in wrenching from David II the lordship for himself and for his heirs. On the fall of the Douglases, the lordship, or Stewardship, fell again to the Crown. About 1500, the Steward was also Keeper of Thrieve Castle. In 1526, the office of Steward of Kirkcudbright was made an hereditary possession of Robert, Lord Maxwell. At the abolition of heritable jurisdictions, Henrietta, Countess-Dowager of Hopetoun and representative of the Maxwells, was allowed £5,000 as compensation for the loss of the Hereditary Stewardship.

Judicially, the office of Steward is analogous to that of Sheriff. Kirkcudbright is now united with the Sheriffdom of Dumfries, but it is an independent administrative county. Kirkcudbright and Wigtown counties form what is now known as Galloway ; but the old Province of Galloway consisted of what are now the counties of Kirkcudbright and Wigtown, together with a part of what is now the county of Dumfries, and a part of the Carrick district of Ayr.

From the title of Steward, or Stewart, the Royal house derived its surname; but that, of course, referred not to the Stewardship of Kirkcudbright, but to the Grand Stewardship of Scotland.

Kennedy

WEATHER

Most people have heard of 'Buchan's Cold Spells,' 'Buchan's Warm Spells,' or, more generally, 'Buchan's Weather.'

Since Dr Alexander Buchan was a Scot, and Secretary of the Scottish Meteorological Society; and since his findings referred to the Scottish temperature, mention of him must be made. Weather is an important thing with us.

Resulting from his scientific examination of the temperature of Scotland, Dr Buchan has shown that 'the following interruptions occur from year to year, with very rare exceptions, in the annual march of the Scottish temperature':

1st Cold Period from February 7th to 10th.
2nd Cold Period from April 11th to 14th.
3rd Cold Period from May 9th to 14th.
4th Cold Period from June 29th to July 4th.
1st Warm Period from July 12th to 15th.
5th Cold Period from August 6th to 11th.
2nd Warm Period from August 12th to 15th.
6th Cold Period from November 6th to 12th.
3rd Warm Period from December 3rd to 9th.

The dates given for these deviations from the normal, are, more or less, approximate.

'One of the best marked of these periods,' says Dr Buchan, ' occurs from about the 11th to the 14th of April. This is the cold weather commonly known as " The Borrowing Days." '

THE BORROWED DAYS

March is represented as borrowing three days from April.

March said to Averil :
I see three hoggs on yonder hill ;
But lend your first three days to me,
And I'll be bound to gar them dee !
The first o' them was wind and weet ;
The second o' them was snaw and sleet ;
The third o' them was sic a freeze,
It froze the birds' feet to the trees.
But when the three borrowed days were gane,
The silly puir hoggs cam hirplin hame.

TRADITIONAL.

Macpherson

THE LAW

It is not too well known, at least out of Scotland, that Scots laws differ considerably from those of her neighbours. The law in Wales runs as in England ; the laws of Ireland are based on the laws forced on Ireland by the English during a seven centuries' occupation of the country, although, as far as The Free State (Saorstat Eireann) is concerned, the English laws are fast being superseded by others more appropriate to the country and the race.

The Scottish legal system is still the system that was in vogue at the time of the Union with England. Recognition of Scots law was an integral part of the Treaty ; and, although certain Scots laws have been superseded, or nullified, by certain statutes of the Westminster Parliament, this part of the Treaty has been honoured to a greater extent than the rest of it.

COURTS

The Supreme Courts, or Authorities, of Scotland are The Court of Session (in which the Court of Exchequer is now merged), and The Court of Justiciary. The supremacy of The Court of Session was, however, disregarded as soon after the signing of the Treaty as 1710, by what can only be described as sharp-practice. I quote from Principal Rait's *The Making of Scotland :* ' The Act of Union had provided that no Court sitting in Westminster Hall should receive appeals from The Court of Session. In 1710 the House of Lords *not sitting in Westminster Hall,* reversed a decision of The Court of Session. . . .'

MARRIAGE

Since the Scots Marriage Laws are likely to be of greater interest to readers living abroad, than reference to any of the other laws, I put this note second in importance to that on the Courts.

Most people of Scottish descent, and any people who are at all interested in Scotland, know that the Marriage Laws of Scotland differ considerably from those of the rest of Europe ; but how, and where, they differ is a matter that is not fully understood even within Scotland itself.

In the law of Scotland marriage is a simple contract, which is completed by nothing more formal than mutual consent. There are no formalities necessary, and any boy over the age of fourteen, and any girl over the age of twelve, may contract a marriage without consent of parents or guardians.

This simple form of marriage, or *Irregular Marriage*, is a survival of modes of marriage at one time general throughout Europe, Scotland having disregarded the decrees of the Council of Trent invalidating such marriages. These irregular marriages are, in Scotland, thoroughly legal, and completely binding, and they can only be dissolved by death or legal divorce.

There are three ways in which an irregular marriage may be contracted : (1) By sincere mutual consent before two witnesses. There need not be anything in writing, and it has even been held that the presence of witnesses is not a necessity if there is anything else to prove the mutual consent to the contract. (2) By promise of marriage followed by intercourse on the faith of that promise. The promise, however, must be definitely proved. (3) By constantly living together as husband and wife, so establishing a consistent repute of marriage. Marriage by the first method (the other two methods obviously not coming into the question) is only valid following a residence in Scotland of not less than three weeks. But it is sufficient if only one of the parties to the marriage has resided in Scotland for three weeks or more. That is to say, a foreigner (see under *Foreigner*) may come to Scotland, live in Scotland for three weeks, and then send for his bride, and marry her immediately she sets foot in Scotland. A native Scot, who has consistently lived out of Scotland for any length of time, is as subject to the residence qualification as a foreigner. The residence qualification is the result of comparatively recent legislation, and is not part of the common law of Scotland.

There is no stigma attached in any way to an irregular marriage, or to those who contract one. Irregular marriages may be registered, if the parties to such a marriage desire it, by their putting in an appearance before the Sheriff within three months. On the Sheriff granting warrant, the Registrar registers the marriage for a fee of 5s. 1d.

A *Regular Marriage* in Scotland is one which is celebrated by a Minister of religion after due notice by publication of banns, or after publication by the Registrar. A regular marriage need not be celebrated in a church : the minister may carry out the marriage ceremony in a private house, or in a room in a restaurant, or public hall, taken for the occasion.

ADVOCATES

Barristers practising before the Supreme Courts of Scotland are called Advocates.

BAIL

All crimes and offences, except murder and treason, are bailable.

BAILLIE, OR BAILIE

A magistrate. Baillies have the same common-law civil jurisdiction as Sheriffs.

BANK NOTES

Bank notes in the form of promissory notes payable to the bearer on demand, are issued by all the important Scottish banks; and these bank notes pass current as money. These bank notes are in general use. They are not accepted in England, but an English bank will change a Scottish note at a commission rate of anything from a few coppers to a shilling. Bank of England notes are not legal tender in Scotland.

BORDER WARRANT

A Border Warrant is a warrant granted by a Sheriff for the detention of a debtor residing on the English side of the Border if found within Scotland. Now in desuetude.

BURGHS, ROYAL

The royal burghs derive their constitution from royal charter, which either exists, or is presumed to have existed at one period, and to have perished ' by the accidents of war and time.' There are sixty-six Royal Burghs, and four Ancient Royal Burghs.

CHURCH OF SCOTLAND

The Roman Church was abolished in Scotland, by statute, at the Reformation. Presbyterian church government was established by Act in 1592, and was again recognised in 1689 by Acts commonly called the Charter of the Church.

CURSING AND SWEARING

Several old Acts dealt with this offence, but they all appear to have fallen into desuetude. The principal statute is one of 1661, which apportioned the penalty according to the following scale : *For a nobleman, £S20 ; for a baron, 20 merks ; for a yeoman, 40s. ; for a servant, 20s. ; and the fifth part of a year's stipend for a minister !*

DEAN OF FACULTY

The President, elected annually, of the Faculty of Advocates in Edinburgh.

DEAN OF GUILD

The President of the guildry, or merchantmen, in a royal burgh. In the burghs of Edinburgh, Glasgow, Perth, Aberdeen, and Dundee, the Dean of Guild has, as such, a seat on the burgh council.

DESUETUDE

Scots statutes, contrary to the practice in most other countries, cease to be law by long non-observance, or by long contrary practice.

DIVORCE

There are two grounds of divorce : Adultery ; and Malicious Desertion for four years.

FOREIGNERS

Anyone who is not a native Scot, or who is not born of Scottish parentage, or who has not a Scottish domicile, is in Scots law a foreigner, and must be cited as such edictally before the Court of Session. It is definitely laid down by an authority that an Englishman and an Irishman are legally foreigners in Scotland.

FUGITATION OR OUTLAWRY

The sentence of the Justiciary Court against a person lawfully cited and failing to appear to answer to a criminal charge. Outlawry carries with it forfeiture of movables, and deprives the outlaw of certain rights. An outlaw may be apprehended without warrant.

HAMESUCKEN

Hamesucken is an assault committed in the dwelling-house of the person assaulted, to which he has fled for safety; or an assault by one who goes to a man's dwelling-house designedly for the purpose. It is not hamesucken to assault a landlord in his inn, nor is it hamesucken to assault an actor in a theatre; nor is it hamesucken to assault a man in an outbuilding, or in his shop or office.

HOLOGRAPH DEEDS

Holograph deeds are deeds written wholly, or in the essential parts, by the signer's own hand. Such deeds do not require to be witnessed. A holograph will, unwitnessed, will stand in law. Incidentally, the term *Will* is not by itself used technically in Scots law. A will may be written in pencil.

INFANCY

The term *Infancy* has no precise meaning in Scots law as it has in English law. With us persons are *Pupils*, or are said to be in *Pupillarity*, until they reach the age of twelve in girls, and fourteen in boys ; they are then *minors*, or *minor-pubes*, until they reach the age of twenty-one, when they become majors, or of lawful age. (See under *Marriage*.)

JUSTICES OF THE PEACE

' Godlie, wyse, and vertuous gentlemen, of good quality, moyen, and report, making residence within their respective shyres, appointed by his majestie for the keeping of his majestie's peace.'—Act 1609.

JUSTICIARY COURT

The supreme criminal court. It consists of the Justice-General, the Justice-Clerk, and all the other Senators of the College of Justice as Lords Commissioners of Justiciary. No appeal is competent from the Justiciary to any other body.

NAME

A change of name is authorised and registered by The Court of the Lord Lyon. The fee is under a pound. But, according to Lord President Boyle, ' By the law of Scotland, there is no need of the authority of court to enable a man to change his name.'

In England change of name is effected by Deed Poll, and the cost may be anything between twenty-five and fifty pounds.

PROCURATOR-FISCAL

The officer at whose instance public prosecutions proceed.

ROMAN LAW

The municipal law of ancient Rome. The Scots Law incorporates its principles in great measure.

SANCTUARY

The Abbey of Holyrood, with its precincts, is now the only place in Scotland having the privilege of sanctuary. The protection does not, however, extend to criminal warrants.

SHERIFF

The office of Sheriff is first noticed in the reign of Alexander I.

STEWARTRY

There are two Stewartries : Orkney and Shetland ; and Kirkcudbright. Judicially, the office of Steward is analogous with that of Sheriff.

WRITERS TO THE SIGNET (W.S.)

A Legal Incorporation by immemorial custom. They are members of the College of Justice, and are eligible after ten years' practice to be Senators, that is, judges in the Supreme Court.

MONEY AND MEASURES

In order to perpetuate the old lie about Scotland's poverty-stricken state prior to the Union, it has been the custom of our traducers—native and otherwise—to go out of their way to explain that the old Scots money bore approximately the proportion of one-twelfth to the money of England : the inference being that the Englishman was twelve times richer than the Scot. This downright falsehood arose from the fact that the Scots ' penny ' was called a SCHILLIN or SGILLINN, and there was a Scots coin called the PUND or POUND, worth about the twelfth of an English coin called the pound. But SCHILLIN and PUND were merely names. If we suddenly decided to call the modern sixpence a florin, the change of name alone would not increase its value or buying power.

Here are the names and comparative values of the old Scots coins :

2 Doits	-	-	-	- 1 Bodle
2 Bodles	-	-	-	- 1 Plack or Groa
3 Placks	-	-	-	- 1 Schillin
40 Placks	-	-	-	- 1 Merk
20 Schillins	-	-	-	- 1 Pund

The following old measures are now obsolete.

Land Measures :

The Ell	-	-	-	- 37.2 inches
The Mile	-	-	-	- 1984 yards
The Acre	-	-	-	- 6150 square yards

Liquid Measures :

4 gills	1 mutchkin :	modern equivalent—1 pint
2 mutchkins	1 choppin :	„ „ —1 quart

2 choppins	1 pint : modern equivalent —2 quarts
2 pints	1 quart : „ „ —1 gallon
4 quarts	1 gallon : „ „ —4 gallons

' *The Scottish pint of liquid measure comprehends four English measures of the same denomination. The jest is well-known of my poor countryman who, driven to extremity by the raillery of the Southern on the small denomination of the Scottish coin, at length answered :* " *Ay, ay ! but the deil tak them that hes the least pint-stoup !* " '

Scott : NOTE TO ' REDGAUNTLET.'

PROVERBS

'... *there are current in society upwards of* 3,000 *proverbs, exclusively Scottish* ... *the Scots are wonderfully given to this way of speaking, and as the consequence of that, abound with proverbs, many of which are very expressive, quick, and home to the purpose ; and, indeed, this humour prevails universally over the whole nation.* ...'

James Kelly (1721).

Some of the following proverbs are translations from the Gaelic ; others, originally in Old Scots, have been modernised or transliterated.

A gangin' fit will ay get something, gin it's naethin' but a thorn or a broken tae.

Reivers shouldna be ruers.

There's nae füle like an auld füle.

A' Stuarts arena sib ta the king.

It's ill wark takin the breeks frae aff a Hielandman.

The deil's no ay the ill chiel he's ca'd.

The deil's bairns hae ay deil's luck.

Raise nae mair deils than ye're able to lay.

Wha wad sup kail wi' the deil wants a lang-shaftit spüne.

Keep your ain fish guts ta your ain sea maws.

A blate cat maks a prood moose.

Better a toom hoose than an ill tenant.

Mony a yin spiers the gait he kens fu' weel.

Him that hes a muckle nose thinks ilka yin speaks o't.

Wha teaches himself hes a füle for a maister.

Ye're nae chicken for a' your cheepin'.

Better be quiet than sing a bad sang.

A black ewe may have a white lamb.

He who waits long at the ferry will get across sometime.

Playing with a pup will end in a howl.

Gentility will never boil the pot.

There's no much guile in the heart that's ay singing.

The deaf man will ay hear the clink o' money.

Even a pig will keep its ain sty clean.

A spark has often kindled a big fire.

If ye canna bite dinna show your teeth.

There's meat and music here, as the fox said when he stole the bagpipes.

Put silk on a stick, and it will look fine.

Better a good wife than plough and land.

Better be dead than be a fat slave.

A light-heeled mother makes a leaden-heeled daughter.

Choose your wife with her night-cap on.

The highest mountain in the land is oftenest covered with mist.

The clan is stronger than the chief.

The tinker's wages—paid beforehand.

Scotland's strength, and England's cunning.

Taking a salmon from the river, a tree from the forest, and a deer from the mountain, are three actions no Gael was ever ashamed of.

TOASTS

A Bottle and a Friend

Here's a bottle and an honest friend
    What wad ye wish for mair, man?
Wha kens, before his life may end,
    What his share may be o' care, man?

Then catch the moments as they fly,
    And use them as ye ought, man;
Believe me, happiness is shy,
    And comes no ay when sought, man!

Burns.

We are supposed to be a ' drukken ' race—but that is an old tale ! However, be that as it may, if we are occasionally ' dour ' we also know how to make the best of convivial moments ; and for these moments our tongue is rich in characteristic toasts.

And every Scot has at least one word of the Gaelic : SLÀINTE !—often slightly mispronounced as ' Slansh,' but that will do.

And so, to quote from Fergusson : ' Let the toast roond gang. . . .'

Freedom an' Whusky gang thegither—tak aff your dram !

Here's ta us ! Wha's like us ?—Deil the yin !

The Land o' Cakes, an' Brither Scots,
Frae Maidenkirk tae Johnny Groats !

Whan we're gaun up the hill o' fortune may we ne'er meet
    a freend comin' doon !

Here's ta mair freends, an' less need o' them !

Here's grand luck, an' muckle fat weans !

Here's health ta the seeck, an' stilts ta the lame ;
Claise ta the back, an' brose ta the wame !

Here's health, wealth, wit, an' meal !

The deil rock them in a creel,
That disna wish us a' weel !

May ye ne'er want a freend, nor a dram ta gie him !

Guid nicht ta ye, an' take your nappy ;
A wully-waught's a guid night-cappy !

A cosy but, an' a canty ben,
Ta couthie women, an' honest men !

May the moose ne'er leave your meal-pock wi' the tear in
its ee !

Up wi' yer glesses, an' deil tak the hindmaist !

Here's the Land o' the Bens, the Glens, an' the Heroes

Blythe may we a' be,
Ill may we never see !

Here's ta them that lo'es us, or lends us a lift !

Here's ta the heath, the hill, and the heather,
The bonnet, the plaidie, the kilt, and the feather !
Here's ta the song that Auld Scotland can boast,
May her name never die !—that's a Highlandman's toast.

And, incidentally, ' Doch an Dorris' is really DEOCH AN DORUIS, and literally means ' The Drink at the Door.'

DEOCH-SLÀINTE is a Toast, and for all ordinary occasions, such as standing in a sawdust-bar in Saxon breeks, where an Englishman would say ' Cheerio !' say SLÀINTE ! or, if the other man has paid for the drink, you might even go so far as to say SLÀINTE-MHÓR ! But for all ceremonial occasions, the kilt and a true knowledge of the old tongue are necessary. Rise to your feet, fling back your chair, leap upon it, leave your left foot on the chair, and plant your right foot on the table, raise aloft your glass, and, with the appropriate gestures, roll out the following :

Suas e, suas e, suas e !

Sios e, sios e, sios e !

A null e, a null e, a null e !

A nall e, a nall e, a nall e !

Na h-uile là gu math duit, a charaid,

Sguab as e !

Then, having drunk :

Agus chan òl neach eile as a' ghloine so gu bràth !

And when that has been said, fling the glass with a mighty gesture over the left shoulder that it may crash to smithereens on the floor.

And the Gaelic of all that may be translated, line for line, as :

Up with it, up with it, up with it !

Down it, down it, down it !

From me, from me, from me!

To me, to me, to me!

May all your days be good, my friend! (*or whatever other sentiment you wish to express*)

Take it down!

And no other shall drink from this glass again ever more!

And that's the Highland way of doing things!

Munro

MEAT AND DRINK

As a mere man, I approach this section with a certain amount of trepidation ; but some reference must be made in this book to our National Dishes and our National Drinks. I trust that my perverted sense of humour will not run away with me.

Miss F. Marian MacNeill, that Master (or is it Mistress ?) of the Art of Scots cookery, has covered the field so adequately that I can only doff my bonnet and hope for the best.

> *O Lord, when hunger pinches sore,*
> *Do Thou stand us in stead,*
> *And send us, from Thy bounteous store,*
> *A tup or wether head ! Amen.*

BARLEY BANNOCKS

> *For me, I can be weel content,*
> *To eat my bannock on the bent,*
> *And kitchen't wi' fresh air. . . .*
> *Allan Ramsay.*

Mix well in a bowl, a pound of barley-meal, four ounces of flour, and half a teaspoonful of salt. Into a pint of buttermilk stir two small teaspoonfuls of bicarbonate of soda, and, as it fizzes up, pour it into the mixed barley-meal and flour. Work into a soft dough, flour, and roll out lightly to the thickness of about half-an-inch. Cut into large rounds and bake on a hot girdle, turning the bannock until each side is a rich brown.

Black Bun

Make a mixture of 1 lb. of stoned Valencia raisins, 1 lb. of stoned big blue raisins, 2 lb. washed and dried currants, ½ lb. blanched and roughly chopped almonds, ½ lb. brown sugar, ½ oz. each of cinnamon, ginger, and Jamaica pepper, 1 lb. of flour and a small teaspoonful of baking soda, and half-a-pound of finely chopped mixed candied peel. Add milk or beaten egg to moisten the mixture.

Grease a cake-tin, and line it evenly with a thin paste made of 1 lb. of flour, ¼ lb. of butter, and half a teaspoonful of baking soda, and buttermilk to mix. Retain sufficient of the paste to cover the top.

Put in the fruit mixture, put on the cover and join to the sides. Prick all over the top with a fork—make a thistle design if you feel that way !—brush over the cover with milk or beaten egg, and bake in a moderate oven for about four hours.

Great stuff ! but only to be eaten in small quantities at a time !

Carrageen Jelly

This is made in the Hebrides : it is made, too, in the Irish Gaeltachd. I have eaten it in Connacht, but I don't recommend it !

Wash all the salt and sand out of sea-weed gathered from the rocks, spread it on a cloth out-of-doors to dry and bleach for several days (no suggestion is offered for drying it in rainy weather !). When thoroughly dry hang up in a warmish place in a bag, or bags (pillow-cases might do !). As, and when, required put two dessert-spoonfuls into a quart of milk. Simmer till the milk begins to thicken, strain, and pour into a bowl to cool and set.

COLCANNON

This is another dish common to the Isles and Ireland. And this is good.

Chop up finely two cabbages that have been parboiled, mash up with well-boiled carrots, two well-boiled turnips, and about a dozen boiled potatoes. Melt some butter in a stew-pan, put in the mixed vegetables, and let them go at it for twenty minutes or so. Season with salt and black pepper ; and don't let the stuff grow cold.

CROWDIE

O that I had ne'er been married,
I wad never had nae care,
Now I've gotten wife an' weans,
An' they cry ' Crowdie ! ' ever mair.

Burns.

There are several kinds of Crowdie : the sort that this book has been written on consists of nothing but milk and coarse oatmeal stirred together. And if the tastiness and food value of this mixture were as well known now, as, apparently, they once were, there would be fewer expensive imported cereals of the ' corn flakes ' type bothered about.

' Crowdie ' is the Lowland name : in the Highlands it is ' Fuarag,' and it is sometimes made of soured cream whipped, and then mixed with toasted oatmeal.

In the Highlands ' Crowdie ' is the term applied to an elementary form of cheese.

CROWDIE (CHEESE)

Heat some sour milk very slowly until it separates. Do not allow it to come anywhere near boiling-point. Strain off the whey. Season the solid matter with salt and a little pepper, and an excellent cheese is the result. To get out the moisture, the cheese should be 'pressed' by being squeezed in a muslin bag. It is, also, the better of being allowed to stand for a day or two.

FORFAR BRIDIES

Make a stiffish paste with flour and water, seasoned with salt. Roll out into ovals. Cover the half of each oval with minced beef, adding a little minced suet. Sprinkle over with minced, or finely chopped, onion. Wet the edges of the paste, fold over and crimp together. Brush over with milk, and bake in a quick oven for about half-an-hour, or until the pastry has turned a golden brown.

GUNDY

This auld-farrant sweetie may be neither meat nor drink, but it is very good ; and it is much better than many of the toffees sold nowadays.

Boil in a saucepan, a pound of brown sugar, two ounces of butter, and a teaspoonful of black treacle—although golden syrup will do. Test at intervals by dropping a little of the boiling mixture into cold water. When the sample comes from the water quite hard, the Gundy is done. At the last minute, flavour with aniseed or cinnamon—or, if you want Gundy that's guid for a sair hoast (*anglice :* bad cold) you can chance putting horehound in. Pour out

thinly into a buttered tin, and, if you can resist its tempta-
tion, give the Gundy a chance to become quite cold and
hard. You will then require a hammer ; but it will respond
to the attentions of a flat-iron.

HAGGIS

> *Fair fa' your honest, sonsie face,*
> *Great chieftain o' the pudden race !*

For this, the greatest of Scots savouries, is required : a
sheep's bag, and the small bag, the pluck complete (lights,
liver, and heart), beef suet, onions, and oatmeal, with
seasoning of salt and black pepper.

Thoroughly clean the bag, and soak in cold salted water
for at least twelve hours. Turn the rough side out. Wash
the pluck and the small bag, cover them with cold water,
and set to boil with the windpipe hanging over the side of
the pot to let out impurities. Boil for an hour and a half,
or two hours. Then take out, and cut away all gristle and
pipes. Half the liver only will be required, grate this, and
mince the heart and lights. Make a mixture of this and
half a pound of minced suet, a couple of finely chopped
onions, and a large cupful of previously toasted oatmeal, all
well moistened with some of the liquid in which the pluck
was boiled. Put the mixture into the large bag, leaving
plenty of room to swell. Sew the bag securely, and
put it to boil in a large pot of hot water. Prick the bag
all over with a darning needle as soon as it begins to
swell, to prevent the possibility of its bursting. Boil
steadily for three hours with the lid off the pot. Serve
immediately.

A form of Haggis may be made without the sheep's bag, by putting the mixture into a buttered basin, and steaming it for about four hours.

HERRINGS—FRIED

> *Wha'll buy ma caller herrin'?*
> *They're bonnie fish an' halesome farin'.*

Split, bone, clean, and dry the herrings. Sprinkle with salt and pepper, and thoroughly coat each fish with coarse oatmeal. Put some dripping in the frying pan, and when it smokes blue, put in the herrings, and fry till they are well browned on either side.

HOTCH-POTCH

> *Then here's to ilka kindly Scot,*
> *Wi' mony guid broths he boils his pot,*
> *But rare hotch-potch beats a' the lot. . . .*

Hotch-potch may be made with any of three or four different kinds of meat—mutton or beef, or even a marrow-bone will do, but the best meat to use is neck of mutton. And vegetables of all kinds are needed—the more varieties the better, and they must be fresh : carrots, turnips, cabbage, green peas, spring onions or leeks, and anything else obtainable. A stick of celery, for those who like it, may be added, and the broth is the better of having a handful of barley added.

Put three pounds of meat into a pot and cover with cold water : the meat should be a solid piece, or a piece that has been securely tied. Bring to the boil and skim. Have all the vegetables cut into small pieces—the turnips and carrots cut into dice. Add the vegetables and the barley to the boiling liquid, and simmer slowly for at least three hours. The peas should be added last of all, and allow them no more time than will just cook them nicely. If they are put in too soon and become ' mushy ' the broth will be ruined. Salt the broth in the process of cooking. Hotch-potch should be served boiling hot, and should be thick.

PORRIDGE

> *The halesome parritch, chief o' Scotia's food.*
>
> *Burns.*

It should scarcely be necessary to give a recipe for the making of porridge, but porridge is one of those simple things—like plain boiled potatoes—that can easily be ruined ; and, with the advent of quick-cooking American rolled oats, and other such novelties, the making of real porridge is becoming almost a lost art.

Use only the best oatmeal, and at that, not too finely ground. Bring water to the boil and let the oatmeal be trickled into it, stirring all the time with a spirtle—a wooden stick about a foot long. Let the porridge cook steadily for about half-an-hour : keep stirring, look out for lumps, and don't give the stuff a chance to burn. Never cook porridge without salt, but don't add the salt until the porridge is more than half-done.

Porridge should be eaten with fresh milk or butter-milk, and *salt*. If you cannot eat porridge without committing the ghastly sin of putting sugar on it, then don't eat it at all. I have terrible recollections of English army messes, and English subalterns gulping down porridge mixed with golden syrup. That was during the war, but I still ' grue ' at the memory.

Incidentally, porridge is not ' it,' it is ' they ' or ' them.' And *they* should be eaten standing. Miss MacNeill mentions this in her excellent *Scots Kitchen*; and I recall the fact that my father always stood to his porridge, but whether he was observing some ancient secret rite, or whether he was just in a plain hurry I never discovered.

STOVIE TATTIES

Cut up into small pieces two or three onions, and fry them together with any small scraps of meat. Peel and cut up into smallish pieces about half-a-dozen large potatoes. Put the pieces of potato into a pan that has in it only sufficient water to cover the bottom. Add small pieces of butter, and when the butter has melted and run through the potatoes, add the fried onions and meat. Salt, and simmer slowly with the lid on until the potatoes are quite soft.

And now :

O Lord, since we have feasted thus,
 Which we so little merit,
Let Meg now take away the flesh,
 And Jock bring in the spirit !   Amen.

It might not be out of place to explain here how POITÌN, or illicitly distilled whisky, is made ; but the GÀID-SEARAN are cunning fellows, and the penalties are stiff. We must be content with paying 12s. 6d. a bottle (8s. 5d. of it tax) or do with something less potent.

HEATHER ALE

> *From the bonny bells of heather,*
> *They brewed a drink langsyne,*
> *Was sweeter far than honey,*
> *Was stronger far than wine.*
>
> *R. L. S.*

Take the heather-bells when the heather is in full bloom. Wash in cold water to remove any dust or small insects that there may be. Then fill a pot with the heather, cover with water, and boil for an hour. Strain the liquid into a clean wooden tub, and for every dozen pints add half-an-ounce of hops, an ounce of ground ginger, and a pound of sweet treacle or honey. Boil again for another twenty minutes. Strain off once more, and when almost cold add five table-spoonfuls of barm. Cover with a cloth and allow the stuff to 'work' undisturbed for at least twenty-four hours. After that, skim carefully, and pour over gently into a tub, leaving all the barmy sediment behind. Put into bottles and cork tightly. Put the bottles away in a dark place for a week. At the end of the week the Heather Ale may be got rid of in the usual manner. There is spirit in Heather.

See the Story of the Heather Ale on page 152.

And now for one or two ways of taking whisky without drinking it neat.

ATHOLL BROSE

> *Aye since he wore the tartan trews,*
> *He dearly lo'ed the Atholl Brose.*
>
> *Neil Gow.*

Stir together half-a-pound of fine oatmeal, half-a-pound

of running honey, and a cupful of cold water. When they are thoroughly mixed, add *slowly* two pints of whisky. Stir briskly till the mixture froths. Bottle and cork tightly. After a day or two remove the cork, and forget all about the whisky-tax.

TODDY

Into a heated tumbler put a spoonful of sugar, and then sufficient boiling water to dissolve it. Add half a glassful of whisky, stir with a silver spoon, pour in more boiling water, and then top with more whisky. A terrible waste of good *uisge-beatha*!

Campbell

FESTIVALS AND QUARTER DAYS

Some of the old Festival Days are now disregarded, but the majority are still kept in some shape or form.

Jan. 1st	New Year's Day
Jan. 5th	Twelfth Night
1st Monday of New Year, O.S.	Auld Handsel Monday
Jan. 25th	Burns Night
Feb. 1st	Candlemas Eve
Shrove Tuesday (Feb.-Mar.)	Fastern's E'en
Sunday before Palm Sunday (Mar.-Apr.)	Car Sunday
Easter (Mar.-Apr.)	Pasch
May 1st	Beltane
June 9th	St Columba's Day
Aug. 1st	Lammas
Sep. 29th	Michaelmas
Oct. 31st	Hallowe'en
Nov. 1st	Hallowmas
Nov. 11th	Martinmas
Nov. 30th	St Andrew's Day
Dec. 25th	Yule (Iol)
Dec. 31st	Hogmanay
Dec. 24th to Handsel Monday	The Daft Days

The Scottish Quarter Days differ from the Quarter Days of England and Ireland, and are :

Candlemas	Feb. 2nd
Whit	May 15th
Lammas	Aug. 1st
Martinmas	Nov. 11th

A CALENDAR FOR ANY YEAR

JANUARY :

   1 Charles II crowned at Scone, 1651.

   5 John Howie, author of *The Scots Worthies*, died, 1793.

   7 Glasgow University founded, 1451.   Allan Ramsay died, 1758.

  11 King David I died, 1153.

  12 Old New Year's Day.

  16 Union with England ratified by Scots Parliament, 1707.

  17 Battle of Falkirk, 1746.

  20 Regent Moray shot, 1570.

  24 Forth Bridge opened, 1890.

  25 Robert Burns born, 1759.   James Hogg born, 1772.

  29 Up-Helly-A Festival in Shetland.

  31 Prince Charles Edward (Charles III) died in Rome 1788.

FEBRUARY :

   2 Candlemas Day.   Battle of Inverlochy, 1645.

   4 James VIII left Scotland, 1716.

   5 Thomas Carlyle died, 1881.

   6 Charles II proclaimed King, in Edinburgh, 1649.

   8 Queen Mary beheaded at Fotheringay, 1587.

   9 First Parliament assembled at Scone, 1292.

  10 Aberdeen University founded, 1494.   Death of Comyn, 1306.

  13 Massacre of Glencoe, 1692.

  15 Caledonian Railway opened, 1848.

FEBRUARY :

16   First Postal Service (Edinburgh to Portpatrick), 1642.

21   James I assassinated at Perth, 1437.

23   King David II died, 1370.

24   Battle of Roslin, 1303.

27   Battle of Ancrum Muir, 1545.

MARCH :

1   National Covenant signed, 1638.

2   Robert II born, 1316.

5   Flora MacDonald died, 1790.

9   Execution of the Duke of Hamilton, 1649.

14   Edinburgh Castle recaptured from the English, 1313.

15   Underground Railway in Glasgow opened, 1886.

16   Alexander III died, 1286.

20   Duncan Bàn Macintyre, Gaelic Poet, born, 1724.

21   King Robert I born, 1274.

24   James VI succeeded to the English throne, 1603.

27   King Robert I crowned, 1306.   James VI died, 1625.

31   Last Mass in St Giles's Cathedral, 1560.

APRIL :

2   John Wilson (' Christopher North ') died, 1854.

4   Robert III died, 1406.

9   Simon, Lord Lovat (*Mac .Shimidh*) executed, 1747.

14   University of Edinburgh founded, 1582.

16   Battle of Culloden, 1746.

17   The Knight of Liddesdale (Douglas) took Edinburgh Castle from the English, 1341.

19   Robert II died, 1390.

24   Queen Mary married the Dauphin of France, 1558.

25 Malcolm III crowned, 1058.

27 Battle of Dunbar, 1296. Alexander I died, 1124.

MAY :

1   Union with England came into force, 1707.

2   Queen Mary escaped from Loch Leven, 1568.

10 Battle of Loudon Hill, 1307.

11 David I died, 1153.

13 Battle of Langside, 1568.

15 Queen Mary married Bothwell, 1567.

17 James V instituted the College of Justice, 1532.

18 Disruption of the Church of Scotland, 1843.

21 Marquis of Montrose executed, 1650.

22 Battle of Inverurie, 1308.

27 Marquis of Argyle executed, 1661.

29 Restoration of Charles II, 1660.

31 Tay Bridge opened, 1878.

JUNE :

1   Battle of Drumclog, 1678.

2   James Douglas, Earl of Morton, beheaded, 1581.

7   King Robert I died, 1329.

9   St Columba died, 597.

10 James VIII born, 1688. Battle of Glenshiel, 1719.

11 Battle of Sauchieburn, 1488.

12 James III killed, 1488.

19 James VI born, 1566. Charles I crowned at Holy-
    rood, 1633.

22 Battle of Bothwell Brig, 1679.

24 Battle of Bannockburn, 1314.

28 Kelso Abbey burned by the English, 1544.

29 Prince Charles landed in the Isle of Skye, 1746.

JULY :

1   Bank of Scotland established, 1695.
8   Alexander II died, 1249.
12 William the Lion made prisoner at Alnwick, 1174.
13 Alexander III crowned, 1249.
15 National Portrait Gallery opened, 1889.
16 Lady Nairne born, 1766.
17 Lady Glamis burned as a witch, Edinburgh, 1537.
18 Treaty safeguarding liberties against the English, 1290.
19 Battle of Halidon Hill, 1333.
21 Robert Burns died, 1796.
22 Battle of Falkirk, 1298.
23 Prince Charles first landed in Scotland, at Eriskay, 1745.
24 Forced abdication of Queen Mary, 1567.
25 Prince Charles landed at Moidart, 1745.
27 Battle of Killiecrankie, 1689.
29 Queen Mary married Darnley, 1565. James VI crowned, 1567.

AUGUST :

2   James II killed at Roxburgh Castle, 1460.
6   English government offered £30,000 for the head of Prince Charles, 1746.
8   The Stone of Destiny stolen by Edward I of England, 1296.
11 National Dress prohibited, 1746.
14 Duncan I assassinated, 1040.
15 Battle of Largs, 1263. Sir Walter Scott born, 1771.
16 Charles II signed the Covenant, 1650.

18 Execution of Lord Balmerino and Lord Kilmarnock, 1746.

19 Battle of Otterburn and death of The Douglas, 1388. Royal Standard raised at Glenfinnan, 1745.

20 Queen Mary returned from France, 1561.

23 William Wallace executed by the English, 1305.

25 Douglas, 'The Good Sir James,' killed in Spain, 1330.

28 St Andrews University founded, 1411.

SEPTEMBER :

3 Battle of Dunbar, 1650.

4 Prince Charles proclaimed his father King, 1745. Alexander III born, 1241.

9 Battle of Flodden, 1513.

10 Battle of Pinkie, 1547. Battle of Cambuskenneth, 1297.

11 Battle of Stirling, 1297.

13 Battle of Philiphaugh, 1645.

14 Battle of Homildon, 1402.

16 Prince Charles and King James proclaimed in Edinburgh, 1745.

20 Prince Charles escaped to Brittany, 1746.

21 Battle of Prestonpans, 1745.

28 ' Chapter of Mitton,' 1319. Scots win a battle under a smoke screen !

OCTOBER :

7 David II made prisoner at Neville's Cross, 1346.

11 ' Trial ' of Queen Mary at Fotheringay, 1586.

15 Allan Ramsay born, 1686.

OCTOBER:

16   Robert Fergusson died, 1774.
19   Union with England proposed and abandoned, 1669.
23   Treaty of Paris between Scotland and France
       against the English, 1295. Caledonian Canal
       opened, 1822.
31   Hallowe'en.

NOVEMBER:

2   First Scottish Settlement in America, 1698.
12   Duncan II killed, 1094.
13   Malcolm Ceanmor killed 1093. Battle of Alnwick,
       1093. Battle of Sheriffmuir, 1715.
21   James Hogg died, 1835.
23   Battle of Solway Moss, 1542.
24   John Knox died, 1572.
30   St Andrew's Day.

DECEMBER:

8   Queen Mary born, 1542.
9   Malcolm IV died, 1165.
14   James V died, 1542.
28   Tay Bridge disaster, 1879.
30   King James VIII died, 1765.
31   Hogmanay.

PART IV

FRAGMENTS

PART IV

A Promise

    He wha tills the fairies' green
      Nae luck again shall hae.
    An' he wha spills the fairies' ring
      Betide him want an' wae.

    But wha gaes by the fairy ring
      Nae dule nor pine shall see ;
    An' he wha cleans the fairy ring
      An easy daith shall dee.   *Traditional.*

Kindness and Courage

    Life is mostly froth and bubble ;
      Two things stand like stone :
    Kindness in another's trouble,
      Courage in your own.   *Adam Lindsay Gordon.*

The Black Douglas

    The following lines are from an old lullaby that is said to have been sung to their children by the women of the English garrisons, during the War of Independence :

    Hush ye, hush ye, little pet ye,
    Hush ye, hush ye, do not fret ye,
    The Black Douglas shall not get ye.

    A story used to be told about the re-capture of Roxburgh Castle. Douglas, leading his men by twos and threes, crept silently through the dusk and effected an entrance.

The first person he encountered was a woman singing her child to sleep.   Suddenly, as she sang ' The Black Douglas shall not get ye,' a steel-gloved hand was laid on her arm, and a voice said : ' I am not so sure of that ! '   It was The Black Douglas himself.

THE HEART OF BRUCE

The dying Bruce commanded his friend, Lord James of Douglas, to carry his heart ' against the enemies of God ' ; and to have it buried in the Holy Land.   The story is well known of how Douglas, mortally wounded in conflict against the Saracens, flung the casket containing the embalmed heart amongst the enemy, so fulfilling an old prophecy that 'after death it should pass once more in fiery fight against the foe.'
The following lines are from ' The Buke of the Howlat ' :

Amang the heathen men the hart hardely he slang,
Said ' Wend thou on as thou was wont,
Thro the battell in front,
Aye formaist in the front, thy foes amang.'

THE COVENANTER'S GRACE

These lines are usually, but erroneously, attributed to Burns.   They were known as ' The Covenanter's Grace ' in Galloway long before Burns was born :

Some hae meat that canna eat,
    An' some wad eat that want it ;
But we hae meat, an' we can eat,
    Sae let the Lord be thankit !

THE MONKS OF MELROSE

The monks o' Melrose made guid kail,
   On Fridays when they fasted;
Nor wanted they guid beef and ale
   As lang's their neighbour's lasted!

THE LORD'S PRAYER IN OLD (MIDDLE) SCOTS

Uor fader quhilk beest i Hevin, Hallowit weird thyne
nam. Cum thyne kinrik. Be dune thyne wull as is i Hevin,
sva po yerd. Uor dailie breid gif us thilk day. And forleit
us uor skaiths, as we forleit them quha skaith us. And leed
us na intill temptatioun. Butan fre us fra evil. Amen.

AN OLD SONG

O Maidens of England sair may ye mourne,
For tint have ye your lemans at Bannockbourne:
         (With *heavy-a-low!*)
What weened the king of England
To have gotten Scotland?
         (With *rumbelow!*)
            From an old song, sung after Bannockburn.

SO LONG AS BUT A HUNDRED OF US STAND....

*Here is an extract from a translation of the famous
Declaration of Arbroath—the letter sent by the Council in
1320 to Pope John XXII:*

. . Through the grace of Him who woundeth and
maketh whole, we have been freed from so many and so
great evils by the valour of our Lord and Sovereign,
Robert. Like Judas Maccabeus or Joshua, he gladly

endured toil, pain, the extremity of want and every danger to save his people and kingdom from their enemies. By reason of his desert as of his rights, the Providence of God, the lawful succession which we will maintain with our lives, and our common and just consent have made him our King, because through him our salvation has been wrought. If he should give up our cause and yield us to England, we would cast him out as the enemy of us all, and choose another king who should defend us, *for so long as but a hundred of us stand, we will never yield to the dominion of England.* We fight not for glory nor for wealth nor honour, but for that freedom which no good man surrenders but with his life.

The Epitaph of Walter Kennedy (1460-1508)

> I will nae priests for me sall sing,
> Nor yet nae bells for me to ring ;
> But ae bag-pype to play a spring.

King James VI to the English Parliament

This I must say for Scotland, and may truly vaunt it. Here I sit and govern it with my pen ; I write and it is done ; and by a clerk of the council I govern Scotland now —which my ancestors could not do by the sword.

Food

A Highland hunter will eat with a keen appetite and sufficient discrimination, but were he to stop in any pursuit because it was meal-time, to growl over a bad dinner or visibly exult over a good one, the manly dignity of his character would be considered as fallen for ever.

Mrs Grant of Laggan (1807).

The Value of a Dram

'Ay, ay—it's easy for your honour, and the like o' you gentle-folks, to say sae, that hae stouth and routh, and fire and fending, and meat and claith, and sit dry and canny by the fireside—but an ye wanted fire, and meat, and dry claise, and were deeing o' cauld, and had a sair heart, whilk is warst ava, wi' just tippence in your pouch, wadna ye be glad to buy a dram wi't, to be eilding and claise, and a supper and heart's ease into the bargain, till the morn's morning ? '   THE ANTIQUARY : CHAPTER XI.

John Knox

What I have been to my country, albeit this unthankful age will not know, yet the ages to come will be compelled to bear witness to the truth.

From the farewell sermon of John Knox (1571).

Followers

Tradition tells of an old minister . . . not of the brightest parts it may be supposed, who, in discoursing from some text in which the word ' follow ' occurred, informed his audience that he would speak of four different kinds of followers : ' First,' said he, ' my friends, there are followers ahint ; secondly, there are followers afore ; thirdly, there are followers cheekie for chow, and sidie by sidie ; and last o' a', there are followers that stand stane-still.'

DISSERTATION ON THE ORIGIN OF THE SCOTTISH
LANGUAGE : *John Jamieson.*

JONAH AND WEE JOSIE

Zachary Boyd, minister of the Barony Church, Glasgow, in the time of Charles I, among other things translated the Bible into verse.   But his piety was greater than his ' poetry.'   Here is a verse from his ' History of Jonah ' :

What house is this, where's neither coal nor candle,
Where I no thing but guts of fishes handle ?—
The like of this on earth no man ever saw,
A living man within a monster's maw.

Boyd, not unnaturally, became the butt of the anti-presbyterian wags, who wrote other equally quaint verses ascribing them to him.   The following is from ' The Whig's Supplication ' by Samuel Colvill :

And Jacob made for his wee Josie,
A tartan coat to keep him cosie ;
And what for no ?—there was nae harm
To keep the lad baith saft and warm.

PORT AND CLARET

John Home detested port—claret was his drink.   The imposition of a tax on claret offended more Scots than the author of the following lines :

Firm and erect the Caledonian stood,
Old was his mutton, and his claret good ;
' Let him drink port ! ' an English statesman cried ;
He drank the poison, and his spirit died !

PRACTICE IN ENGLAND

It happened at a small country town that Scott suddenly required medical advice for one of his servants, and, on

enquiring if there was any doctor at the place, was told that there was two—one long established, and the other a new comer. The latter gentleman, being luckily found at home, soon made his appearance ;—a grave, sagacious-looking personage, attired in black, with a shovel hat, in whom, to his utter astonishment, Sir Walter recognised a Scotch blacksmith, who had formerly practised, with tolerable success, as a veterinary operator in the neighbour-hood of Ashestiel.—' How, in all the world ! ' exclaimed he, ' can it be possible that this is John Lundie ? '—' In troth is it, your honour—just *a' that's for him.*'—' Well, but let us hear ; you were a *horse*-doctor before ; now, it seems, you are a *man*-doctor ; how do you get on ? '—
' Ou, just extraordinar weel ; for your honour maun ken my practice is vera sure and orthodox. I depend entirely upon twa *simples.*'—' And what may their names be ? Perhaps it is a secret ? '—' I'll tell your honour,' in a low tone ; ' my twa simples are just *laudamy* and *calamy* ! '—
' Simples with a vengeance ! ' replied Scott. ' But John, do you never happen to *kill* any of your patients ? '—' Kill ? Ou ay, may be sae ! Whiles they die, and whiles no ; but it's the will o' Providence. *Ony how, your honour, it wad be lang before it makes up for Flodden !* '

LIFE OF SIR WALTER SCOTT : *John Gibson Lockhart.*

THE CURSE OF SCOTLAND

Several cards in the pack have, at different times, been called ' The Curse of Scotland.' Grose says :

' The Curse of Scotland ' is the nine of diamonds . . . it is from its similarity to the arms of Argyle ; the Duke of Argyle having been very instrumental in bringing about the Union (with England) which, by some Scottish patriots, has been considered as detrimental to their country. . . .

Others say the ' Curse ' is the nine of spades ; and give as the reason that news of a great defeat was once brought to the capital written on the back of such a card. Another story connects the Dalrymple arms with the ' Curse,' linking up the Dalrymples and Argyle on the basis of a saying of King Charles II :

There never was a rebellion in Scotland without either a Campbell or a Dalrymple at the bottom of it.

LEADERSHIP

In leadership there is a tincture of the miraculous . . . I should define the miraculous element as a response of spirit to spirit. There is in all men, even the basest, some kinship with the divine, something which is capable of rising superior to common passions and the lure of easy rewards, superior to pain and loss, superior even to death. The true leader evokes this. The greatness in him wins a response, an answering greatness in his followers. . . . The test of leadership is not to put greatness into humanity, but to elicit it, for the greatness is already there.

MONTROSE AND LEADERSHIP : *John Buchan.*
(Walker Trust Lecture, 27/1/30.)

THE SOLDIER-POET

He either fears his fate too much,
    Or his deserts are small,
That dares not put it to the touch
    To gain or lose it all.
      James Graham, Marquis of Montrose (1612-1650).

THE LAY OF THE LAST MINSTREL

The Reply of Sir Harry Englefield to a critic ' who made himself conspicuous by the severity of his censure on the verbal inaccuracies and careless lines of The Lay.'

' My dear sir,' said the Baronet, ' you remind me of a lecture on sculpture, which M. Falconet delivered at Rome, shortly after completing the model of his equestrian statue of Czar Peter, now at Petersburg. He took for his subject the celebrated horse of Marcus Aurelius in the Capitol, and pointed out as many faults in it as ever a jockey did in an animal he was about to purchase. But something came over him, vain as he was, when he was about to conclude the harangue. He took a long pinch of snuff, and eyeing his own faultless model, exclaimed with a sigh—*Cependant, Messieurs, il faut avouer que cette vilaine bête là est vivante, et que la mienne est morte.'*

LIFE OF SIR WALTER SCOTT : *Lockhart.*

SCOTT IN THE DOCK

The following appeared in ' The Inverness Courier' of December the 10th, 1834.

A meeting of the Skene Reading Society was held on Monday last for the approving or disapproving of the Waverley Novels as forming part of their library. . . . The arguments of the first party were that the books were full of oaths . . . that the works tended to debase Christianity, to uphold worldly motives of action, and that they were to the mind what cholera and pestilence were to the body. . . . The argument on both sides being finished . . . a member, to procure unanimity, proposed to remit the forty-eight volumes to a committee to consider them. . . . A committee of eleven was then appointed, and thus . . . are eleven of the good men of the parish of Skene to sit in judgement on the works of the master spirit of the age. . . .

THE SCOTS GUARD OF FRANCE

The institution of the Scots Guard was an acknowledgement of the service the Scots rendered to Charles VII in reducing France to his obedience, and of the great loyalty and virtue he found in them.

LETTERS OF GENERAL NATURALIZATION FOR
THE WHOLE SCOTTISH NATION IN FRANCE:
Louis XII.

MAIS LES ECOSSAIS!

At Brussels, and wherever I went in the Netherlands when the English troops were mentioned . . . the natives always returned to the Scotch with ' *mais les Ecossais!*— they are good and kind as well as brave. . . .'

. . . On the Continent, the Highland regiments are not called *Montagnards*, or Highlanders, but Scotch; which is really their appellation.

James Simpson, Advocate (1816).

The love and admiration of the whole people for the Highlanders are most remarkable. Whenever they heard them mentioned, they exclaimed : ' *Ah ! ces braves hommes, ces bons Ecossais ! Ils sont si doux—et si aimables—et dans la guerre—ah Mon Dieu ! comme ils sont terribles !* ' They never speak of them without some epithet of affection or admiration.

WATERLOO DAYS : *Mrs C. E. Eaton.*

THE GRIEVANCE

... On the insults and injuries which had been unsparingly flung on Scotland and Scotsmen, he (Argyle) spoke like a high-minded and high-spirited man. ... This bold orator came nearest to speaking out the real cause of the universal discontent ... the sense of the habitually insulting and injurious manner in which they were treated by the English ... as if the representatives of some inferior and subjugated province.

TALES OF A GRANDFATHER : *Scott.*

THE FIERCE DE BOHUN

In the year 1818, the workmen engaged in clearing the foundations for a new church among the ruins of Dunfermline Abbey, came upon the tomb of Robert the Bruce. ... Men looked with wonder and awe upon the skull where once had dwelt counsel so sage and high, and upon the mouldering bone which had once been the strong right arm that struck down the fierce de Bohun.

HISTORY OF SCOTLAND : *Mackenzie.*

THE SOUL OF FREEDOM

Thee, Caledonia ! thy wild heaths among,
Fam'd for the martial deed, the heaven-taught song,
    To thee I turn with swimming eyes ;
Where is that soul of Freedom fled ?—
Immingled with the mighty dead,
    Beneath that hallowed turf where Wallace lies !

Burns.

Wallace

All this may be, the people's voice is odd;
The Scots will fight for Wallace as for God.

Pope.

Genealogy

. . . And so ye see, auld Pittoddles, when his third wife dee'd, he got mairrit upon the laird o' Blaithershins' aughteenth dochter, that was sister to Jemima, that was mairrit till Tam Flumexer, that was first and second cousin to the Pittoddleses, whase brither becam laird efterwards, an' mairrit Blaithershins' Baubie—an' that way Jemima becam in a kind o' a way her ain niece an' her ain aunty, an', as we used to say, her guid-brither was mairrit to his ain grannie.

BOOK OF SCOTTISH ANECDOTE : *Hislop.*

An Epitaph

Here lie I, Martin Elginbrod.
Hae mercy on my soul, Lord God;
As I would do, were I lord God,
And Ye were Martin Elginbrod.

Mons Meg

Of the old cannon at Edinburgh Castle, known as '*Mons Meg,*' *Robert Chambers says :*

The history of this cannon being obscure, tradition has stepped forward with a story regarding it. At Carlingwark, now Castle Douglas, there once lived a smith named Mouncey, who had six stout sons of his own profession, and a noisy wife. In his forge was prepared this huge engine, for the purpose of battering the neighbouring castle of Thrave, then in the possession of the Douglas family. The neighbours gave it the name of *Mouncey's Meg*, in jocular allusion to the roaring habits of the fabricator's wife. To support this tale, the people allege that the stone bullets belonging to Meg can be identified with a kind of rock found on Lourin Hill near Carlingwark.

JOHNIE ARMSTRANG: THE BORDER REIVER

In 1529 James V, with a strong cavalcade, visited the Borders, for the purpose of curbing the activities of some of the Border Chiefs. Among those who suffered the death penalty was Johnie Armstrang, whose proud boast it was that he harried only the English and never his fellow-countrymen.

The old ballad tells us :

> John murdered was at Carlinrigg,
>   And all his gallant companie ;
> But Scotland's heart was ne'er sae wae,
>   To see sae mony brave men dee ;
>
> Because they saved their countrie dear
>   Frae Englishmen : nane were sae bauld,
> While Johnie lived on the Borderside,
>   Nane o' them durst come near his hauld.

THE ARCHBISHOP'S VISITOR

Archbishop Sharpe, presiding in the Privy Council, was earnest to have Janet Douglas brought before that board, accusing her of sorcery and witchcraft. When she was brought, she vindicated herself, for she was endeavouring to discover those secret hellish plots, and to countermine the kingdom of darkness. The Archbishop insisted she might be sent away to the King's plantations in the West Indies. She only dropt one word to the Bishop : ' My Lord,' says she, ' who was with you in your closet on Saturday night last, betwixt twelve and one o'clock ? ' upon which the Bishop changed his countenance, and turned black and pale, and then no more was said. When the council rose up, the Duke of Rothes called Janet into a room, and inquired at her privately ' who that person was that was with the Bishop ? ' She refused at first ; but he promising upon his word of honour to warrant her at all hands, and that she should not be sent to America, she says : ' My Lord, it was the meikle black devil ! '

ANALECTA : *Robert Wodrow* (1679-1734).

FAIR MAIDEN LILLIARD

In 1545 the Battle of Ancrum Muir was fought a mile and a half north of the village of Ancrum. The English were defeated. According to tradition, the bravest of the Scottish warriors was a woman, Lilliard, who fought beside her lover. A stone erected on the spot bears the following gruesome explanatory inscription :

Fair Maiden Lilliard lies under this stane ;
Little was her stature, but great was her fame ;
Upon the English loons she laid mony thumps,
And when her legs were cuttit off, she focht upon her
    stumps !

Ever since the battle, the site has been known as Lilliard's Edge.

SOME COUNTY ROXBURGH RIVERS

The Ettrick and the Slitterick,
The Leader and the Feeder,
The Fala and the Gala,
The Aill and the Kale,
The Yod and the Jed,
The Blackatter and the Whitatter,
The Teviot and the Tweed.   *Traditional.*

CANNIE FISHER JAMIE

This charming and simple little thing is contributed by a Border correspondent.   A slightly different version appears in ' The Northern Muse.'   Mr John Buchan recalls it from his early youth.

Cannie Fisher Jamie, comin' hame at e'en,
Cannie Fisher Jamie, whaur hae ye been ?
Mony lang miles laddie, ower the knowes sae green.
Fishin' doun Ale Water ?   *Na, laddie, nae—*
Juist a wee bit burnie rinnin' doun a brae,
Fishin' doun a burnie nae bigger nor a sheuch.
Gat ye mony troot, Jamie ?   *Aye, I gat eneuch—*
Eneuch tae buy ma baccie, snuff, an' pickle tea,
An' leave's tippence for a gill, an' that'll dae for me !

THANKSGIVING

All labourers draw hame at even,
And can till other say,
Thanks to the gracious God of heaven,
Whilk sent this summer day.
          Alexander Hume.

EDINBURGH AFTER FLODDEN

Immediately news of the tragic defeat of Flodden reached the capital, most of the women, and all the men who had been left, were impressed into service for the strengthening of the city's defences.

The fear of invasion and attack on the capital was met with dignity and courage, as is shown by the following transcript of the Municipal Proclamation issued on September the 10th, 1513.

Forasmuch as there is great rumour now lately risen within this town, touching our Sovereign Lord and his army, of which we understand there has come no verity as yet, wherefore we charge strictly and command in our said Sovereign Lord the King's name, and in that of the Presidents for the Provosts and Baillies within this burgh, that all manner of persons, townsmen within the same, have ready their arms of defence and weapons for war, and appear therewith before the said Presidents at the tolling of the common bell, for the keeping and defence of the town against them that would invade the same. And we also charge that all women, and especially vagabonds, that they pass to their labours, and be not seen upon the street clamouring and crying, under the pain of banishing of their persons without favour, and that the other women of better sort pass to the kirk and pray, when time requires, for our Sovereign Lord and his army, and the townsmen who are with the army ; and that they hold them at their private labours off the streets within their houses, as becometh.

THIRTY THOUSAND POUNDS

Captured after Culloden, and reminded of the fact that a reward of thirty thousand pounds was being offered for the body of Prince Charles, one, Donald MacLeod, a simple clansman, delivered himself of the following :

What then ? Thirty thoosan' pounds ! Though I had gotten't I could not enjoy it eight and forty hours. Conscience would get up upon me—that money could not keep it down. And though I could get all Scotland and England for my pains, I would not allow a hair of his body to be touched if I could help it !

EPITAPH ON LORD BALMERINO

Lord Balmerino, for his loyalty to the Stuart cause, was beheaded in London on August the 18th, 1746.

Here Arthur lies—the rest forbear :
There may be treason in a tear !
Yet this bold soger may find room
Where sceptered tyrants dare not come.

THE MOONLIGHT AND THE WIND

The herring loves the merry moonlight,
    The mackerel loves the wind,
But the oyster loves the dredging sang,
    For they come of a gentle kind.

Scott.

THE NOBLE HOUSES OF SCOTLAND

The clouds of pride and madness and mysterious sorrow that hang more heavily on the noble houses of Scotland than on any other of the children of men. . . .

G. K. Chesterton.

MY NAME IS NORVAL

*These lines from John Home's tragedy ' Douglas ' recall
that it was on the first production of the play that an enthu-
siastic Scot hurled out the now-famous challenge to the
English : ' Whaur's your Wullie Shakespeare noo ? '*

My name is Norval ; on the Grampian Hills
My father feeds his flocks ; a frugal swain,
Whose constant cares were to increase his store,
And keep his only son, myself, at home ;
For I had heard of battles, and I longed
To follow to the field some warlike lord. . . .

*The lines also gave rise to another retort : schoolboys all
over the country, disregarding the semi-colon in the first
line, used to read : ' Ma name is Norval on the Grampian
Hills,' which gave dominies all over the country the opportunity to inquire sarcastically : ' Oh, and what would your
name be on the Cheviots ? '*

LOVE

He that can love unlov'd again
Hath better store of love than brain.

Sir Robert Ayton.

A GALLOWAY GRACE

Bless the sheep for Dauvid's sake, he herdit sheep himsel ;
Bless the fish for Peter's sake, he gruppit fish himsel ;
Bless the soo for Satan's sake, he was yince a soo himsel.

GALLOWAY GOSSIP : *Dr Trotter.*

INVOCATION

Frae Witches, Warlocks, an' Wurricoes,
An' Evil Spirits, an' a' Things
That gang Bump i' the nicht,
Guid Lord, deliver us!

'THINGS THAT GANG BUMP I' THE NICHT'

GOOD FOR HOGS—AND SAMUEL JOHNSON

'Do you like our Scots broth, Dr Johnson?'
'*Uh. Very good for hogs, I believe.*'
'Then let me help you to a little more!'

A Recipe for Cramp

The most extraordinary recipe was that of my Highland piper, John Bruce, who spent a whole Sunday in selecting twelve stones from twelve *south-running* streams, with the purpose that I should sleep upon them, and be whole. I caused him to be told that the recipe was infallible, but that it was absolutely necessary to success that the stones should be wrapt up in the petticoat of a widow who had never wished to marry again ; upon which the piper renounced all hope of completing the charm.

Scott, in a letter to the Duke of Buccleuch.

Chess

A certain Judge, whenever he went on a particular circuit, was in the habit of visiting a gentleman of good fortune in the neighbourhood of one of the assize towns, and staying at least one night, which, being both of them ardent chess-players, they usually concluded with their favourite game. One Spring circuit the battle was not decided at daybreak, so the Judge said—' Weel, Donald, I must e'en come back this gate in the harvest, and let the game lie ower for the present ; ' and back he came in October, but not to his old friend's hospitable house ; for that gentleman had, in the interim, been apprehended on a capital charge (of forgery), and his name stood on the *Porteous Roll*, or list of those who were about to be tried under his former guest's auspices. The laird was indicted and tried accordingly, and the jury returned a verdict of *guilty*. The Judge forthwith put on his cocked hat (which answers to the black cap in England), and pronounced the sentence of the law in the usual terms—' To be hanged by the neck until you be dead ;

and may the Lord have mercy upon your unhappy soul ! '
Having concluded this awful formula in his most sonorous
cadence, the Judge, dismounting his formidable beaver,
gave a familiar nod to his unfortunate acquaintance, and
said to him, in a sort of chuckling whisper—' And now,
Donald, my man, I think I've checkmated you for ance.'

LIFE OF SIR WALTER SCOTT : *John Gibson Lockhart.*

An Epitaph

Here lies Andra Macpherson,
Who was a peculiar person :
He was six foot two
Without his shoe,
And he was slew
At Waterloo.

The Weariness of a Ghost

Wae's me, wae's me !—
The acorn's no' yet
Fa'en frae the tree
That's to grow the wood,
That's to mak the creddle,
That's to rock the bairn
That's to grow a man
That's to lay me.

The Kailyarders

. . . Then came the Kailyarders, and said that . . . they
alone could draw the Scottish type. England believed them,
and their sales and cheap editions clinched it, and to-day a
Scotchman stands self-confessed a sentimental fool, a

canting cheat, a grave sententious man, dressed in a ' stan' o' black,' oppressed with the tremendous difficulties of the jargon he is bound to speak and, above all, weighted down with the responsibilities of being Scotch.

R. B. Cuninghame Graham.

A GORDON ! A GORDON ! *BYDAND !*

The reply of George Gordon, second Marquis of Huntly, to ' certain Noblemen, Gentlemen, and Covenanters of Scotland when they bade him to assist their designs, or be carried to prison ' :

Whereas you offer me liberty, I am not so bad a merchant as to buy it with the loss of my conscience, fidelity, and honour. I have already given my faith to my Prince, upon whose head this crown, by all laws of nature and nations, is justly fallen. I am in your power, and resolved not to leave that foul title of traitor as an inheritance upon my posterity. You may take my head from my shoulders, but not my heart from my sovereign.

A FEW SHORT EXTRACTS FROM SCOTT

THE BORDER LAW

'Hout, there's nae great skill needed ; just put a lighted peat on the end of a spear, or hayfork, or siclike, and blaw a horn, and cry the gathering-word, and then it's lawful to follow gear into England, and recover it by the strong hand, or to take gear frae some other Englishman, providing ye lift nae mair than's been lifted frae you. That's the auld

Border law, made at Dundrennan in the days of the Black
Douglas. Deil ane need doubt it. It's as clear as the sun.'
THE BLACK DWARF : CHAPTER VII.

The Highland Law

' But in the thicket of the wilderness, and in the mist of
the mountain, Kenneth, son of Eracht, keep thou unsoiled
the freedom which I leave thee as a birthright. Barter it
not neither for the rich garment, nor for the stone roof, nor
for the covered board, nor for the couch of down—on the
rock or in the valley, in abundance or in famine—in the
leafy summer, and in the days of the iron winter—Son of the
Mist ! be free as thy forefathers. Own no lord—receive
no law—take no hire—give no stipend—build no hut—
enclose no pasture—sow no grain ;—let the deer of the
mountain be thy flocks and herds—if these fail thee, prey
upon the goods of our oppressors—of the Saxons, and of
such Gael as are Saxons in their souls, valuing herds and
flocks more than honour and freedom. Well for us that
they do so—it affords the broader scope for our revenge.
Remember those who have done kindness to our race, and
pay their services with thy blood, should the hour require
it.'   THE LEGEND OF MONTROSE : CHAPTER XXII.

Parliaments

' Aweel after the Commons' Parliament had tuggit, and
rived, and ruggit . . . till they were tired o't, the Lords'
Parliament they behoved to hae their spell o't. In puir
auld Scotland's Parliament they a' sate thegither, cheek by
choul, and than they didna need to hae the same blethers
twice ower again.'   ROB ROY : CHAPTER XIV.

SOMETHING TO FIGHT FOR

' *Me* no muckle to fight for, sir ?—Isna there the country to fight for, and the burnsides that I gang daundering beside, and the hearths o' the gudewives that gie me my bit bread, and the bits o' weans that come toddling to play wi' me when I come about a landward town ? '

THE ANTIQUARY : CHAPTER XLIV.

A WARNING

' But fare ye weel—fare ye weel, for ever and a day ; and, if you quarrel wi' a Scot again, man, say as mickle ill o' himself as ye like, but say nane . . . of his countrymen, or it will scarce be your flat cap that will keep your lang lugs from the sharp abridgement of a Highland whinger, man.'

THE FORTUNES OF NIGEL : CHAPTER IX.

SCOTT ON THE DESTRUCTION OF SCOTLAND

He was earnest and serious in his belief that the new rulers of the country were disposed to abolish many of its most valuable institutions ; and he regarded with special jealousy certain schemes of innovation with respect to the courts of law and the administration of justice, which were set on foot by the Crown Officers for Scotland. At a debate of the Faculty of Advocates on some of these propositions, he made a speech much longer than any he had ever before delivered in that assembly ; and several who heard it have assured me, that it had a flow and energy of eloquence for which those who knew him best had been quite unprepared. When the meeting broke up, he walked across *The Mound*, on his way to Castle Street, between Mr. Jeffrey and another of his reforming friends, who compli-

mented him on the rhetorical powers he had been display-
ing, and would willingly have treated the subject-matter of
the discussion playfully.   But his feelings had been moved
to an extent far beyond their apprehension : he exclaimed,
' No, no—'tis no laughing matter ; little by little, whatever
your wishes may be, you will destroy and undermine, until
nothing of what makes Scotland Scotland shall remain.'
And so saying, he turned round to conceal his agitation—
but not until Mr. Jeffrey saw tears gushing down his cheek
—resting his head until he recovered himself on the wall of
The Mound.   Seldom, if ever, in his more advanced age, did
any feelings obtain such mastery.

    LIFE OF SIR WALTER SCOTT : *John Gibson Lockhart.*

Fraser

PART V

PROSE AND LETTERS

Stirling Castle

PART V

BANNOCKBURN

Sir Edward's division, Douglas's, and Randolph's, marched out of the wood, then, with their banners flying : the King had asked for a brave show of these, for knowing men he knew how imagination, and resolution, are stimulated by a material sign. They came down from the wood in an inverted wedge, Douglas between but a little behind the others. The English trumpets sounded the alarm. Edward's men mounted in haste and some confusion : it was vital they should get up from the carse, and their confusion would not be amended by the fact that they had looked for a night raid, and the dawn would just have made them feel safe from attack, and convinced them the Scots were going to keep the defensive.

Edward was in a post whence he saw the advance—on the slope at the mouth of the gorge, very probably—and they say that he cried out to Umfraville, ' What, will these Scots fight ? ' perplexed, perhaps, that footmen should challenge knights, and mocking at such a contemptible little army. Umfraville, who was a Baliol Scot, knew they meant business, and said so, advising Edward to fall back and adopt the old tactic of a feigned retreat. Edward would not—from arrogance, Barbour says, and may be right : but in any case, his position being what it was, it would have been difficult to take the advice.

The Scots came down on the plain between wood and carse, and there they halted, dropped on their knees, and

said a Paternoster. Edward mistook the gesture, and cried
out joyfully, ' They are asking mercy,' and Umfraville, who
was a Scot after all, told him curtly, ' True enough. But not
of you. I tell you certainly, those men will win or perish.'

The English, as many as could, swarmed up the slope,
but betweeen the haste and the ground, the pressure of
those behind, and the latter's difficulty in seeing what was
happening, their deployment was clearly confused : and the
confusion was rapidly made worse. Someone had got the
archers into action, posting them, probably, strung out
along the north side of the gorge, where they poured a hot
fire on the advancing Scots schiltroms and incidentally
sprinkled their own front ranks as well, which would not
cheer these, since to find oneself under the fire of one's own
side does not strengthen confidence in one's higher command.

The archers were a grave danger to the Scots. The
whole battle depended on the unbroken schiltrom. King
Robert, remembering Falkirk, was ready for them, and sent
Keith and the cavalry out by his right. The rise where the
St Ninians-Bannockburn road runs now would conceal
them almost until the moment of impact. They drove
down on the flank of the English archers, who could not
have seen them in time to make a stand, and who were not
armed to meet horsemen at close quarters. The archers
broke, flying to the deploying English line, and causing
further confusion and shock to morale, while some of them
were struck down by their own comrades.

The advancing schiltroms narrowed the ' hard ground,'
cramping the English, who were cramped still more by the
rushing pressure of their own advancing rear, who, remem-

ber, would many of them be unable to see precisely what was happening on their front, though they could hear the sounds of beginning action. Someone ordered a counter-charge of cavalry: it was probably this that caught the archers' fire, since the first moves of the general engagement were of course going on simultaneously with Keith's attack. It might have held up the Scots advance a little, and given the English time and room to deploy. But the chance was missed. . . . The English van . . . crashed against Edward Bruce's advancing schiltrom, the Scots right. The English right seems to have tried to charge too, for to break the schiltroms, get the ground clear to form for an attack in mass, was their obvious counter, and King Robert had seen that the night before, when he implored the schiltroms to keep formation and not to break their ranks whatever happened. Randolph, well away to Sir Edward's left, met them full, let them shatter against his front like a wave on a rock, and drove on into the confused mass of the English . . . and into the gap between the two Scottish wings came Stewart and Douglas, closing the moving wall.

The whole note of the orders is ' Press, press.' The gorge pinned the English helpless on their left. Their right and rear were held up by their own front : many men never struck a blow that day, and two hundred knights never even drew their swords, not for cowardice—the panic came much later—but simply because they never had the chance.

The eddying confusion in middle and rear grew worse as remorseless pressure drove in the front, and the Scots archers, from the slope behind their own line, poured in a short-range fire above the schiltroms. Their arrows would go down too in the mass on the carse, of men and horses

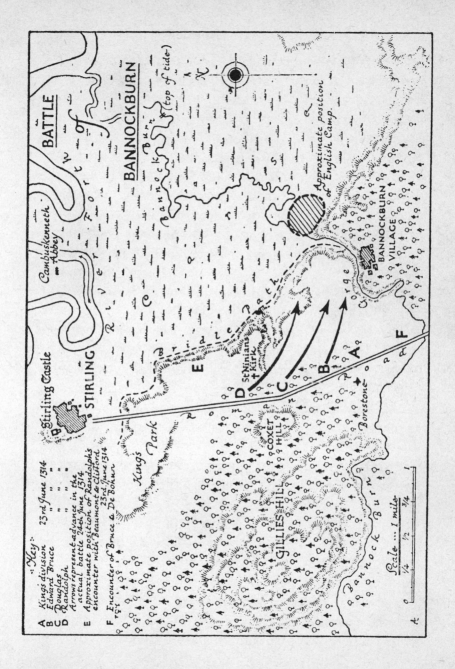

BATTLE

of

BANNOCKBURN

:: Key ::

A   King's division   23rd June 1314
B   Edward Bruce   "   "   "
C   Douglas   "   "   "
D   Randolph   "   "   "
     Arrows represent advance in the
E   actual battle 24th June 1314
     Approximate position of Randolph's
     encounter with Beaumont & Clifford
     23rd June 1314
F   Encounter of Bruce & De Bohun
     23rd June 1314

Scale ... 1 mile
0   ¼   ½   ¾   1

Cambuskenneth Abbey

Stirling Castle

STIRLING

King's Park

GILLIES HILL

COXET HILL

St Ninian's Kirk

Bannock Burn

Borestone

Bannock Burn

BANNOCKBURN VILLAGE

Approximate position of English Camp.

(top of tide)

River Forth of Forth

struggling to reach the plateau, and not able to see what they could hear in front. Then, out from the wood, the King led in his reserve. It seems to have struck in upon the flank, alongside the rest, pinning the English wing and buckling their line still further. It was probably under the stress of this new impact that an appalling thing happened. The muddled men and the maddened horses broke : the steady pressure drove them left on the gorge, whose bank goes down steep and suddenly from the plain, and a flood of men and squealing, kicking stallions poured over the edge, where *chescun cheoit sur autre*—mailed men and their crazy beasts in one awful confusion, helpless. No wonder that Bannockburn ' was in English mouths for many years thereafter,' because of that horror. To look at the place, and think of it, makes one sick. And yet one can see exactly how it would happen.

Panic spread, and now a shout rose from the schiltroms, ' On them ! They fail ! ' The pressure grew fiercer yet : and then there was more shouting from a fresh quarter, and from the dark obscurity of the wood there appeared another division of the Scots. It was the ' small folk,' from behind Coxet Hill. Schoolbook tradition says they came of themselves. It is much more likely that they were part of the plan, for . . . no discipline could keep Highlanders out of a fight unless they were given a clear strategic reason . . . and a general who tackles a force three times his own will certainly want every able-bodied man, though not necessarily, if some are ill-drilled, for shock-troops.

They came pouring from the wood, in rough formation, and remembering the King's words overnight, they had made banners out of the camp blankets. The sight of them

struck on the broken English nerves : there was no knowing
what more the wood might hold, on top of the devils it had
let loose already.   There was excuse, for King Edward's
staff threw their hand in, and tried to get their master clear
of the field, making for Beaumont's and Clifford's track by
the slope.   The sight of the royal banner in visible flight,
with a new force advancing yelling from the wood, completed the demoralization of the English.   They broke
hideously, in a tangled fleeing mob without formation,
while here and there men more stubborn than the rest
fought on singly or in small groups till they went down.
They fled all ways. . . .

ROBERT BRUCE KING OF SCOTS : *Agnes Mure Mackenzie.*

OTTERBOURNE

Knights and squires were of good courage on both
parties to fight valiantly ; cowards there had no place, but
hardiness reigned with goodly feats of arms, for knights
and squires were so joined together at hand strokes, that
archers had no place of neither party.   There the Scots
shewed great hardiness, and fought merrily, with great
desire of honour : the Englishmen were three to one ; how-
beit, I say not but Englishmen did nobly acquit themself,
for ever the Englishmen had rather been slain or taken in
the place than to fly.   Thus as I have said the banners of
Douglas and Percy and their men were met each against
other, envious who should win the honour of that journey.
At the beginning the Englishmen were so strong, that they
recoiled back their enemies : then the Earl Douglas, who
was of great heart and high of enterprise, seeing his men

recoil back, then to recover the place and to shew knightly valour, he took his axe in both his hands, and entered so into the press, that he made himself way in such wise that none durst approach near him, and he was so well armed that he bare well of such strokes as he received : thus he went ever forward like a hardy Hector, willing alone to conquer the field, and to discomfit his enemies ; but at last he was encountered with three spears all at once ; the one strake him on the shoulder, the other on the breast, and the stroke glinted down to his belly, and the third strake him in the thigh, and sore hurt with all three strokes, so that he was borne perforce to the earth, and after that he could not be again releved : some of his knights and squires followed him, but not all, for it was night and no light but by the shining of the moon. The Englishmen knew well they had borne one down to the earth, but they wist not who it was, for if they had known that it had been the Earl Douglas, they had been thereof so joyful and so proud, that the victory had been theirs : nor also the Scots knew not of that adventure till the end of the battle, for if they had known it, they should have been so sore despaired and discouraged, that they would have fled away. Thus as the Earl Douglas was felled to the earth he was stricken into the head with an axe, and another stroke through the thigh : the Englishmen passed forth and took no heed of him : they thought none otherwise but that they had slain a man of arms. On the other part, the earl George de la Marche and of Dunbar fought right valiantly, and gave the Englishmen much ado, and cried : Follow Douglas and set on the sons of Percy : also Earl John of Moray with his banner and men fought valiantly, and set fiercely on the Englishmen, and gave them so much to do, that they wist not to whom to attend.

Of all the battles and encouterings that I have made mention of here before in all this history, great or small, this battle that I treat of now, was one of the sorest and best foughten, without cowards or faint hearts : for there was neither knight nor squire but that did his devoir and fought hand to hand : this battle was like the battle of Becherell, the which was valiantly fought and endured. The earl of Northumberland's sons, Sir Henry and Sir Ralph Percy, who were chief sovereign captains, acquitted themself nobly, and Sir Ralph Percy entered in so far among his enemies that he was closed in and hurt, and so sore handled that his breath was so short that he was taken prisoner by a knight of the earl of Moray's, called Sir John Maxwell. In the taking the Scottish knight demanded what he was (for it was in the night, so that he knew him not) : and Sir Ralph was so sore overcome and bled fast, that at last he said, I am Ralph Percy. Then the Scot said, Sir Ralph, rescue or no rescue, I take you for my prisoner ; I am Maxwell. Well, quoth Sir Ralph, I am content ; but then take heed to me, for I am sore hurt ; my hosen and my greaves are full of blood. Then the knight saw by him the Earl Moray and said, Sir, here I deliver to you sir Ralph Percy as prisoner ; but, sir, let good heed be taken to him, for he is sore hurt. The earl was joyful of those words, and said, Maxwell, thou hast well won thy spurs. Then he delivered sir Ralph Percy to certain of his men, and they stopped and wrapped his wounds ; and still the battle endured, not knowing who had as then the better, for there were many taken and rescued again that came to no knowledge.

Now let us speak of the young James earl of Douglas, who did marvels in arms or he was beaten down. When he was overthrown the press was great about him, so that he could not releve, for with an axe he had his death's wound. His men followed him as near as they could, and there came to him Sir James Lyndsay his cousin, and Sir John and Sir Walter Saint Clair, and other knights and squires ; and by him was a gentle knight of his, who followed him all the day, and a chaplain of his, not like a priest, but like a valiant man of arms : for all that night he followed the earl with a good axe in his hands, and still skirmished about the earl there as he lay, and recoiled back some of the English-men with great strokes that he gave. Thus he was found fighting near to his master, whereby he had great praise, and thereby the same year he was made archdeacon of Aberdeen. This priest was called Sir William of North Berwick : he was a tall man and a hardy, and was sore hurt. When these knights came to the Earl, they found him in an evil case, and a knight of his lying by him, called Sir Robert Hart : he had a fifteen wounds in one place and other. Then Sir John Saint Clair demanded of the earl how he died. Right well, cousin, quoth the earl ; but thanked be God there hath been but a few of mine ancestors that hath died in their beds ; but cousin, I require you think to revenge me, for I reckon myself but dead, for my heart fainteth often times : my cousin Walter and you, I pray you raise up again my banner which lieth on the ground, and my squire Davy Collemnie slain ; but, sirs, shew neither to friend nor foe in what case ye see me in, for if mine enemies knew it they would rejoice, and our friends discomforted. The two brethren of Saint Clair and Sir

James Lyndsay did as the earl had desired them, and raised up again his banner, and cried Douglas. Such as were behind and heard that cry, drew together and set on their enemies valiantly, and recoiled back the Englishmen and many were overthrown, and so drave the Englishmen back beyond the place where as the Earl lay, who was by that time dead, and so came to the earl's banner, the which Sir John Saint Clair held in his hands, and many good knights and squires of Scotland about him : and still company drew to the cry of Douglas.

. . . .

Whereto should I write long process : This was a sore battle, and well foughten, and as fortune is always changeable, though the Englishmen were more in number than the Scots, and were right valiant men of war, and well expert, and that at the first front they recoiled back the Scots, yet finally the Scots obtained the place and victory, and all the foresaid Englishmen taken, and a hundred more, saving Sir Matthew Redman, captain of Berwick, who when he knew no remedy nor recoverance, and saw his company fly from the Scots, and yielded them on every side, then he took his horse and departed to save himself. The same season about the end of this discomfiture, there was an English squire called Thomas Felton, a goodly and a valiant man, and that was well seen, for of all that night he would neither fly nor yet yield him ; it was said he had made a vow at a feast in England, that the first time that ever he saw Englishmen and Scots in battle, he would so do his devoir to his power, in such wise, that either he would be reputed for the best doer on both sides, or else to die in the pain ; he was called a valiant man and a hardy man, and did so much by his prowess, that under the banner of the earl of Moray, he did such valiantness in arms, that the Scots had marvel thereof, and so was slain in fighting ; the Scots would gladly have taken him alive, but he would never yield : he hoped ever to have been rescued ; and with him there was a Scottish squire slain, cousin to the King of Scots, called Simon Glendinning ; his death was greatly complained of the Scots. This battle was fierce and cruel till it came to the end of the discomfiture, but when the Scots saw the Englishmen recoil and yield themself then the Scots were courteous, and set them to their ransom and every man said to his prisoner ; Sirs, go and unarm you and take your ease, I am your master ; and so made their prisoners as good cheer as though they had been brethren, without doing to them any damage.

FROISSART'S CHRONICLES : *Translation of John Bourchier, Lord Berners* (1467-1533).

HOMILDON

The family of Swinton is very ancient, and was once very powerful, and at the period of this battle the knight of Swinton was gigantic in stature, unequalled in strength, and a sage and experienced leader to boot. In one of those quarrels which divided the kingdom of Scotland in every corner, he had slain his neighbour, the head of the Gordon family, and an inveterate feud had ensued ; for it seems that powerful as the Gordons always were, the Swintons could then bide a bang with them. Well, the battle of Halidon*

* *Scott wrote* Halidon, *but the incident described in this letter occurred at the Battle of Homildon* (*1402*) *and not at Halidon Hill* (*1333*).

began, and the Scottish army, unskilfully disposed on the side of a hill where no arrow fell in vain, was dreadfully galled by the archery of the English, as usual ; upon which Swinton approached the Scottish General, requesting command of a body of cavalry, and pledging his honour that he would, if so supported, charge and disperse the English archery—one of the manœuvres by which Bruce gained the battle of Bannockburn.—This was refused, out of stupidity or sullenness, by the General, on which Swinton expressed his determination to charge at the head of his own followers, though totally inadequate for the purpose. The young Gordon heard the proposal, son of him whom Swinton had slain, and with one of those irregular bursts of generosity and feeling which redeem the dark ages from the character of utter barbarism, he threw himself from his horse, and kneeled down before Swinton.—' I have not yet been knighted,' he said, ' and never can I take the honour from the hand of a truer, more loyal, more valiant leader, than he who slew my father : grant me,' he said, ' the boon I ask, and I unite my forces to yours, that we may live and die together.' His feudal enemy became instantly his godfather in chivalry, and his ally in battle. Swinton knighted the young Gordon, and they rushed down at the head of their united retainers, dispersed the archery, and would have turned the battle, had they been supported. At length they both fell, and all who followed them were cut off ; and it was remarked, that while the fight lasted, the old giant guarded the young man's life more than his own, and the same was indicated by the manner in which his body lay stretched over that of Gordon.

From a Letter written by Scott to Joanna Baillie.

FLODDEN

Often as I have wished for your company, I never did it more earnestly than when I rode over Flodden Edge. I know your taste for these things, and could have undertaken to demonstrate that never was an affair more completely bungled than that day's work was. Suppose one army posted upon the face of a hill, and secured by high grounds projecting on each flank, with the river Till in front, a deep and still river, winding through a very extensive valley called Milfield Plain, and the only passage over it by a narrow bridge, which the Scots artillery, from the hill, could in a moment have demolished. Add that the English must have hazarded a battle while their troops, which were tumultuously levied, remained together; and that the Scots, behind whom the country was open to Scotland, had nothing to do but to wait for the attack as they were posted. Yet did two thirds of the army, actuated by the *perfervidum ingenium Scotorum*, rush down and give an opportunity to Stanley to occupy the ground they had quitted, by coming over the shoulder of the hill, while the other third, under Lord Home, kept their ground, and having seen their king and about 10,000 of their countrymen cut to pieces, retired into Scotland without loss.

From a Letter written by Scott to his friend
William Clerk : August the 26th, 1791.

BONNIE DUNDEE: KILLIECRANKIE

When we look at the portrait of Claverhouse, and survey the calm, melancholy, and beautiful features of the devoted soldier, it appears almost incredible that he should ever have suffered under such an overwhelming load of misrepresentation. But when—discarding modern historians, who in too many instances do not seem to entertain the slightest scruple in dealing with the memory of the dead—we turn to the writings of his contemporaries who knew the man, his character appears in a very different light. They describe him as one who was stainless in his honour, pure in his faith, wise in his council, resolute in action, and utterly free from that selfishness which disgraced many of the Scottish statesmen of the time. No one dares question his loyalty, for he sealed that confession with his blood ; and it is universally admitted, that with him fell the last hopes of the reinstatement of the house of Stuart. . . .

Imitating the example, and inheriting the enthusiasm of his great predecessor Montrose, he invoked the loyalty of the clans to assist him in the struggle for legitimacy,—and he did not appeal to them in vain. His name was a spell to rouse the ardent spirits of the mountaineers ; and not the Great Marquis himself, in the height of his renown, was more sincerely welcomed and more fondly loved than ' Iain Dubh nan Catha,'—dark John of the Battles,—the name by which Lord Dundee is still remembered in Highland song. In the meantime the Convention, terrified at their danger, and dreading a Highland inroad, had despatched Mackay, a military officer of great experience, with a considerable body of troops, to quell the threatened insurrection. He was encountered by Dundee, and compelled to evacuate the high country and fall back upon the Lowlands, where he subsequently received reinforcements, and again marched northward. The Highland host was assembled at Blair, though not in great force, when the news of Mackay's advance arrived ; and a council of the chiefs and officers was summoned, to determine whether it would be most advisable to fall back upon the glens and wild fastnesses of the Highlands, or to meet the enemy at once, though with a far inferior force.

Most of the old officers, who had been trained in the foreign wars, were of the former opinion—' alleging that it was neither prudent nor cautious to risk an engagement against an army of disciplined men, that exceeded theirs in number by more than a half.' But both Glengarry and Lochiel, to the great satisfaction of the General, maintained the contrary view, and argued that neither hunger nor fatigue was so likely to depress the Highlanders as a retreat when the enemy was in view. The account of the discussion is so interesting, and so characteristic of Dundee, that I shall take leave to quote its termination in the words of Drummond of Balhaldy :—

' An advice so hardy and resolute could not miss to please the generous Dundee. His looks seemed to heighten with an air of delight and satisfaction all the while Lochiel was speaking. He told his council that they had heard his sentiments from the mouth of a person who had formed his judgment upon infallible proofs drawn from a long experience, and an intimate acquaintance with the persons and subject he spoke of. Not one in the company offering to contradict their general, it was unanimously agreed to fight.

' When the news of this vigorous resolution spread

through the army, nothing was heard but acclamations of joy, which exceedingly pleased their gallant general ; but before the council broke up, Lochiel begged to be heard for a few words. " My Lord," said he, " I have just now declared, in presence of this honourable company, that I was resolved to give an implicit obedience to all your Lordship's commands ; but I humbly beg leave, in name of these gentlemen, to give the word of command for this one time. It is the voice of your council, and their orders are that you do not engage personally. Your Lordship's business is to have an eye on all parts, and to issue out your commands as you shall think proper ; it is ours to execute them with promptitude and courage. On your Lordship depends the fate, not only of this little brave army, but also of our king and country. If your Lordship deny us this reasonable demand, for my own part I declare, that neither I, nor any I am concerned in, shall draw a sword on this important occasion, whatever construction shall be put upon the matter."

' Lochiel was seconded in this by the whole council ; but Dundee begged leave to be heard in his turn. " Gentlemen," said he, " as I am absolutely convinced, and have had repeated proofs, of your zeal for the King's service, and of your affection to me as his general and your friend, so I am fully sensible that my engaging personally this day may be of some loss if I shall chance to be killed. But I beg leave of you, however, to allow me to give one *shear darg* (that is, one harvest-day's work) to the King, my master, that I may have an opportunity of convincing the brave clans that I can hazard my life in that service as freely as the meanest of them. Ye know their temper, gentlemen ;

and if they do not think I have personal courage enough, they will not esteem me hereafter, nor obey my commands with cheerfulness. Allow me this single favour, and I here promise, upon my honour, never again to risk my person while I have that of commanding you."

' The council, finding him inflexible, broke up, and the army marched directly towards the Pass of Killiecrankie.'

Those who have visited that romantic spot need not be reminded of its peculiar features, for these, once seen, must dwell for ever in the memory. The lower part of the Pass is a stupendous mountain-chasm, scooped out by the waters of the Garry, which here descend in a succession of roaring cataracts and pools. The old road, which ran almost parallel to the river and close upon its edge, was extremely narrow, and wound its way beneath a wall of enormous crags, sur-mounted by a natural forest of birch, oak and pine. An army cooped up in that gloomy ravine would have as little chance of escape from the onset of an enterprising partisan corps, as had the Bavarian troops when attacked by the Tyrolese in the steep defiles of the Inn. General Mackay, however, had made his arrangements with consummate tact and skill, and had calculated his time so well, that he was enabled to clear the Pass before the Highlanders could reach it from the other side. Advancing upwards, the passage becomes gradually broader, until, just below the House of Urrard, there is a considerable width of meadow-land. It was here that Mackay took up his position, and arrayed his troops, on observing that the heights above were occupied by the army of Dundee.

The forces of the latter scarcely amounted to one-third of those of his antagonist, which were drawn up in line without any reserve. He was therefore compelled, in making his dispositions, to leave considerable gaps in his own line, which gave Mackay a further advantage. The right of Dundee's army was formed of the M'Lean, Glengarry, and Clanranald regiments, along with some Irish levies. In the centre was Dundee himself, at the head of a small and ill-equipped body of cavalry, composed of Lowland gentlemen and their followers, and about forty of his old troopers. The Camerons and Skyemen, under the command of Lochiel and Sir Donald Macdonald of Sleat, were stationed on the left. During the time occupied by these dispositions, a brisk cannonade was opened by Mackay's artillery, which materially increased the impatience of the Highlanders to come to close quarters. At last the word was given to advance, and the whole line rushed forward with the terrific impetuosity peculiar to a charge of the clans. They received the fire of the regular troops without flinching, reserved their own until they were close at hand, poured in a murderous volley, and then, throwing away their firelocks, attacked the enemy with the broadsword.

The victory was almost instantaneous, but it was bought at a terrible price. Through some mistake or misunderstanding, a portion of the cavalry, instead of following their general, who had charged directly for the guns, executed a manœuvre which threw them into disorder ; and when last seen in the battle, Dundee, accompanied only by the Earl of Dunfermline and about sixteen gentlemen, was entering into the cloud of smoke, standing up in his stirrups, and waving to the others to come on. It was in this attitude that he appears to have received his death-wound. On returning from the pursuit, the Highlanders found him dying on the field.

It would be difficult to point out another instance in which the maintenance of a great cause depended solely upon the life of a single man. Whilst Dundee survived, Scotland at least was not lost to the Stuarts, for, shortly before the battle, he had received assurance that the greater part of the organised troops in the north were devoted to his person, and ready to join him; and the victory of Killiecrankie would have been followed by a general rising of the loyal gentlemen in the Lowlands. But with his fall the enterprise was over.

THE LAYS OF THE SCOTTISH CAVALIERS : *Wm. Edmond-ston Aytoun.*

JAMES IV, THE HERO OF FLODDEN

The King is twenty-five years and some months old. He is of noble stature, neither tall nor short, and as handsome in complexion and shape as a man can be. His address is very agreeable. He speaks the following foreign languages : Latin, very well; French, German, Flemish, Italian, and Spanish. . . . His own Scottish language is as different from English as Aragonese from Castilian. The king speaks besides the language of the savages (!) who live in some parts of Scotland and on the islands. It is as different from Scottish as Biscayan is from Castilian. His knowledge of languages is wonderful. He is well read in the Bible and some other devout books. He is a good historian. He has read many Latin and French histories, and has profited by them, as he has a very good memory. . . .

He says all his prayers. Before transacting any business he hears two masses. After mass he has a cantata sung, during which he sometimes despatches very urgent business. He gives alms liberally ; but is a severe judge, especially in the case of murderers. . . .

Rarely, even in joking, a word escapes him that is not the truth. He prides himself upon it, and says it does not seem to him well for kings to swear their treaties as they do now. The oath of a king should be his Royal Word, as was the case in bygone days. . . . He is courageous, even more so than a king should be. I am a good witness of it. I have seen him often undertake most dangerous things in the last wars. . . . He is not a good captain because he begins to fight before he has given his orders . . . he does not think it right to begin any warlike undertaking without being himself the first in danger. His deeds are as good as his words. For this reason, and because he is a very humane prince, he is much loved. . . . He loves war so much that I fear, judging by the provocation he receives, the peace will not last long. . . .

> *From the translation of a letter written by Pedro di Ayala, the Spanish Ambassador to the Court of King James, to Ferdinand and Isabella of Spain (July the 25th, 1498.)*

THE DEATH OF QUEEN MARY

The warrant and sentence the Earl of Kent held in his hand. The Great Seal of the Crown of England was thereon. Then the Queen replied that she would as lief die as live any longer. As she turned round she perceived her most distinguished servitor, Melville, and said to him : ' My faithful servant Melville, though thou art a Protestant and I a Catholic, there is nevertheless but one Christendom and I am thy Queen. . . . And so I adjure thee before God that thou give this command to my son : I beg him to serve God, and the Catholic Church, and to rule and keep his country in peace and to submit (as I have done) to no other Master. Although I had the right good will to unite the kingdoms of this island, I renounce this. May he do likewise ; and do not let him put overmuch trust in the presumptions of the world. . . . Let him speak no evil of the Queen of England ; and thou, Melville, art my witness that I die like a true Scotswoman, Frenchwoman, and Catholic, which belief has ever been mine.' These words and such like did she repeat. . . .

When the executioner wished to assist her, she said to him that it was not her wont to be disrobed in the presence of such a crowd, nor with the help of such handmaidens. She herself took off her robe and pushed it down as far as the waist. . . .

As she knelt down she repeated the 70th Psalm. . . . When she had said this to the end, she, full of courage, bent down with her body and laid her head on the block, exclaiming: ' *In manus tuas, Domine, commendo spiritum meum.*' Then one of the executioners held down her hands, and the other cut off her head with two strokes of the chopper.

Thus ended her life.

The executioner took the head and showed it to the people, who cried : ' God spare our Queen of England ! '

THE FUGGER NEWS LETTERS : *From the Report of the Execution given by Samuel Tomascon, who was present.*

SCOTLAND'S MISFORTUNES

It is beyond the reach of Man to assign Reasons for the good or bad Fate that attends Kingdoms, Families, or single Persons (for the ways of God are past finding out) ; yet there are two Considerations that I have often reflected on to have had a great share in bringing down those Judgments which have of late fallen upon the Kings and Kingdom of Scotland : For since the Union of the two Crowns many and heavy have been the misfortunes of both. The first is, the mean spirited behaviour of King James VI in not revenging his Mother's Murder. Ought he, with a View of not irritating Queen Elizabeth, been guilty of such an unnatural Submission ? And was it not a servile Acknowledgment of England's Dominion to suffer the sacred Person of the Queen of Scotland to be Tried, Condemned, and Executed, without so much as daring to say it was ill done ? And was it not a Connivance at the greatest Violation and Encroachment that was ever offered to the Divine Rights of crowned Heads, thus silently to see her treated after such a manner, who was accountable to none but God ? How much was he degenerated from the illustrious and generous Stock from whence he sprung ? And which of his Royal Progenitors would not have

resented it with Fire and Sword ?   For my part, I'm afraid
the Indignation of God was stirred up upon this Account
against his Posterity, and that particularly in the Case of his
Son, Charles I ;   God visited the Iniquity of his Father,
committed by shewing so little Duty and natural Affection
to his Mother, and regard and value for the sacred Rights
of Crowned Heads.   For tho' we often read of Conquerors
having dispatched conquered Kings, and Subjects murder-
ing their Sovereigns, yet she was the first Instance of a
Royal Pannel, and the only Precedent to the hard Fate of
her Grandson.

MEMOIRS CONCERNING THE AFFAIRS OF SCOTLAND
(1714) : *George Lockhart of Carnwath* (1673-1731).

THE SCOTS TONGUE AND THE LAW

It may seem a Paradox to others, but to me it appears un-
deniable, that the Scottish idiom . . . is more fit for pleading,
than either the English idiom, or the French tongue ;   for
certainly a pleader must use a brisk, smart and quick way
of speaking ;   whereas the English, who are a grave nation,
use a too slow and grave pronunciation, and the French a
too soft and effeminate one.   And therefore, I think the
English is fit for haranguing, the French for complement-
ing, but the Scots for pleading.   Our pronunciation is like
ourselves, fiery, abrupt, sprightly and bold ;   their greatest
wits being employed at Court, have indeed enrich'd very
much their language as to conversation ;   but all ours bend-
ing themselves to study the law, the chief science in repute
with us, hath much smoothed our language as to pleading.
. . . Their language is invented by courtiers, and may be

softer, but ours by learn'd men, and men of business and so must be more massie and significant; and for our pronunciation, beside what I said formerly of its being more fitted to the complexion of our people than the English accent is; I cannot but remember them that the Scots are thought the nation under Heaven, who do with most ease learn to pronounce best the French, Spanish and other foreign languages; and all nations acknowledge that they speak the Latin with the most intelligible accent; for which no other reason can be given, but that our accent is natural, and hath nothing, at least little, in it that is peculiar. I say not this to asperse the English, they are a nation I honour, but to reprove the petulancy and malice of some amongst them, who think they do their country good service when they reproach ours.

PLEADINGS IN SOME REMARKABLE CASES BEFORE THE SUPREME COURTS OF SCOTLAND (1673): *Sir George MacKenzie.*

MacKenzie

THE MASSACRE OF GLENCOE

To Captain Robert Campbell of Glenlyon ' For Their Majesties' Service.'

Sir,—You are hereby ordered to fall upon the rebels, the M'Donalds, of Glencoe, and putt all to the sword under seventy. You are to have special care that the old fox and his sons doe upon no account escape your hands. You are to secure all the avenues, that no man escape. This you are to put in execution att five o'clock in the morning precisely, and by that time, or very shortly after it, I'll strive to be att you with a stronger party. If I doe not come to you att five, you are not to tarry for me, but to fall on. This is by the king's special command, for the good and safety of the country, that these miscreants be cutt off root and branch. See that this be putt in execution without feud or favour, else you may expect to be treated as not true to the king's government, nor a man fitt to carry a commission in the king's service. Expecting you will not faill in the ful-filling hereof as you love yourself, I subscribe these with my hand.

ROBERT DUNCANSON.

Ballacholis, 12th February, 1692.

The ' king ' mentioned in this letter, was, of course, the usurping William, Prince of Orange.

THE UNION WITH ENGLAND

I think I see a free and independent kingdom delivering up that which all the world hath been fighting for since the days of Nimrod ; yea, that for which most of all the empires, kingdoms, states, principalities, and the dukedoms of Europe are at this time engaged in the most bloody and cruel wars ; to wit, a power to manage their own affairs by themselves. . . .

. . . I think I see our ancient mother, Caledonia, like Caesar, sitting in the midst of our senate, ruefully looking round about her, covering herself with her royal garment, attending the fatal blow, and breathing out her last with an *et tu quoque mi fili !* . . .

My Lord Chancellor, the greatest honour that was done unto a Roman was to allow him the glory of a triumph ; the greatest and most dishonourable punishment was that of a parricide. He that was guilty of parricide was beaten with rods upon his naked body till the blood gushed out of all the veins of his body ; then he was sewed up in a leathern sack . . . with a cock, a viper, and an ape, and thrown headlong into the sea. . . .

My Lord, patricide is a greater crime than parricide, all the world over. . . .

> *From the Speech delivered by John Hamilton, Lord Belhaven, to the Scottish Parliament on November the 2nd, 1706.*

PRINCE CHARLES EDWARD

Do not the pulpits and congregations of the clergy, as well as your weekly papers, ring with the dreadful threats of popery, slavery, tyranny, and arbitrary power, which are now ready to be imposed upon you by the formidable powers of France and Spain ? Is not my royal father represented as a bloodthirsty tyrant, breathing out nothing but destruction to all who will not immediately embrace an odious religion ? Or have I myself been better used ? But listen only to the naked truth.

I, with my own money, hired a small vessel. Ill-supplied with money, arms, or friends, I arrived in Scotland attended by seven persons. I publish the King my father's declaration, and proclaim his title, with pardon in one hand, and in the other liberty of conscience, and the most solemn promises to grant whatever a free parliament shall propose for the happiness of a people. I have, I confess, the greatest reason to adore the goodness of Almighty God, who has in so remarkable a manner protected me and my small army through the many dangers to which we were at first exposed, and who has led me in the way to victory, and to the capital of this ancient kingdom, amidst the acclamations of the King my father's subjects. Why, then, is so much pains taken to spirit up the minds of the people against this my undertaking ?

The reason is obvious ; it is, lest the real sense of the nation's present sufferings should blot out the remembrance of past misfortunes, and of outcries formerly raised against the royal family. Whatever miscarriages might have given occasion to them, they have been more than atoned for since ; and the nation has now an opportunity of being secured against the like in the future.

That our family has suffered exile during these fifty-seven years, everybody knows. Has the nation, during that period of time, been the more happy and flourishing for it ? Have you found reason to love and cherish your governors as the fathers of the people. . . . Has a family, upon whom a faction unlawfully bestowed the diadem of a rightful prince, retained a due sense of so great a trust and favour ? . . . Have their ears been open to the cries of the people ? . . . Have you reaped any other benefit from them than an immense load of debt ? If I am answered in the affirmative, why has their government been so often railed at in all your public assemblies ? Why has the nation been so long crying out in vain for redress against the abuse of parliaments, upon account of their long duration, the multitude of placemen, which occasions their venality, the introduction of penal laws, and, in general, against the miserable situation of the kingdom at home and abroad ?

It is now time to conclude ; and I shall do it with this reflection : Civil wars are ever attended with rancour and ill-will. . . . I, therefore, earnestly require it of my friends to give as little loose as possible to such passions : this will prove the most effectual means to prevent the same in the enemies of my royal cause. And this my declaration wil vindicate to all posterity the nobleness of my undertaking, and the generosity of my intentions. . . .

From the Edinburgh Declaration of Prince Charles Edward, issued on the 10th of October, 1745.

BURNS'S BEGINNING WITH LOVE AND POETRY

You know our country custom of coupling a man and woman together as partners in the labours of the harvest. In my fifteenth summer my partner was a bewitching creature, a year younger than myself. . . . She was a bonnie, sweet, sonsie lass. . . . Among her love-inspiring qualities, she sang sweetly ; and it was her favourite reel to which I attempted giving an embodied vehicle in rhyme. I was not so presumptuous as to imagine that I could make verses like printed ones, composed by men who read Greek and Latin ; but my girl sang a song, which was said to be composed by a country laird's son, on one of his father's maids with whom he was in love ; and I saw no reason why I might not rhyme as well as he ; for, excepting that he could shear sheep, and cast peats, his father living in the moorlands, he had no more scholarcraft than myself.

Thus with me began love and poetry. . . .

Robert Burns.

BURNS

To his Father

Honoured Sir,—I have purposely delayed writing, in the hope that I should have the pleasure of seeing you on New-Year's Day ; but work comes so hard upon us, that I do not choose to be absent on that account, as well as for some other little reasons, which I shall tell you at meeting. My health is nearly the same as when you were here, only my sleep is a little sounder ; and, on the whole, I am rather better than otherwise, though I mend by very slow degrees. . . .

BURNS AND HIS PARTNER

As for this world, I despair of ever making a figure in it. I am not formed for the bustle of the busy, nor the flutter of the gay. I shall never again be capable of entering into such scenes. Indeed, I am altogether unconcerned at the thoughts of this life. I foresee that poverty and obscurity probably await me. I am in some measure prepared, and daily preparing to meet them. I have but just time and paper to return you my grateful thanks for the lessons of virtue and piety you have given me, which were too much neglected at the time of giving them ; but which, I hope, have been remembered ere it was too late. Present my dutiful respects to my mother . . . and with wishing you a merry New-Year's Day, I shall conclude.

I am, honoured sir, your dutiful son,

ROBERT BURNS.

P.S.—My meal is nearly out, but I am going to borrow till I get more.

Irvine, December 27, 1781.

SCOTT

In truth, I have long given up poetry. I have had my day with the public ; and being no great believer in poetical immortality, I was very well pleased to rise a winner, without continuing the game till I was beggared of any credit I had acquired. Besides, I felt the prudence of giving way before the more forcible and powerful genius of Byron. If I were either greedy, or jealous of poetical fame—and both are strangers to my nature—I might comfort myself with the thought, that I would hesitate to strip myself to the

contest so fearlessly as Byron does ; or to command the
wonder and terror of the public, by exhibiting, in my own
person, the sublime attitude of the dying gladiator. But
with the old frankness of twenty years since, I will fairly
own, that this same delicacy of mine may arise more from
the conscious want of vigour and inferiority, than from a
delicate dislike to the nature of the conflict. At any rate,
there is a time for everything, and without swearing oaths
to it, I think my time for poetry has gone by.

My health suffered horridly last year, I think from over
labour and excitation ; and though it is now apparently
restored to its usual tone, yet during the long and painful
disorder (spasms in the stomach), and the frightful process
of cure, by a prolonged use of calomel, I learned that my
frame was made of flesh, and not of iron—a conviction
which I will long keep in remembrance, and avoid any
occupation so laborious and agitating, as poetry must be
to be worth anything.

In this humour, I often think of passing a few weeks on
the continent—a summer vacation if I can—and of course
my attraction to Gratz would be very strong. I fear this is
the only chance of our meeting in this world—we, who once
saw each other daily ! for I understand from George and
Henry, that there is little chance of your coming here. And
when I look around me, and consider how many changes
you would see in feature, form, and fashion, amongst all
you knew and loved ; and how much, no sudden squall, or
violent tempest, but the slow and gradual progress of life's
long voyage, has severed all the gallant fellowships whom
you left spreading their sails to the morning breeze, I really
am not sure that you would have much pleasure.

The gay and wild romance of life is over with all of us. The real, dull, and stern history of humanity has made a far greater progress over our heads ; and age, dark and unlovely, has laid his crutch over the stoutest fellow's shoulders. One thing your old society may boast, that they have all run their course with honour, and almost all with distinction ; and the brother suppers of Frederick Street have certainly made a very considerable figure in the world, as was to be expected, from her talents under whose auspices they were assembled.

From a Letter written by Scott to the Countess of Purgstall (formerly Jane Anne Cranstoun), 1821.

TOURISTS AT ABBOTSFORD

On returning to Abbotsford, we found Mrs. Scott and her daughters doing penance under the merciless curiosity of a couple of tourists who had arrived from Selkirk soon after we set out for Melrose. They were rich specimens—tall, lanky young men, both of them rigged out in new jackets and trowsers of the Macgregor tartan ; the one, as they had revealed, being a lawyer, the other a Unitarian preacher, from New England. These gentlemen, when told on their arrival that Mr. Scott was not at home, had shown such signs of impatience, that the servant took it for granted they must have serious business, and asked if they would wish to speak a word with his lady. They grasped at this, and so conducted themselves in the interview, that Mrs. Scott never doubted they had brought letters of introduction to her husband, and invited them accordingly to partake of her luncheon. They had been walking about the house and grounds with her and her daughters ever since that time, and appeared at the porch, when the Sheriff and his party returned to dinner, as if they had been already fairly enrolled on his visiting list. For the moment, he too was taken in—he fancied that his wife must have received and opened their credentials—and shook hands with them with courteous cordiality. But Mrs. Scott, with all her overflowing good-nature, was a sharp observer; and she, before a minute had elapsed, interrupted the ecstatic compliments of the strangers, by reminding them that her husband would be glad to have the letters of the friends who had been so good as to write by them. It then turned out that there were no letters to be produced;—and Scott, signifying that his hour for dinner approached, added, that as he supposed they meant to walk to Melrose, he could not trespass further on their time. The two lion-hunters seemed quite unprepared for this abrupt escape; but there was about Scott, in perfection, when he chose to exert it, the power of civil repulsion; he bowed the overwhelmed originals to his door, and on re-entering the parlour, found Mrs. Scott complaining very indignantly that they had gone so far as to pull out their note-book, and beg an exact account, not only of his age—but of her own. Scott, already half relenting, laughed heartily at this misery. He observed, however, that, ' if he were to take in all the world, he had better put up a sign-post at once—

" Porter, ale, and British spirits,"

painted bright between two trees; and that no traveller of respectability could ever be at a loss for such an introduction as would ensure his best hospitality.' Still he was not quite pleased with what had happened—and as we were about to pass, half an hour afterwards, from the drawing-room to the dining-room, he said to his wife, ' Hang the Yahoos, Charlotte—but we should have bid them stay dinner.' ' Devil a bit,' quoth Captain John Fergusson, who had again come over from Huntly Burn, and had been latterly assisting the lady to amuse her Americans—' Devil a bit, my dear, they were quite in a mistake I could see. The one asked Madame whether she deigned to call her new house Tullyveolan or Tillytudlem—and the other when Maida happened to lay his nose against the window, exclaimed *pro-di-gi-ous!*   In short, they evidently meant all their humbug not for you, but for the culprit of Waverley, and the rest of that there rubbish.' ' Well, well, Skipper,' was the reply,—' for a' that, the loons would hae been nane the waur o' their kail.'

LIFE OF SIR WALTER SCOTT : *John Gibson Lockhart.*

FOOTBALL MATCH (1815)

On Monday, 4th December, there was played, upon the extensive plain of Carterhaugh, near the junction of the Ettrick and Yarrow, the greatest match at the ball which has taken place for many years. It was held by the people of the Dale of Yarrow, against those of the parish of Selkirk ; the former being brought to the field by the Right Hon. the Earl of Home, and the Gallant Sutors by their Chief Magistrate, Ebenezer Clarkson, Esq. Both sides were joined by many volunteers from other parishes ; and the appearance of the various parties marching from their different glens to the place of rendezvous, with pipes playing and loud acclamations, carried back the coldest imagination to the old times when the Foresters assembled with the less peaceable purpose of invading the English territory, or defending their own. The romantic character of the scenery aided the illusion, as well as the performance of a feudal ceremony previous to commencing the games.

His Grace the Duke of Buccleuch and Queensberry came upon the ground about 11 o'clock, attended by his sons, the young Earl of Dalkeith and Lord John Scott ; the Countess of Home ; the Ladies Ann, Charlotte, and Isabella Scott ; Lord and Lady Montagu and family ; the Hon. General Sir Edward Stopford, K.B. ; Sir John Riddell of Riddell ; Sir Alexander Don of Newton ; Mr. Elliot Lockhart, member for the county ; Mr. Pringle of Whytebank, younger ; Mr. Pringle of Torwoodlee ; Captain Pringle, Royal Navy ; Mr. Boyd of Broadmeadows and family ; Mr. Chisholm of Chisholm ; Major Pott of Todrig ; Mr. Walter Scott, Sheriff of Selkirkshire, and family,—and many other gentlemen and ladies.—The ancient banner of the Buccleuch family, a curious and venerable relique, emblazoned with armorial bearings, and with the word ' Bellendaine,' the ancient war-cry of the clan of Scott, was then displayed, as on former occasions when the Chief took the field in person, whether for the purpose of war or sport. The banner was delivered by Lady Ann Scott to Master Walter Scott, younger of Abbotsford, who attended suitably mounted and armed, and riding over the field displayed it to the sound of the war-pipes, and amid the acclamations of the assembled spectators, who could not be fewer than 2000 in number. That this singular renewal of an ancient military custom might not want poetical celebrity, verses were distributed among the spectators, composed for the occasion by Mr. Walter Scott and the Ettrick Shepherd.—

Mr. James Hogg acted as aide-de-camp to the Earl of Home in the command of the Yarrow men, and Mr. Robert Henderson of Selkirk to Mr. Clarkson, both of whom contributed not a little to the good order of the day.

The ball was thrown up between the parties by the Duke of Buccleuch, and the first game was gained, after a severe conflict of an hour and a half duration, by the Selkirk men. The second game was still more severely contested, and after a close and stubborn struggle of more than three hours, with various fortune, and much display of strength and agility on both sides, was at length carried by the Yarrow men. The ball should then have been thrown up a third time, but considerable difficulty occurred in arranging the voluntary auxiliaries from other parishes, so as to make the match equal ; and, as the day began to close, it was found impossible to bring the strife to an issue, by playing a decisive game.

Both parties, therefore, parted with equal honours, but, before they left the ground, the Sheriff threw up his hat, and in Lord Dalkeith's name and his own, challenged the Yarrow men, on the part of the Sutors, to a match to be played upon the first convenient opportunity, with 100 picked men only on each side. The challenge was mutually accepted by Lord Home, on his own part, and for Lord John Scott, and was received with acclamation by the players on both sides. The principal gentlemen present took part with one side or other, except the Duke of Buccleuch, who remains neutral. Great play is expected, and all bets are to be paid by the losers to the poor of the winning parish. We cannot dismiss the subject without giving our highest commendation to the Earl of Home, and to Mr. Clarkson for the attention which they showed in promoting the spirit and good order of the day. For the players themselves, it was impossible to see a finer set of active and athletic young fellows than appeared on the field. But what we chiefly admired in their conduct was, that though several hundreds in number, exceedingly keen for their respective parties, and engaged in so rough and animated a contest, they maintained the most perfect good humour, and showed how unnecessary it is to discourage manly and athletic exercises among the common people, under pretext of maintaining subordination and good order. We have only to regret, that the great concourse of spectators rendered it difficult to mention the names of the several players who distinguished themselves by feats of strength or agility ; but we must not omit to record, that the first ball was *hailed* by Robert Hall, mason in *Selkirk*, and the second by George Brodie, from *Greatlaws*, upon *Aill-water*.

The Selkirk party wore slips of fir as their mark of distinction—the Yarrow men, sprigs of heath.

Refreshments were distributed to the players by the Duke of Buccleuch's domestics, in a booth erected for the purpose ; and no persons were allowed to sell ale or spirits on the field.

> *From the report in* BALLANTYNE'S NEWSPAPER :
> *probably written by Scott.*

Then up with the banner, let forest winds fan her,
She has blazed over Ettrick eight ages and more ;
In sport we'll attend her, in battle defend her,
With heart and with hand, like our fathers before.

> *Scott.*

A HOUSEBREAKER'S FEE

From this pleasant tour, so rich in its results, Scott returned in time to attend the autumnal assizes at Jedburgh, on which occasion he made his first appearance as counsel in a criminal court ; and had the satisfaction of helping a veteran poacher and sheepstealer to escape through some of the meshes of the law. ' You're a lucky scoundrel,' Scott whispered to his client, when the verdict was pronounced. ' I'm just o' your mind,' quoth the desperado, ' and I'll send ye a maukin the morn, man.' I am not sure whether it was at these assizes or the next in the same town, that he had less success in the case of a certain notorious housebreaker. The man, however, was well aware that no skill could have baffled the clear evidence against him, and was, after his fashion, grateful for such exertions as had been made in his behalf. He requested the young advocate to visit him once more before he left the place. Scott's curiosity induced him to accept this invitation, and his friend, as soon as they were alone together in the *condemned cell*, said—' I am very sorry, sir, that I have no fee to offer you—so let me beg your acceptance of two bits of advice which may be useful perhaps when you come to have a house of your own. I am done with practice, you see, and here is my legacy. Never keep a large watchdog out of doors—we can always silence them cheaply—indeed if it be a *dog*, 'tis easier than whistling —but tie a little tight yelping terrier within ; and secondly, put no trust in nice, clever, gimcrack locks—the only thing that bothers us is a huge old heavy one, no matter how simple the construction,—and the ruder and rustier the key, so much the better for the housekeeper.' I remember hearing him tell this story some thirty years after at a

Judges' dinner at Jedburgh, and he summed it up with a rhyme—' Ay, ay, my lord,' (I think he addressed his friend Lord Meadowbank)—

> ' Yelping terrier, rusty key
> Was Walter Scott's best Jeddart fee.'

LIFE OF SIR WALTER SCOTT : *John Gibson Lockhart.*

A NATION'S WEALTH

So many hundred thousands sit in workhouses : and other hundred thousands have not yet got even workhouses ; and in thrifty Scotland itself, in Glasgow or Edinburgh City, in their dark lanes, hidden from all but the eye of God, and of rare Benevolence the minister of God, there are scenes of woe and destitution and desolation, such as, one may hope, the Sun never saw before in the most barbarous regions where men dwelt. Competent witnesses, the brave and humane Dr. Alison, who speaks what he knows, whose noble Healing Art in his charitable hands becomes once more a truly sacred one, report these things for us : these things are not of this year, or of last year, have no reference to our present state of commercial stagnation, but only to the common state. Not in sharp fever-fits, but in chronic gangrene of this kind is Scotland suffering. A Poor-law, any and every Poor-law, it may be observed, is but a temporary measure ; an anodyne, not a remedy : Rich and Poor, when once the naked facts of their condition have come into collision, cannot long subsist together on a mere Poor-law. True enough :—and yet, human beings cannot be left to die ! Scotland too, till something better come, must have a Poor-law, if Scotland is not to be a byword among the nations. O, what a waste is there ; of noble and thrice-noble national virtues ; peasant Stoicisms, Heroisms ; valiant manful habits, soul of a Nation's worth,—which all the metal of Potosi cannot purchase back ; to which the metal of Potosi, and all you can buy with *it*, is dross and dust !

PAST AND PRESENT : *Carlyle*.

COMMERCIAL VISION

That the Scot is largely endowed with the commercial imagination his foes will be ready to acknowledge. Imagination may consecrate the world to a man, or it may merely be a visualising faculty which sees that, as already perfect, which is still lying in the raw material . . . he has the forecasting leap of the mind which sees what to make of things —more, sees them made and in vivid operation. To him there is a railway through the desert where no railway exists, and mills along the quiet stream. And his *perfervidum ingenium* is quick to attempt the realising of his dreams. . . . Indeed, so flushed and riotous can the Scottish mind become over a commercial prospect that it sometimes sends native caution by the board, and a man's really fine idea becomes an empty balloon, to carry him off to the limbo of vanities.

There is a megalomaniac in every parish of Scotland. Well, not so much as that. . . . But in every district, almost, you may find a poor creature who for thirty years has cherished a great scheme by which means to revolutionize the world's commerce, and amass a fortune in mon-

strous degree.   He is generally to be seen shivering at the
Cross, and (if you are a nippy man) you shout carelessly in
going by, ' Good morning, Tamson ; how's the scheme ? '
And he would be very willing to tell you, if only you would
wait to listen.   ' Man,' he will cry eagerly behind you, ' if I
only had anither wee wheel in my invention—she would do,
the besom !   I'll süne have her ready noo.'
    Poor Tamson !

THE HOUSE WITH THE GREEN SHUTTERS :
George Douglas Brown.

' AULD LANG SYNE '

Heavy feeding, a careless collocation of guests, dull and
rambling speeches, bad singing, an inferior piano, a poor
accompanist, and a negligent chairman have their fitting
culmination in a mumbled and mangled rendering of Burns's
immortal Song of Friendship.   The dragging tune, the
self-conscious stare, the fish-like hand extended to the
trusty ' friend ' (*sic*), the ghastly galvanism of the prestis-
simo, proclaim the feast a fiasco.   The end is all.   Let us
get ' Auld Lang Syne ' right and make the feast lead up to
it.   Let us get it into our noddles that there are no ' days
of auld lang syne ' in the song ; that ' And surely ye'll be
your pint-stowp, And surely I'll be mine,' means ' You'll
pay for one pint and I'll pay for another ' (treat about or no
treating) ; that ' dine ' means noon ; that the last verse
begins, ' And there's a hand (not " haun "), my trusty
fiere,' ' fiere ' meaning crony ; and that ' a right gude-
willy waught ' means a right full-of-goodwill long draught.
Finally, let us follow the example of the ' fifty-niners ' and

entrust each of the first four stanzas to one of four picked
and reliable vocalists, and the last stanza to the four vocalists singing in parts, reserving our united energies for the
recurrent and final chorus and the breaking-off 'three
cheers.' Fortune gave us the greatest of the world's song-
writers, who gave the world its best convivial songs. Why
not show ourselves worthy of the honour ?

ROBERT BURNS AND OTHER ESSAYS : *William Power.*

THE CAIRNGORMS

It is fitting to take leave of the Cairngorms with the
crumbling desolation of the Archer's Corrie as last impression. For after days of sunshine, days of colour, days of
gloom and storm, enjoyed amongst them in as many various
moods, the summary of our thoughts of them, more than of
other hills, is inevitably serious, and even sad. Only a
stranger from lands farther from the sky can think of ' the
eternal hills ' as so much less mortal than ourselves ; but
most of them have found ways to hide that they too are
slowly dying. When we look at the scarred sides of Loch
Avon, or at Braeriach, which in the piling up of centuries has
worn to so thin a shell that each successive vertical section
of granite as it falls must now steal something also from the
height, they seem almost to be in suffering, and the venerable thought is again borne in upon us that nothing is im-
perishable—not even time itself, of whose power their condition is the vast evidence. We may be tempted to imagine
their story told, and no sooner told than reduced to insigni-
ficance by some celestial Gibbon, in a passage to compare
with that (speaking of those ' sixty phantoms of kings,

which have passed before our eyes and faintly dwell on our remembrance ') with which his forty-eighth chapter closes —or, I suppose, a period yet more tremendous, if that could be conceived.

But of all the vanities, time alone needs, and will endure, no monument.

WALKING IN THE GRAMPIANS : *Charles Plumb*.

GLOSSARY

INTRODUCTION

THIS glossary has been specially compiled : it is not a reprint of any other glossary with necessary emendations or additions; but, as a matter of interest—in order to carry out the general conception of this book right to the end—many of the words are glossed in a more general way than is necessary merely to explain the meanings of the words in the text.

All the Gaelic words in the book are explained in, or by, the text ; so that this glossary contains only Scots words (there are one or two archaisms) ; but a few examples of Gaelic and other cognates are shown, as are also pronunciations according to English phonetics.

Scots is not in the true sense a language, but it could be made into one—after all, the Dutch *manufactured* a literary language out of their several Low German dialects, and they had not the ground to work on that there is in Scots. Anyhow, Scots is much more than a mere dialect ; and it is certainly not a dialect of English. There are old English (Anglo-Saxon) words in Scots, but there are, too, many more words of Scandinavian, French, Flemish, and other Gothic origins ; and the base of the tongue—most of the idioms, and over forty per cent. of the words, are of Celtic derivation : Gaelic (Irish) and Cymric (Welsh, or Brythonic).

Scots has certainly become terribly anglicized of recent years ; and the blame cannot entirely be attributed to books, newspapers, films, and the radio. We are, as a race, good linguists, capable of separating words and idioms with ease. Half the trouble of the debasement of Scots has been due to our native writers and poets, who, professing to write in Scots, have merely written in bad English splattered with a few Scots words. And this, no doubt, was occasioned as much by sheer laziness as by ignorance. It was so much easier to substitute an English word, or words, for the sake of rhyme, metre, or euphony, than to delve into their brains for the right expression in Scots. If, on the other hand, they were writing with an eye to the English market (and who

shall blame them for that, things being as they were, and are ?)
why did they not write in ' straight ' English instead of doing
their worst to commit linguistic suicide ?

Anyhow, it is very doubtful if there are now more than a
dozen people left in Scotland capable of carrying on a pro-
tracted conversation in Scots. I certainly can't. I am not
indeed so interested in Scots as I am in the true language of
Scotland—and I recognise that the use of three different
tongues is altogether too much in one small land ; but, as it
is, I will fight for Scots as I will for the Gaelic, or for anything else that will militate against the complete denational-
ization of my country.

And now, whilst I am riding the high-horse, let me make
a plea against the use of the term ' Braid Scots.' Surely
Scots should be sufficient. To an Englishman ' Broad
English ' means a provincial and debased form of his language. Is, then, the use of the expression ' Braid Scots '
anything other than a further degradation of the tongue ?

So, too, it is, with the lavish and ridiculous use of apostrophes to which we are accustomed. To pepper a page with
apostrophes indicative of supposed omissions is to admit that
what is written is written not as anything other than the
merest dialect. Throughout this book, for obvious reasons,
and particularly when dealing with the work of other people,
I have had to transcribe in the usual orthodox manner—with
apostrophes by the hundred ; but I deprecate the method for
all that.

The Scots word for English *all* should be written *aw* or *au*,
which does give the correct sound. To write *a'* is to write
something that looks like nothing, and that can be extremely
misleading. So, too, with the Scots equivalent for the English
terminal *ing*. To write *in'* is not even to indicate the correct
sound. What is wrong with the use of the Old Scots suffix,
an, or *and* ? That (with the *a* scarcely heard) would indicate
the true sound, and would give us *bydand*, or *bydan* (not
bidin') for ' staying ' ; and *gloman* (not gloamin') for ' twilight.' And why, usually, *'d* in such words as *reek'd* and
thirl'd ? Even *ed* is not right. Why not give a true indication of the real sound, and write *reekt* and *thirlt* ? Scots
written differently, and a little more logically, would at anyrate look and read something like a language.

It is time some of us got together to put this thing right. Yes, I know there is a Dictionary in process of compilation ; but I would hate to count the apostrophes that will be in it !

In this glossary I have given rough indications of certain pronunciations. These indications are shown in brackets and in ordinary type immediately after the Scots word.

The *u* sound of words like *lufe*, *cuif*, and *pulé*, I have shown as *ü*. This sound does not exist in English. It is something like a cross between the sound of English *i* in *ink*, and the way an Englishman pronounces the *u* in *burn*. There is another *u* sound as in *puir* that is not unlike the English pronunciation of the *e* in *where*. But English readers should note that the ordinary *u* as in Scots *burn* is sounded as in *gun*, and never as *bern*. An *i* standing without another vowel beside it is always sounded as in English *drink* : *thirl*, *birl*, and not *therl*, *berl*. And do try to sound the *r*, although not with the exaggerated trill usually given to it by so-called Scotch comedians. But, and this again to my English readers, don't even attempt to get the guttural sounds of *ach*, and *loch*. You will only strangle yourselves. To say *ach !* correctly you need generations of Scots blood behind you, and you must have been born with the peat-reek in your nostrils, and the sight of the hills as the first thing ever you clapped your eyes on.

Abbreviations

G.—Gaelic ; Ir. G.—Irish Gaelic ; Icel.—Icelandic ; Fr.—French.

a' (aw, au) : all.
ablach (*G. ablach*) : a dwarf ; an insignificant person.
aboon or abune (abüne) : above, over.
abread (abreed) : abroad ; in breadth.
acquent : acquainted.
ae (yeh) : one.
aff-lufe (aff-lüfe) : off-hand ; at once.
afore : before ; in front.
aft : often.

agley (aglee) : aslant ; not straight.
ahint : behind.
aiblins (aiblins *or* yiblins) : perhaps.
aidle : foul water.
aik : oak.
aiken : made of oak.
ain : own.
aince (aince *or* yince) : once.
airles : earnest-money ; a deposit to secure a bargain.
airm : arm.

airn : iron.

airt (*G. àirde*) : direction ; point of the compass.

airtit : directed.

aits (aits *or* yits) : oats.

aizle or eizel : a red ember ; hot cinder.

ajee : half-open ; to one side.

a'maist (awmaist) : almost.

ane (ain *or* yin) : one.

aneth : beneath.

aneuch : enough.

antrin : occasional.

atweel : in truth ; certainly.

atweel na : by no means.

aucht (aucht *or* echt) : eight.

aught (ocht) : anything.

auld : old.

auld-farrant : old-fashioned ; sagacious.

auld lang syne : long ago.

Auld Reekie : Edinburgh (Old smoky).

aumous : alms ; a gift to a beggar.

ava (avaw) : at all ; of all. (*nane ava*—nothing at all.)

awee : a little. (*bide awee*—wait awhile.)

ay or aye (eye) : yes ; always.

ayont : beyond ; behind. (*ayont yon knowe*—behind that hill.)

ba' (baw) : ball ; a ball.

bailie : Municipal Official, equivalent to Eng. alderman.

bairn : child.

bairned : pregnant, or made pregnant.

baith : both.

bakes : biscuits.

ballants : ballads.

ban : to swear.

bandster : a binder of sheaves.

bane : bone.

bannock (*G. bannag*) : a flat cake of bread.

barkit : dirtied ; encrusted with dirt.

barley-bree : whisky (lit. juice of the barley).

barra : a barrow.

baudrons : generic term for a cat.

bauld : bold.

bawbee : a half-penny.

bawds : hares.

beet : to feed ; to warm.

begood : began.

ben : in ; inner room ; inside. (*c'wa ben*—come away inside.)

benmaist : innermost.

bent : coarse grass ; open field of rough grass.

bere : barley.

beuk : a book.

bide : stay.

bield : shelter.

bieldy : sheltered.

big : to build.

biggs : builds.

bike : a nest. (*a bummie's bike* —a wasp's nest.)

bing : a heap.

birk : the birch tree.

birl : turn.

birn : burden.

birse : impudence.

bizzem : a bad girl ; a randy woman.

blackmail (*G. màil-dubh*) : money levied to secure protection, equivalent to a modern gangster's demands.

blae : livid.

blate : bashful ; shy.

blaw : to blow ; to boast.

bleer : to smear.

bleeze : flame.

blether : to talk idly.

blethers : idle talk ; nonsense.
blicht (*Icel. blitha*) : blithe ;
happy.
blude or bluid : blood.
bocht : bought.
bock (boke): to gush forth; to
vomit. (*the bock*—sickness).
bodach (*G. bodach*) : an old
man.
bogle : a hobgoblin ; a ghost.
bonnie : beautiful (*not* as English usage : well-fleshed,
stout.)
boo'er : a bower.
bool : a marble ; to bowl.
bools : the game of bowls.
boortree : the shrub-elder.
bore : a hole ; a nook. (*benmaist bore*—farthest corner.)
boune (boon) (*Icel. búinn*) : get
ready ; prepare ; till.
bounes : ' wherever thou
bounes ' (p. 37)—*wherever
thou makest ready* : poss.
wherever thou art bound.
bour (boor) : a bower.
brae (*G. braighe*) : slope or
upper part of a hill.
braid : broad.
brander : to grill.
braw (*G. brèagha*) (*N. brav,
bra*) : handsome ; fine ;
good.
brawlie : finely ; very well.
(*daein brawlie*—doing fine.)
braxie : a sheep that has died
of disease, or has been killed
in consequence of disease.
bree : juice ; liquid.
breeks (*G. briogais*) : breeches ;
trousers.
breenge (breenj) : plunge forward rashly.
breist (breest) : breast.
bricht : bright.
brock (*G. broc*) : a badger.

brogue (*G. bròg*) : shoe.
brogue (*Ir. G. barróg*) : This
word really refers not to
English spoken with a Scots
or Irish accent, but to Scots
or Gaelic spoken with an
English accent.
brose (*G. brochan*) : porridge;
gruel ; oatmeal and water.
bucht : a sheep-pen.
buirdly : stoutly built ; broad-
shouldered.
buit (büt) : a boot.
bunemaist (bünmaist) : highest.
burn : a stream ; a brook.
busk : to dress. (*busk an'
boune*—dress and get ready.)
but-an-ben : small cottage ;
house with only two rooms.
but or bot : without. (*but the
breeks*—without trousers) ;
outer (*but-an-ben*—outer and
inner room.)

caird (*G. cèard*) : a tinker ; a
sturdy beggar.
cairn (*G. càrn*) : a heaped-up
pile of stones.
caller : fresh ; cool.
cam : came.
canna : cannot.
cannas : canvas.
cannie or canny : gentle (*not* as
English usage : mean, cunning.)
cantie : cheerful, lively.
cantrip : a spell ; a charm.
carle : an old man.
carlin : a strong old woman.
ca's : calves.
cauld : cold.
cauper : a turner.
caur : a calf ; a car.
chanter : the tune-pipe of bagpipes, also a single pipe for
practice.

chap : to knock ; to rap.
chapman : a pedlar ; a packman.
cheek for chow : side by side.
cheep : chirp.
chiel : a youth.
clachan (*G. clachan*) : a small village ; a hamlet.
claes : clothes.
claik, clash : gossip.
claith : cloth.
claut : scrape ; a little of anything. (*a claut*—a handful.)
claw : to scratch.
claymor (*G. claidheamh-mor*) : a big sword ; a broadsword.
cled : clothed.
cleedin : clothing.
cleek (*G. clìchd*) : a hook.
cleekit : linked or hooked together ; strung-up.
cleekit-shalt : a pony suffering from string-halt.
clegs : gad-flies.
clishmaclaver : idle conversation.
cloker : a broody hen.
cloot : the hoof.
clootie : the Devil.
clout (cloot) : a rag. (*a bit clout*—a piece of rag.)
clud (clood) : a cloud.
coft : bought.
cog or coggie : a wooden dish ; a small basin.
connached : abused ; wasted ; destroyed.
cooser : a stallion.
corbies : carrion crows ; ravens.
corrie (*G. coire*) : a circular hollow on a hill-side.
coulter : plough blade.
coup (cowp) : to heel over ; to tip up.
coup-cairt : a tip cart.
couthie or couthy : kind ; gentle ; loving.

cowshus : cautious.
crack : a chat. (*a guid crack*— a good chat ; *crack thegither* —talk together.)
craft : a small farm ; a croft.
cranreuch : hore-frost.
cratur : creature. (*a puir bit cratur*—a poor, useless person.)
creel : a basket ; a shallow wicker container for fish, peats, corn, etc.
croun (croon) : a crown.
crounes (croons) : pieces of money ; crown-pieces ; wealth.
crouse (croose) : proud ; cocksure.
cruives (*G. craobh*) : branches ; lattice-work ; fish-traps.
cuddy : a donkey or small horse.
cuif (cüf) : a ninny ; a blockhead.
curch : a kerchief worn on the head ; head-dress.
cutty : short.

dabbit : dabbed ; aimed at.
dae : do.
daffin : merriment.
daimen : rare ; occasional.
daith : death.
dander : wander ; walk slowly.
dang : drove.
danton : subdue.
darg : work ; a measure of work. (*sair darg*—hard work.)
daur : dare.
deasal (*G. deiseil*) : sun-wise ; from east to west.
deid : dead.
deil : the Devil ; a devil.
dicht : to wipe.
ding : to push ; to excel ; to press down.
dinna : do not.
dochter or dother : daughter.

doitit : stupid ; bewildered.

douce : sober ; prudent.

doukit (dookit) : ducked.

doun (doon) : down.

doup (dowp) : the buttocks ; the behind ; a fag-end.

dour (*G. dùr*) : stubborn.

dowie (*G. dubhach*) : sad ; sorrowful ; melancholy.

dree : to suffer ; to endure.

dreid : dread.

drooth : a thirst.

drukken : drunken.

drumlie : muddy.

duddie : ragged.

dule : sorrow.

dyke : a stone dividing wall.

dyvor : a bankrupt.

ee (pl. een) : eye.

eident : busy ; diligent ; industrious.

eizel or aizel : a red ember ; hot cinder.

eldrich : ghostly ; frightful.

lle : an old, and now obsolete, measure.

ell-wan : a measuring stick ; a yard-stick.

ellys : else.

clshin, : an awl.

eneuch : enough ; sufficient.

ettle : to try ; intent.

fa' (faw) : fall ; try.

fae : foe.

faem : foam.

fail-dyke : stone and turf wall.

fan' : found.

fan (Aberdeen dialect) : when.

far (Aberdeen dialect) : where.

farl : an oatcake.

farrant : fashioned.

fash (*Fr. facher*) : trouble ; annoyance. (*dinna fash yersel* —don't trouble yourself.)

fasheous : troublesome.

faucht : fought.

fause : false.

fay or fey : psychic ; other-worldly.

fecht : to fight ; a fight.

feck : the greater quantity. (*the feck o't*—most of it.)

feckless : puny ; senseless.

ferlies : oddities ; things to wonder at.

feucht : fought.

fiere (*G. fear*) : man ; comrade ; friend.

flair : floor.

flang : flung ; danced wildly.

fleer (Aberdeen dialect) : floor.

fley'd : frightened.

flit, flittin' : to move ; a removal.

flüre (flür) : floor ; to floor.

forfochen : worn out ; done for ; wearied.

fou or fu' : full ; drunk.

frae : from.

füle (fùl) : a fool ; to fool ; to mislead.

fur : a furrow.

fushion : pith ; vigour.

fye : an exclamation signifying haste.

fye-gar : make haste ; hurry to do.

fyou (fyow) : a few.

gab (*G. gob*) : the mouth ; talk (*haud yer gab !*—shut your mouth !).

gabbin : talking ; mouthing.

gae : go ; to go.

gaed : went.

gait or gate : way ; manner of doing a thing.

gane : gone.

gang : go ; to go. (*gang yer ain gait*—go your own way.)

gar : make ; force ; compel.

garr'd : compelled.

gat : got ; obtained.

gaun : going.

gear : goods ; belongings ; wealth.

gey (gye) : very. (*gey-dowie*— very sorrowful.)

gie : give ; to give.

gied : gave.

gie's : give us, or give me. (*gie's't*—give me it.)

gin : if.

gird : a hoop.

girse : grass.

glaikit : foolish ; thoughtless.

glaives (*G. claidheamh*): swords.

gleades (*G. gléidh?*): glowing embers ; remains of a fire kept in from the night before.

gleg : sharp ; quick.

gloamin (*G. glóamainn*) : twilight ; evening.

gouans or gowans : mountain or wild daisies.

goud or gowd : gold.

grat : wept.

grauvit : cravat.

greet : to weep.

greetin' : weeping ; crying.

gress : grass.

groat : an old coin, worth fourpence.

guid or gude (güd) : good.

guidman : husband ; master ; a petty title, as : *The Guidman o' Ballengeich*—The Master, or owner, of B.

guid-willie-waucht : a good long drink.

ha' (haw) : hall.

hae : have ; or, as a command : hae ! (h-yeh) meaning *Here, take this !*

hairst : harvest.

hale : whole ; healthy ; well.

hansel : a first gift ; a gift in token of something special.

happed or happit : wrapped ; covered.

harn : a coarse linen cloth.

haud : hold.

haughs : low-lying lands ; meadows.

hauld : hold.

hert : heart.

het : hot.

hicht : height.

hie : high.

hirple : to walk haltingly or lamely.

hirplin' : limping.

hoast : a cough.

hod : hid.

hogg (*G. òg*) : young castrated sheep.

hogmanay : the festival of Old Year's Night.

hosen : stockings.

hout ! (howt) : an exclamation of impatience.

howes : hollows.

humpit : carried.

hurdies : the hips.

hurl : to roll over ; to drive ; a drive.

ilk or ilka : each ; every.

ingle (*G. aingeal*) : the fire ; the fireside.

intil : into ; unto.

Janiveer : January.

jimp : slender.

juist (jüst) : just ; only.

kail : colewort ; broth ; Hotchpotch soup.

kebars (*G. cabar*) : rafters ; tree-trunks when cut ; poles.

keek : a sly look ; a peep.

keel : red chalk.

kelpie : a water-horse ; a demon of the lochs.

ken : to know. (*ken ye ocht ?*— do you know anything ?)

kerne (*G. ceathairne*) : a warring man ; a fighting peasant.

kirk : church.

kirkit : churched ; married in a kirk ; appeared at the kirk for the first time after an event.

kirn : a churn ; to churn.

kist (*G. ciste*) : a box ; a chest ; a coffin.

kittle (*G. ciotach*) : difficult ; awkward ; to tickle.

kittled : gave birth to kittens.

knicht : a knight.

knowe (now) (*G. cnoc*) : a hillock.

kye : cows.

laigh : low.

laird : a landowner. (*bonnet-laird*—a small proprietor : one whose land is so small that his bonnet might cover it ?)

lane : lone. (*ma lane*—alone, by myself.)

lang syne : long since ; long ago.

lanwart : urban.

lapstane : a stone on which a shoemaker beats his leather.

lauch : laugh.

lave : the rest ; the remainder. (*the lave*—the others.)

law : a hill.

lawin' : the score ; the reckoning.

lear : learning ; lore.

leglen : a milking stool.

leem (Aberdeen dialect) : a loom.

leister : an implement for spearing fish.

lemans : lovers ; paramours.

lest : last.

lettergae : precentor.

lickit : beaten ; thrashed.

licks : thrashings. (*yer licks*— your punishment.)

lift : the sky.

linn (*G. linne*) : a cascade ; a pool.

lippen : to trust.

loan (*G. lonaidh*) : a narrow road ; a path through a field.

loch : a lake ; an arm of the sea ; an inlet.

lo'ed : loved.

loon : a boy ; a young fellow. (*The Lossie Loon*—the lad from Lossiemouth.)

loot : let.

loup or lowp : jump ; leap.

lowe : a flame.

luckie : a dame ; a middle-aged woman.

lufe (lüf) : the palm of the hand ; the hand.

lug : the ear.

lum : chimney. (*yon reekin lum*—that smoking chimney.)

lunt : a column of smoke ; to smoke.

luve (lüv) : love.

lyart (*G. liath*) : grey ; grey-headed.

mair : more.

Mairch : March.

mairrit : married.

mane : moan.

manse : a minister's house.

mansuet : gentle.

maukin : a hare.

maun : must.

maunna : must not.

mirk : dark ; darkness.

mools or mouls : earth ; the grave.

moudiwart : a mole.

muckle : big ; much. (*muckle gab*—big mouth ; *no muckle* —not much.)

muir : a moor.

na : no ; a negative suffix.

neist or niest (neest) : next.

neive : fist ; hand. (*a neivefu* —a handful.)

neuk (*G. niùc*) : a corner ; a nook.

nicht : night.

nickum : a little devil ; a mischievous boy.

niffer : exchange.

nocht : nothing. (*nocht ava*— nothing at all.)

nott : required.

och ! or ochone ! (*G. ochòin*) : exclamations of sorrow or longing.

onie or ony : any.

oot-bye : outside.

orra : odd ; extra. (*orraman*— an odd job man.)

outspeckle or kenspeckle : standing out ; different.

ower or owre : over.

pang, panged : to cram ; crammed ; full.

paughty (pauchty) : proud ; haughty.

paukie or pawky : sly ; artful.

peel : a tower ; a turret.

pet : coddle. (*mak a pet o masel*—coddle myself.)

pibroch (*G. pìobaireachd*) : a martial bagpipe tune.

pickle : a few ; a small quantity.

pike : pick out ; dig out.

pirn : a spool ; a thread-reel.

plaid (plaed *not* plad) : a covering ; a tartan blanket.

plat : pleated ; twisted or twined together.

pleuch or pleugh : a plough.

pliskie or plisky : a trick.

poind or poined : to seize ; to distrain ; distrained.

poke : bag or wallet. (*mealpoke*—oatmeal-sack.)

poleist : polished.

poortith or puirtith : poverty.

pow : the head.

pree or prie : to taste ; to kiss.

pree'd : tasted ; kissed.

preen : a pin.

puckle or pickle : a few ; small quantity.

pu'd : pulled.

puddock : a frog ; a toad.

puir : poor.

püles (püls) : pools.

quaich (*G. cuach*) : a drinking cup ; a dish ; a bowl.

quean or queyn : a young woman ; a lass.

queel (Aberdeen dialect) : cool.

quhair : a sheaf of papers ; a quire ; a 'script or book.)

rade : rode.

rant : an unskilled song ; to rollick.

ratton : a rat.

raukle : rash ; fearless.

raw : a row ; a line of things.

rax : to stretch. (*rax-owre*— stretch across.)

ream : cream ; froth.

reamin' : brim full ; frothing.

reck : heed.

redd : to tidy ; to clear up.

rede : to advise ; to counsel.

reek : smoke ; to smoke.

reemish : a hefty blow ; a weighty stroke.

reivers : warrior cattle-lifters.

richt : right.

rickle : a heap.

rin : run.

rive : to tear ; to burst.

riven : torn.

roup : sale by auction.

routh : plenty.

rowed : rolled ; wrapped.

ruggit : pulled and tugged ; wrenched.

ruit (rüt) : root.

rung : a staff ; a cudgel.

runt : stalk of a cabbage ; an undersized, dried-up, little man.

sae : so.

sair : sore ; hard. (*sair ta dae* —hard to do.)

sall : shall.

sark or serk : a shirt ; a vest or a chemise.

saul : soul.

saut : salt.

saw, sawis : sow ; to sow ; sows.

sax : six.

scaith : hurt ; damage.

scaur (*G. sgòrr*) : a jutting cliff ; a sharp rock.

schiltrom : a military formation.

scunner : to sicken with disgust. (*gied me a scunner*— made me sick.)

shalt, sheltie : a pony.

shaw : a wooded dell. (*birkenshaw*—a wood of birch trees.)

shaw or schaw : show ; a show (*wapponschaw* — a showing of weapons and accoutrements.)

sheuch (*G. siùch*) : a ditch ; a rivulet.

shieling : a hut ; a small cottage ; a hill pasture hut.

shoon or shune (shün) : shoes.

shouther (shoother) : shoulder.

sbue (shoo or shü) : sew ; to stitch.

shure (shür) : sure ; steady.

sib : kin ; akin.

sic : such.

sic-like : such as ; such a. (*sic-like yin*—such a one.)

sicht : sight ; a sight.

siller : silver ; money in general.

sizzens : seasons.

skaith or scaith : hurt ; damage.

skelp (*G. sgealb*) : run ; dash ; dash against ; slap.

skirl : shriek ; cry out.

skirtit : ran round ; ran quickly.

slock, sloken : quench ; to quench thirst.

smooring, smoor (*G. smúradh*) : the act of burning to the embers ; damp down (*not* from English : smothering).

smytrie : a huddled collection.

snool : to cringe ; to sneak.

snoove : creep forward.

snowk : to sniff.

sodger (*G. saighdear*) : a soldier.

sonsie or sonsy : plump ; jolly.

soo : a sow.

sooter or soutar : a cobbler ; a shoemaker.

spae : to foretell. (*spaewife*—a fortune-teller.)

spak : spoke ; spake.

spate : a sudden flood.

speir or spier (speer) : to inquire ; to ask.

spence : the parlour ; the best room.

spirtle : a stick for stirring.

spleuchan (*Ir. G. spliúchán*) : a purse ; a tobacco-pouch.

spune (spün) : a spoon.

spunk (*G. spong*) : mettle ; fire ; a match ; tinder.

spunkie : fiery ; a goblin ; the will o' the wisp.

stane : a stone.

stang : pole ; tongue of jaws-harp.

stank : a pool of standing water.

staw : stole.

steek : a stitch ; to shut ; to lock.

steeked or steekit : locked ; bolted.

stents : dues ; assessments.

stern, stern light : stars ; star-light.

stey : steep.

stirk : a young bullock or heifer.

stot : an·ox ; to bounce. (*a stottie*, or *stottin ba*—a bouncing ball.

stoup : a measure ; a drink container.

strae : straw.

streek : to stretch.

streen : yesterday.

strype : a small rill.

sugarolly : sweet stuff ; a stick of rock ; liquorice.

suld or sud : should.

sumph : someone soft and stupid.

sune (sün) : soon.

swank : tall and lithe (*not* as modern English usage.)

swankie : a strapping youth.

swap (*G. suaip*) : exchange, barter (taken into English slang).

swatch : a sample ; a pattern-piece.

sweer, sweir or sweirt : lazy ; extremely averse from.

swither : to hesitate.

sybow or syba : a young onion ; a spring-onion.

syne : then ; since. (*lang syne* —long ago.)

ta : to ; toward.

tack : lease.

tackets : shoe-nails ; hob-nails.

tackitty-buits : hobnailed boots.

tae : toe.

taen : taken.

taet : a small quantity ; a little piece.

tane : the one. (*tane an tither* —the one and the other.)

tassie : a drinking cup.

taupie : a witless, or slovenly, young woman.

teen : provocation ; vexation.

tent : to heed ; to mark. (*tak tent*—take care.)

teuch : tough.

teuk (tük) : took.

thack : thatch.

thae : those.

theek : thatch, cover.

thegither : together.

thick : familiar. (*gey thick thegither*—very friendly with each other.)

thirled : bound ; tied.

thole : to suffer ; to endure.

thoom : thumb. (*to thoom*— to finger.)

thrang (*G. trainge*) : busy ; crowded ; intimate.

thrapple : the throat.

thrawn : twisted, stubborn ; contentious.

threap : argue ; assert.

thummles (Aberdeen dialect) : thimbles.

till : to ; toward. (*gang till't*— go to it.)

timmer : timber ; wood ; a tree ; trees.

tint : lost. (*tint yer lemans*— lost your lads.)

tirl : to ring. (*tirl at the yett*— ring at the door.)

tocher : dowry.

tod : the fox.

toom : empty.

toun (toon) : a town ; a farm house. (*a ferm-toun*—a collection of farm buildings considered together.)

tousie (toosie) : shaggy ; unkempt.

tow : a rope ; flax.

trams : shafts.

trews (*G. triubhas*) : trousers ; 'shorts' ; cloth pants worn beneath a kilt—but not by Scotsmen !

troke, troch : rubbish ; odds and ends ; to barter.

tromp or trump : a jaws-harp.

troot : trout.

trow : to believe.

tulyie, tulzie : a squabble, a fight.

tume (tüm) : empty.

twa, twae : two.

twa-three (twa-hree) : two or three ; a few.

tyauve : an effort. (*wi a tyauve*—with a struggle.)

unco : strange ; uncouth ; very. (*unco thrawn*—very stubborn.)

usquabae (*G. uisge-beatha*— literally 'water of life') : whisky.

verra : very.

wab : a web.

wabster : a weaver.

wad : would ; wager.

wadna : would not.

wadset : a mortgage.

wae : woe.

wae worth ! : woe befall !

wale : choice ; to pick ; choose.

walie ! or waly ! : an exclamation of distress.

wame : the belly.

wark : work.

warl or warld : the world.

warlock : a wizard.

warsle : to wrestle (usually meaning with a problem.)

wast : west.

waster (waaster) : western.

wat : wet.

waucht or waught : a copious drink.

wauken : awake ; to awaken.

waukin' : waking.

waukrife : wakeful.

waur : worse ; to worst.

weans (wains) : children.

wecht : weight.

wede (*Ir. G. uidhe*) : gone ; marched ; taken.

weeda : a widow.

ween : think.

weet : wet ; to wet ; rain.

werna : were not.

wha, wham : who, whom.

whang : a thong ; a slice. (*a whang o kebbuck*—a slice of cheese.)

wha's : whose.

whaur : where.

whiles : sometimes.

whilk, quhilk : which.

whinger : a dirk ; a short sword.

whingin' (wheenjin) : fretting ; complaining.

whings, whungs : thongs ; shoe-laces.

whip-the-cat : the tailor.

whit : what.

wimple : to meander ; to wander.

win : obtain ; gain objective. (*win hame*—get home.)

winna : will not.

winnock (*G. uinneag*) : a window.

won (wun) : to dwell. (*wons yon*—lives there.)

wow ! : an exclamation of surprise or pleasure.

wud : mad ; wild.

wyte : blame ; to blame ; reproach.

yate, yett : gate ; but more usually a door.

yeld : dried up ; not giving milk.

yestreen : last night.

yill : ale.

yin : one.

yince : once.

yont : beyond.

youl : yule ; Christmas.

yow : you.

yowe : a ewe.

INDEX OF AUTHORS

INDEX OF FIRST LINES

(PART I : POETRY SECTION)

GENERAL INDEX

Abbotsford, Tourists at, 326
Aberdeen, 100, 146, 212
Aberdeen (County), 193, 198, 205, 222
Aberdeen, Marquis of, 193
Adams, The, 193
Adamsons, The, 193
Advocates, 234
Advocates, Faculty of, 234
Airlie, Earl of, 205
Ale, Heather, 152
Alexander I, 261
Alexander II, 206, 220, 262
Alexander III, 155, 193, 194, 197, 203, 260, 262, 263
Analecta (Wodrow), 280
Ancrum, Battle of, 220, 280
Ancrum, Earl of, 195
Ancrum Muir, 280
Ancrum, Scotts of, 207
Andersons, The, 206
Angus (County), 196, 216, 222
Angus, Earls of, 191, 205, 220
Angus the Absolute, 200
Annan, 145
Annandale, 188
Annandale, Johnstons of, 194
Antiquary, The, 48, 271, 290
Arbroath, Declaration of, 269
Archers, 295
Ardgour, Macleans of, 201
Ardlamont, Lamonts of, 195
Argyle (County), 189, 192, 203, 205, 222
Argyle, Duke of, 49, 189, 273
Arkleton, Elliotts of, 191
Armstrang, Johnie, 279
Armstrongs, The, 210
Arran, 196
Assynt, MacLeods of, 202

Atholl (District), 51, 192, 205
Atholl Brose, 256
Atholl, Duke of, 211
Auchinshellich, Lamonts of, 195
Auld Alliance, 167
' Auld Clootie,' 106
' Auld Lang Syne,' 335
Avondale, Earls of, 191
Ayr, 212
Ayr (County), 204, 222, 229

Babbity Bowster, 142
Badenoch (District), 116, 149, 197, 200, 203
Badges, Clan, 213
Bail, 235
Bailie, or Baillie, 235
Baillie, Joanna, 305
Bairns' Rhymes, 139
Balcarres, Lindsays of, 196
Ballantyne's Newspaper, 331
Balmerino, Lord : Epitaph on, 283
Balnagown, Rosses of, 206
Baltic, 102
Balwearie, Scotts of, 206
Banff (County), 222
Banff, MacDuffs of, 198
Bank Notes, 235
Bannockburn, Battle of, 191, 220, 269, 294
Bannocks, Barley, 248
Barbour, John, 77, 155, 294
Barra, 223
Barra, MacNeills of, 203
Bartholf of Leslie, 196
Battles, 220
Beaton, Marie, 89
Beauly, 190, 193

357